Rose Douglas: Or, Sketches of a Country Parish, by S.R.W.

Sarah R. Whitehead

ROSE DOUGLAS

OR,

SKETCHES OF A COUNTRY PARISH:

BEING THE

Autobiography of a Scotch Minister's Daughter.

BY

S. R. W.

IN TWO VOLUMES.

VOL. II.

LONDON:

SMITH, ELDER, AND CO., 65 CORNHILL.

—

1851.

ROSE DOUGLAS.

CHAPTER I.

The stranger's foot alone will now trouble thy rest,
And let in the daylight upon thy dark windows;
They are far far away who loved thee and knew thee,
In the old, old time.

WE journeyed on slowly. The cart was so heavy,
and the parish roads in such bad repair, that we made
small progress. We left at eight o'clock in the morning, and it was near eleven before we reached Lanark.
The day was grey and chilly, and I remember, as we
crept wearily over the moor, feeling the raw morning air penetrating into the cart, and shrinking back
into my corner with cold as well as with sorrow. I
did not venture to look out, till certain we were long
past all familiar objects. How many anxious hearts,
I knew, were following me that morning on my road!

At length we entered Lanark, and rumbled on
through its streets.

In a short time we cleared the town, and found our-

selves descending the steep hill which leads down the
valley.   It is a lovely journey down the vale of the
Clyde: corn-fields, orchards where the fruit hangs
temptingly in autumn over the very road, as if to
entice the traveller, are mingled with rich overhang-
ing woods, grey rocks, and picturesque mansions.
Then the noble river itself, the finest object in the view,
winds on amidst the greenest banks that ever poet
sang of, or the feet of fairies prest.   At another time
such a journey would have afforded me the highest
delight.   It would have served, with my dear father
and myself, for a subject of pleasant conversation, for
months afterwards.   We should never have been
weary of recalling the many points of view in the exquisite and ever-varying scenery.   But now, though
I could not but admire, it was with a cold passive
admiration, while the heart was too burdened to allow
the mind to be properly impressed.

We had to stop about half-way to feed the horse.
The day wore gradually on.

I was sorely fatigued by my long tedious journey.
In spite of the variety of the scenery through which
we had passed, I had found the hours very wearisome.   Every mile I felt was taking me farther and
farther away from my old home.   I was entering
a strange country, not knowing the things which
would befall me there.   The world was as a wilder-
ness to me, empty, unknown, and friendless.   And
to add to all this, I was not devoid of apprehension
about the termination of the day's travel.   I had never

slept at an inn in my life, and what to those of this day
of mail-coach travelling, and of something hereafter
even swifter (if all tales be true which reach us), is perfectly easy and customary, was to me in prospect most
alarming. Now every one travels, and all are accustomed to live in inns. But I was a simple country
girl, and except once during my childhood, I had
never travelled more than eight miles in one direction
in my life. I pictured to myself what my landlady
would be like; and as I was only familiar with that
class of persons as they are represented in the pages of
Don Quixote or Gil Blas, now slumbering undisturbed
among the dust of the old library shelves, I could
scarcely arrive at a satisfactory idea, for Spain, I
knew, must not be confounded with our own island.

We at last entered Hamilton, and jingled on through
several narrow crooked streets, until we emerged into a
steep broad one, only partially built up, with houses
here and there situated among small gardens, called
the Muir.

Eglinton's house of public entertainment for man
and beast was one of a small row of houses in a line
with some old almshouses, which are still standing.
The horse, wearied with his long exertions, dragged
the cart slowly up the hill; but at length he did accomplish it, and John willingly drew rein before the
little sign which projected across the pathway. A
number of idle neighbours immediately gathered round
to scrutinize the cart. I stepped out with a little difficulty (for my limbs trembled both from agitation

and fatigue), by means of a chair, for which some hanger-on about the place had run into the kitchen. I was looking round rather bewildered, and hardly knowing where to proceed to, when Mrs Eglinton herself came hurrying out to receive me. She was a tall smart-looking woman, and when I saw her, I understood Mrs M'Whirter's animadversions on her dress, for though it was now winter, she was attired in a white wrapper. She welcomed me very civilly, saying that a room had been kept for me, and that she would show me to it immediately. With many smiles and remarks on my journey, and the fatigue it must have cost me, all uttered with the usual vivacity of an Englishwoman, she conducted me into the house. John was busy getting out my boxes. " I shall see you again before you return, John," I said hurriedly, as I prepared to follow my landlady. He merely nodded in answer.

Mrs Eglinton led me along a little cleanly sanded passage, and then up a narrow staircase. She threw open a door to the right of the small landing-place. " This is your room, Miss," she said, " and I hope you will find it comfortable."

It was a small neat parlour and bedroom in one. There was a bed in a recess in the wall, covered with a snowy quilt. The walls of the room were stained green,—the furniture was dark mahogany, heavy in form, but bright in polish,—a carpet partially concealed the floor, and a clear fire burned in the little grate. It was not at all like my idea of a room in an inn. Every thing was as neat and clean as I had been accustomed to at home. Home! the word, I felt, would always suggest the reality to me.

"Thank you," I forced myself to say to my attentive hostess, who hastened to stir the fire, and to perform other offices about the room; "every thing looks very nice indeed."

"And what will you take, Ma'am?" she now inquired; "you must be worn out and cold."

"Thank you," I said, "I shall be glad to have some tea as soon as convenient."

As I did not require any assistance in removing my travelling equipments, she left the room to get tea prepared for me.

There were two windows facing each other in the apartment; the room occupying the whole width of the house. Having laid aside my wrappings, I went first to one and then to the other. The one to the back looked out merely on a small straggling garden belonging to the house, and on similar ones pertaining to the neighbourhood. As there was nothing in them to attract my attention beyond a moment, I crossed the little room to the other. An experienced traveller would have found even this window dull enough, for except the small group gathered round the house-door, the street was quiet and empty. A servant-girl or a workman would occasionally pass along the opposite side of the way, and once a soldier from the neighbouring barracks, for Hamilton has always a troop quartered there, varied the view while

I looked out. The cart still stood at the door, but the horse was now in the stable, and John was not visible. No one was indeed, but a collection of ragged urchins of both sexes, and a few idle dissolute-looking men.

It was the first time I had been left quietly to myself since morning; for owing to the excitement produced by the sense of constant motion amidst new scenery, I could scarcely think on any subject; at least my ideas had been capable of no arrangement. I sat down in the window with a sense of pleasure in feeling myself alone, and of finding my fears concerning my unknown landlady vain. I had still, however, the morrow before me, with its entrance upon new scenes and untried friends, to shake my spirit;—but yet there was the night between. For one night I was still my own mistress, and it was a temporary consolation to feel this. I determined not to think of the dreaded to-morrow.

Among my many bad habits, I had one, resulting principally from my solitary education and retired life —a great tendency to reverie. The habit had gained on me since my father's death. It was a disadvantage to me at this crisis of my fortunes, for I had lived too much in a world of my own thoughts to please mere strangers, and with such only I was hereafter to associate. I preferred solitude at any time to conversation. I fell now into one of my customary musing fits. My thoughts wandered naturally back to the home I had left. How was it looking now?

What was taking place there? It was probably shut up by this time, and the keys lodged with my dear old friend at the Craiglands till John's return. What were Nanny and Peggy feeling? Then, in imagination, I wandered through all the old familiar rooms. I sat in my own peculiar place in the parlour. I visited my father's room and my own, and was awed by their emptiness and desolation. The quiet solitary road—the ancient churchyard with its trees—the garden—the shrubbery, dank and dripping as it was when I made my way through it that morning—the little green gate which had closed with a prophetic clang behind me, as like Eve I issued sorrowfully from my paradise—they were all present before me. All the sweet seclusion of my old home life came back, and I was at Auchtermuir again.

I was roused from this sweet sad dream by the noise my landlady made in attempting to push open the room door with the tea-tray in her hands. It brought me suddenly and roughly back to the realities I had now to grasp with. I rose hastily and affected to be occupied by looking from the window, that I might, unobserved by her, wipe away the traces of the tears I had been shedding from my cheeks.

Mrs Eglinton placed the tray on the table, having first removed the green baize cover and dusted the table carefully. She then vanished, and reappeared with a plate of bread and butter, some newly-made wheaten *scones*, reeking hot through the snowy napkin that covered them, a pot of marmalade, and then the tea. · All was nice, and arranged with neatness. I asked where the old man who had accompanied me was, and she told me he was sitting in the kitchen. I requested that some supper should be given him, and she withdrew for the purpose, after showing me the position of the bell, that I might ring if I wanted anything.

I was timid about giving trouble, and though I soon finished tea, I did not like to summon Mrs Eglinton to remove the things, as I expected she would do so when convenient for herself. But she did not return for a long time, nor till it was quite dark. I sat patiently by the fire till then, sometimes occupied in tracing familiar spots in the red embers on which I gazed, and sometimes amused by the novelty of the sounds which struck my unpractised ear, proceeding from the street or the kitchen of the little inn. Everything was strange to me. People seemed to come and go often below, and I heard the rumble of a cart leaving the inn. At last the clock down stairs struck six, and sometime after my hostess re-entered the room.

" Bless my heart!" she exclaimed as she made her appearance, " and you have been sitting all this time in the dark! Well, to be sure, I have been very forgetful, but a neighbour dropt in, and there have been so many people coming and going to-night."

It was of no consequence, I said.

" But it is of consequence, my dear Miss, to leave you so long in the dark. What could I have been thinking of ?—and you by yourself too !" and she went on blaming herself.

I answered her that I did not mind about being in the dark, as I was too fatigued either to read or work. But she could not believe that any one could like darkness, or to be left alone.

" It was such a pity," she said, " that I did not arrive earlier in the day, or that I could not wait another day. That would be best, as I had had so long a journey; and then I could have seen the palace, and walked through the policy. She knew the housekeeper very well, and she might have managed to go with me herself; and then, though it was not just the time of year for it, we could have gone, too, and seen the wild cattle—strangers all liked to see the wild cattle. To be sure," she added on reflection, " to-morrow was the term-day, and it might not have been quite convenient for her; but she hoped I would come back some other time, and she would have much pleasure in showing me all these sights."

All this time she was going backwards and forwards removing the tea-things, having first of all, however, procured me candles, which were set in enormous brass candlesticks, ornamented round the sockets with fancifully cut paper of a green colour. She then mended the fire and swept the hearth, talking busily all the time, as if she thought it wrong to let one member lie idle while others were employed. She evidently considered it her duty to entertain me, and as, in her eyes, I most probably appeared a shy, ignorant, simple, country girl, her efforts were very praiseworthy, and as long as they lasted, served at least to divert my thoughts from painful retrospects. But at last I grew somewhat weary of her volubility, for as if to make amends for forgetting me so long, she showed no inclination (though everything was put in order) to leave the room.   She remained standing, too, beside the table, and I was in a fidget, from my want of experience, to decide whether (the room being at present mine) I should ask her to sit down, or whether that was unnecessary in her own house.

At last, as a means of getting rid of her, though I also wished to see John, I mentioned him, and requested her to bring the old man up stairs.   But here a sad disappointment awaited me, and one which so strongly affected me at the time, that I could not conceal it from my hostess.   John had stolen away with the horse and cart without my knowledge, unwilling, I suppose, to undergo the pain of parting from me. The cart I had heard leave the inn had been his.   He had rested the horse for about an hour and a half, and fed him carefully, and then he had set off, forbidding them to let me know, as he said there was no occasion to disturb me.   He had promised, he told them, to wait all night at Dalserf, where he had formerly fed the horse, meaning to return to Auchtermuir early in the morning, as the horse would require a night's rest before he could travel.   My hostess said that she thought the old man looked dull and was anxious to leave, but neither she nor her husband supposed he was stealing a march. She tried to comfort me when she saw my distress at losing the last link to home in this sudden manner: and at length, ashamed of having exhibited this emotion before a stranger, I wiped away my tears, and tried to appear composed.

She ultimately apologized for leaving me, saying she would be required below, and I was glad to see her take her departure. A fresh burst of grief followed her exit. I felt solitary—desolate. Poor old John! I could so well understand his feelings, his unwillingness to witness my distress or to expose his own. I leant my head upon the table, and wept till I could weep no longer from exhaustion. In imagination I followed him along the dark road we had lately travelled, sad at heart, retracing his steps to that home which was now so altered to him. " Poor old man!" thought I, " kind-hearted though rough in exterior, shall I never see thee again?" I had seen the last of Auchtermuir in him—now and hereafter I was to be among strangers!

Afraid at last that my hostess might re-enter the room, I endeavoured to compose myself, that she might not again see me in a state of agitation. But as she did not soon appear, I ventured to ring the bell, feeling as if I was taking a liberty in doing it, and when she hastily answered it, I told her I meant to go to bed, as I felt much fatigued. I inquired at what hour the caravan left in the morning, and learned it was at eight. Mrs Eglinton promised that I should be roused in good time, so that I might have breakfast comfortably before starting.

"I shall take care, too," she said, "that you get the topmost seat in the caravan, and then you wont be troubled with people getting in or out, but sit comfortable all the way. But on account of that you must be stirring early, and you are quite right to go to bed, though I am afraid the old man, foolish fellow, has troubled you a bit."

She prepared the bed for me, and brought in towels and water, and then assuring me again that I would be called in good time, she bade me a cordial good night, and left the room.

The bed was most invitingly clean, and I was so worn out both in body and mind, that I was not long of occupying it. But in spite of fatigue I did not soon fall asleep. The peculiarity of my situation—a stranger in a strange inn, left entirely to my own guidance—the various noises which at times ascended from below—all conspired to occupy my attention and arrest sleep. But at length, after a long interval, these murmurs seemed all to die away. I heard footstep after footstep leave the little inn, and pass beneath my window, till at last the house door was closed and soon all was silence. I fell asleep in the end, with the tears still wet upon my cheeks, and dreamed that I was at Auchtermuir.

CHAPTER II.

Still down the vale the eye enraptured sees
Green sloping fields and clumps of aged trees,
With many a quiet and lowly cot beside
The flowing waters of the crystal Clyde;
Afar the city's smoke pollutes the air.

I WAS awakened in the morning by a noise in my room, and, looking confusedly out of bed, I saw my hostess occupied in opening my shutters. The grey light breaking in as she did so made me more fully awake, and I sat up in bed.

"Ah! good morning, miss," said Mrs Eglinton cheerfully, when she saw I was roused. "I hope you have had a good rest. It is only half-past six at present; but I thought it best to waken you in good time, that you may not be hurried in the end. How did you sleep?"

"Very well, indeed," I answered; "and I am much obliged to you for calling me so early. I shall rise immediately."

But she would not let me do so till she had kindled a fire; after which she left the room, asking me to touch the bell when I was ready, and she would bring my breakfast.

I was not long in dressing, for I feared to be late; but, before I thought it necessary to ring for my landlady, I had time to read a few verses, as was my morning custom, in my little pocket Bible, a birth-day gift of my father's, and earnestly to commend my future course to the protection of God. She came up immediately, and made the room as tidy as a few minutes would allow her. She then brought me my breakfast. In a short time she returned, and with many smiles and curtsies she placed my bill (which I had asked for) on the table beside me, and then withdrew. I opened it with some trepidation, for I had an idea that inn charges were enormous things, and that I should probably have to pay very high, even for the simple fare I had had. I was agreeably surprised, therefore, to find that the charge made for the lodging, food, and attendance I had had, was very moderate. My seat to Glasgow was charged separately, and cost me little more than a shilling. It was a relief to my mind; for I now saw, that when all expenses were paid, I should have still a small surplus over to meet any wants that might arise.

I thanked Mrs Eglinton sincerely for her kindness, and begged her, whenever she had an oppor-

tunity, to let Mrs M'Whirter know how much
indebted I felt myself to her. Mrs Eglinton received my thanks very graciously. She told me that
the caravan had just been brought to the door, and
that Mr Eglinton had seen my boxes placed in it.
The passengers had not yet arrived, she said, but she
would advise me to take my place in it, even though
I had to wait some time. I thought it as well to follow her advice.

The bustle at the door made itself apparent as we
descended the stairs. The man was fastening some of
the horse's harness, and there was a similar group,
though the hour was early, gathered round the door,
as there was on our arrival the previous night. More
than one lazy-looking burgher, too, stood leaning,
with folded arms, in their doorways, in the neighbourhood of the inn, as Mrs Eglinton and I stept out.
Their red Kilmarnock cowls were still on their heads,
as if the wearers had not long risen from bed, and
their unwashed, unbraced-looking appearance, was a
contrast to the fresh clearness of the morning. They
were indolently watching the progress of the man in
preparing the cart. A half-dressed woman, too, would
occasionally show herself at one or other of the doors
in the row, and, with a loud yawn, would perhaps
carelessly fling out a pailful of dirty water, half into
the gutter and half along the street. The morning
was crisp and fair, and promised to keep so.

The caravan in which I was to perform the rest of
my journey was a large unwieldy concern : ours was

small, and even elegant in comparison. In outward shape they were nearly similar; but within, instead of the seats being laid across, they here extended down each side, so that the passengers sat opposite to one another. My boxes were placed under the two seats, at the upper end of the cart. A chair was brought out by the landlord, who was on the spot, and by it, and Mrs Eglinton's assistance, I managed to climb into this Mammoth vehicle, and, after shaking hands with her, grope my way to the farthest corner. Here I seated myself, and patiently awaited the arrival of my fellow-passengers and the moment of starting. I was not long seated when some of them appeared to come into sight.

"Here comes Miss Strang and her niece, Tam," I overheard Mr Eglinton say to his servant. "I hope she 'll no begin to scold,—for they 'll be ill pleased at no getting the twa tap seats. We maun tell them they were owre late o' securing them."

The man answered something which I did not hear, as he was still occupied about the horse, and then they both broke out into a suppressed laugh.

In a few moments, the person alluded to seemed to come up, and greeted Mr Eglinton,—his wife had hastily retreated into the house. "How are ye the day, Mr Eglinton?" I heard her say in a loud masculine tone of voice. "We 're in good time, ye see?"

The owner of the cart returned her greeting in a somewhat hesitating manner, which she, however, took no notice of, but without more words, advanced straight to the vehicle, and put up her foot on the chair, in act to ascend, looking just carelessly in, as if expecting to see no one. I had a distinct view of her. She was a very tall, spare, raw-boned looking woman, very stiff and erect in her figure. This austere-looking personage was attired in a somewhat shabby-genteel fashion. Her clothes looked faded and worn. From what I had heard the landlord remark to his servant, I began to feel a little afraid of having encroached on her prerogative, and shrunk back into the corner to avoid her observation as much as possible. The gloom which reigned in the extremity of the capacious caravan deceived her eye for a moment; but she immediately detected me, and a change came over her face. She drew her foot hastily back, nearly overturning another female, her niece, who stood just behind her, by doing so.

" Did I not tell you, John Eglinton," she said in a loud angry voice, which scorned concealment, " that I wanted the twa tap seats for mysel' and my niece, and there 's a woman in already ?"

" Deed did ye, Miss Strang," said the landlord, fidgetting uneasily from one foot to the other, as he stood directly fronting the cart, on the step of his own door, yet with a malicious twinkle, I thought, perceptible in his eye. " But ye see, the young leddy was stopping all night in our house, and we were bound like to gie 't to her; but ye 'll get the ither end, and Miss Janet here can sit next ye."

"Humph!" uttered the discontented spinster. But as she knew that the landlord had the power as well as the right to place any one where he chose in his cart, she was compelled to acquiesce, though unwillingly. She turned round, therefore, and after darting a keen ireful glance at me, prepared for the second time to ascend.

"Take care o' that umbrella, Janet Strang," she exclaimed, wrathfully looking back, " and dinna be pokin' the end o 't into the dirt, and glawrin' my claise whan ye come in. I wonder folk shute themselves forrit in this manner, and force their betters out o' their proper places."

This I felt was addressed to me; but I only cowered the closer into my corner, and drew my veil tighter over my face in silence. She made her way up the cart, stooping so much on account of her tall figure, that she seemed literally bent in two, grumbling all the while, and holding her petticoats half leg up, in case they might trip her, exhibiting a formidable extent of coarse black woollen stockings, and somewhat masculine-like boots, as she did so. She at last set herself down with a bang in the corner opposite to me; but unfortunately she chanced to knock her heels against the trunk which was stowed beneath, and which protruded a little, I acknowledge, beyond the confines of the seat.

"What's this, John Eglinton? what's this?" she instantly demanded; " am I to be fashed wi' other folk's things? Is't your's?" she asked, severely addressing me.

Before I could answer, the driver, who was assist-ing her niece to mount, diverted her attention from me, and I was relieved.

" Sit down the cart a bit, Miss Strang," he said, grinning openly; " and I 'se warrant it 'll no trouble ye."

This immediately produced a retort from the lady concerning his impertinence, and a threat of complain-ing to his master (who had withdrawn himself), which, however, fell upon deaf ears. She next tried to move the trunk, and did succeed in pushing it farther down the cart; and this apparently satisfied her; for she afterwards settled herself in her corner, and began to examine me. But failing to get a view of my face through my thick veil, she at length turned her atten-tion to the other passengers, who had mostly all arrived by this time. Her niece was seated by her side, and seemed a stupid heavy girl of two or three and twenty, with mouth and eyes constantly open, and gaping at every thing. She carried a large shabby cotton um-brella in one hand, and in the other a pretty capacious hand-basket, whose broken handle was mended with a dirty ribbon.

Various individuals now entered the cart, both men and women. Most of the women were of the class of servants, and I suppose were going home to places. They were each more or less accompanied by friends, who took leave of them after helping them into the cart, with a hearty, " God bless you," and a shake of the hand.

I was interested by the appearance of one pair, who
seemed father and daughter. They were both decently
attired, but had an indescribable air of poverty and
suffering, principally the man, I thought. He was
evidently a mechanic, and had a pale, wasted, care-
worn face, which excited my sympathy. They paused
within a short distance of the cart, when they arrived;
and the man spoke earnestly to the girl, as if enforcing
something upon her attention. She listened attentively, and seemed to make some promise, and I could
observe tears trickling down her young cheeks. She
did not appear more than eighteen at the most. She
was probably leaving her father's roof for the first
time, for servitude. I felt my heart warm towards
them both. The girl's lot somewhat resembled my
own, I thought. She was going like me to earn her
bread among strangers. After a few minutes' conversation they both approached the cart, the girl carrying a little bundle, the only thing she had with her.
But I noticed the man suddenly start back as he
caught sight of some one within. I could not help
thinking it was my grim friend opposite. The girl
observed her father's movement, and stepped after
him. I saw him whisper something hastily to her,
then taking her hand, he pressed it, and went away.
She was obliged to hurry to the cart, as the man
summoned her, but I saw that there was a deep flush
now on her formerly pale face, and that she looked
timid and irresolute. The only vacant seat was on
my side; and, unfortunately, in full view of the virago

opposite to me. Though the young girl hastily averted her face the moment after entering, the lynx eyes of the old lady had caught a sight of it.

" So, Mary Lowrie," she exclaimed in a voice that arrested every one's attention, and made the poor girl herself start as if a pistol had been discharged at her ear; " so this is you; and can ye tell me when that puir gude for naething creature of a faither of yours means to pay my rent? If it 's no ready by the time I come back, out ye 'll a' tramp, bag and baggage; and that 's what I tell ye."

She looked fiery red as she said this. The frightened girl's head sunk on her bosom at this address, while all eyes were directed to her. I felt sorry at heart to witness her distress.

" Hout for shame, Miss Strang," said the driver, who was now putting in the small sliding piece of wood at the bottom of the cart. " Ye shouldna say sic things. James Lowrie is a decent working man, as we a' ken; and were it no that he has had a sair fecht wi' his dwining wife and his large family, he wad owe no man onything.—Cheer up, Mary," he continued, addressing the girl, whom he evidently knew, in a lower tone; " never mind what the auld rudas says,—your faither 's an honest man, and your penny fee will gang far to help him."

Poor Mary lifted her head and tried to smile, but it would not do, and she turned away her face to hide her tears. The man went away, as all things were ready, and chirruping to his horse, the cart began to

be in motion. We moved slowly up the hill on
which the street is built, the caravan steadied by the
weight of its occupants: the driver walked by the
side. We all now began to settle ourselves in our
respective places. Those who had bundles, if they
could not get them beneath the seats, managed to
place them at their feet; but all in my neighbourhood,
I observed, carefully eschewed coming in contact with
Miss Strang. I was in the worst seat, I found, in the
vehicle. Sympathizing looks were furtively thrown
by more than one individual at the weeping girl at
the bottom of the cart. One sturdy motherly-like
woman seemed, however, quite unawed by the presence
of the old lady, and did not hesitate to speak kindly
to the poor young thing, inquiring earnestly after her
mother's health, and then concerning the situation she
herself was bound for. But the girl's voice was so
broken and indistinct when she answered, that I did
not hear what she said. The sympathy expressed
by her neighbour appeared, however, to revive her,
though I could see that an air of dejection, unusual at
her years, was natural to her. To me it seemed to
tell a tale of early sorrow and helpless struggling for
others.

By the time we had proceeded a little way, my
opposite neighbour to my great joy fell fast asleep,
atoning for her broken morning slumbers by a series
of deep snores. She occasionally nodded forwards, as
if she would inevitably lose her balance; her bonnet
almost touching mine, keeping me in a constant state

of apprehension in case her person would suddenly deposit itself upon me.

My fellow-travellers were none of them of a very refined class. There was one man, who from his remarks to his neighbour I found to be a grocer, going down to Glasgow to purchase stores. He was earnest about the ruinous prices of the times, and seemed to think that trade was in a very sad condition indeed. Another man was a spirit-dealer, with an inflamed and pimpled face, which betokened, I fear, too intimate an acquaintance with the commodity he dealt in. These were the only specimens of the male sex present, with the exception of a young lad of fourteen, who, from the answers he made to the grocer's questions, seemed to be going to Glasgow, for the purpose of being bound apprentice there.

We reached the famous Bothwell Bridge before long. Of course I did not know the localities, though I was aware we must cross it soon after leaving Hamilton; but the name of the bridge uttered by one of the passengers attracted my attention, and warned me to be on the outlook. I had so often heard details of the battle fought here from some of the descendants of the very men who had shared in the fight, that it was a spot of much interest to me. Bending forward, I managed, as we crossed it, to obtain a glimpse of the blue waters of the Clyde and the wood-fringed banks; but it was only a passing look, for as none of the others were sensible of my interest, their heads and arms sadly obstructed my view. The little town of Bothwell lies a short way beyond this, and by and bye we passed through its street. Here Miss Strang unfortunately roused herself, and continued awake during the remainder of our journey.

We proceeded very slowly. I think we advanced about the rate of two miles and a half in the hour; consequently, as Glasgow is distant ten miles from Hamilton, it was about twelve when we reached our destination. The road was a good one however, and as the caravan was heavily loaded, we did not suffer much from jolting. Part of the way lay by the bank of the Clyde; but of course from my corner I could see little or nothing of the scenery we were passing through. My opposite neighbour was very troublesome, and I would have been heartily glad that she had fallen asleep again, even at the risk of having her person lodged upon me by some unlucky jolt. She had something caustic to say to every body around her, sometimes about themselves, sometimes about their friends; but no one presumed to contradict her, except the publican, who waxed very wroth at some allusions she made, muttering to himself for minutes afterwards. She at last got up a quarrel with her niece (if that can be called a quarrel which was all on one side) about some message that the latter had forgot to deliver to the servant. It referred to the washing of a certain lilac gown belonging to the old lady, and she could not get over it.

Poor Janet,—she just looked bewildered under the torrent of words. She was evidently hardened to scolding. Winks and smiles passed among the other travellers during the scene. Miss Strang had a pair of very troublesome legs : this might be partly owing to their unusual length, which did not allow them to be easily stowed. They were a sad inconvenience to me, for to give them sufficient room mine were squeezed against the side of the cart into the smallest possible space that would hold them. I looked forward to the end of my journey as to a moment that was to afford me inexpressible relief.

The most wearisome situation must, however, have an end. As minute succeeded minute, and hour hour, I felt I was always getting nearer the time of relief. At length we approached the suburbs of the town we were bound for. Occasional rows of mean houses made their appearance, and the atmosphere, which till then had been pure and clear, began to grow thick and hazy ;—all testified our approach to the even then great manufacturing city of the west. We stopped twice to allow passengers to descend, and then proceeded at the same snail pace. Streets at last began to appear, all more or less dirty and mean however, and occasionally a huge shapeless brick building, with a high chimney, varied the uniformity of the houses. We at last turned into the Gallow-gate, as one of the women called the street in answer to a question of mine on the subject; and speedily emerged from it into the Trongate, a wide noble street, which filled me with admiration when I alighted. But while I remained in the caravan, I of

course could observe little or nothing; and from the
time we entered the town, the rumbling of carts,
the noise made by venders of various commodities,
and the hurry of the foot-passengers, had nearly stupi-
fied me.

We rumbled on for a short way further, passing the
cross with its equestrian statue of King William, of
happy memory, and at length halted just opposite the
steeple of the Tron Kirk. One by one the passengers
got out, till at last my grim neighbour moved off also.
I heard her secure seats for the evening, and she then
walked away with her niece, still grasping her umbrella and basket. My limbs were almost powerless
from their long confinement, but at length I did
manage to descend also; and now I experienced the
dreary uncomfortable feeling creeping upon me of
being a solitary stranger in a large town. The
poor young girl, my fellow-traveller, who was standing forlornly on the pavement gazing about her
before attempting to proceed, drew my attention from
myself. I felt great pity for her; she was so young
and timid-looking. I could not refrain from going up
to her, and, in a kind tone, asking her if she knew the
way to her destination, or had any friend to guide her
to it. She coloured when I spoke to her, as if surprised, and then recovering herself, thanked me in a
grateful manner.

"You are very kind, Mem," she said, "to think o'
me; but Tam the driver promised to my father to see
me safe, and I'm just waitin' till he's ready."

" Have you got a situation?" I inquired.

" Yes, Mem," she said, casting down her eyes, and her bosom swelling at the remembrance, I suppose, of the home she had left, and of the new untried servitude before her. She turned away, and wiped her eyes stealthily with the corner of her shawl. I felt my heart yearn to my poor sister in affliction. I put my hand in my pocket and half drew my purse out. I hesitated, and put it back. Was it right, I questioned myself, on account of mere sympathy with a poor struggling family, however deserving, to deprive myself of what I might erelong feel the need of? " Give, and it shall be given thee," came into my mind with all the force and authority of the divine precept in answer. I pulled out my purse and took five shillings (it was all I could venture to take) from it. I put them gently into the poor girl's hand. She looked up into my face with simple surprise as I did so.

" Send that to-night to your father by the man," I said, " and I trust it will prove an earnest of good to come."

She first glanced at the money in her hand, and then a bright flush glowed on her cheek as she raised her eyes to me.

" Oh, Mem," she said at length in a trembling agitated voice, " ye are owre kind. But if ye ken't our distress ——"

" God will provide for you all, if you trust in him," I answered ;—" Good bye."

I turned away to seek the man.   He was speaking
to one of the passengers.   When he turned from her,
I ventured to remind him of my boxes, and to ask
him to recommend some one to guide me and carry
them.   But just as he was scratching his head in
perplexity, while trying to recollect whom to send
with me, a smart servant girl came up, and after
bestowing an inquisitive look upon me, inquired at
the driver if this was the Hamilton caravan.   Being
answered in the affirmative, she next demanded, with
another shrewd glance at me, if one Miss Douglas
had come by it this morning.

"I am Miss Douglas," I answered, relieved by the
question.

" Are you Miss Douglas?" she said glibly and
without surprise; "I thought sae.   Then I've just
come to show ye the way.   Have ye ony boxes?"

"I had two in the cart," I said.

" Then ye 're to leave them here wi' the man, and
Mr Dalgleish's porter will ca' for them in about an
hour.   Ye 'll tak the things," she continued, turning
to the driver, "into the office there, and let them
stand till we send for them.   Come this way, Miss ;"
and without more words, she prepared to lead the
way down the street.   I followed her as she daintily
picked her steps through the passengers who thronged
around us.   This being the term-day, the streets were
unusually busy, though, of course, I fancied they were
always the same.   I soon grew confused and giddy
with the noise and bustle, but did not like to ask my

companion to pause till I recovered myself, as she seemed indifferent to my accommodation, and perhaps forgot that I was a stranger. She offered me no assistance in carrying the small articles I had brought along with me. I followed her as closely as I could. She went for a short way along the street the cart had come, passing the cross again, and then changed over to the other side. When she did this, she just looked back for a moment to be sure that I observed her, and then led the way on as before. We at last got into a quieter street, along which we walked for a short way; and from it we turned into another, somewhat formal in point of architecture, but handsome and imposing. The houses on either hand were built on nearly the same plan, and were adorned on the summit with stone vases, which had a good effect. The street terminated, I saw, with an iron railing, beyond which appeared trees and green grass. My guide walked down this street for a few yards, and at length paused at one of the houses.

"This is Mr Dalgleish's," she said, speaking for the first time since we left the Trongate.

She drew a latch-key from her pocket and applied it to the lock; the door opened, we walked in, and I found myself at last in my aunt's house.

CHAPTER III.

For life to me had oped its page ; and grief, alas ! had shed
Its dark and chilling bitterness on my devoted head :
I felt this world had other scenes than those I once had known,
And I must share in others' cares if I would shun my own.

MY heart was beating quickly, and a mist seemed over my sight, as I first stood in my aunt Dalgleish's lobby. The rapid manner in which I had been compelled to walk from the Trongate, together with the rush of a thousand painful thoughts into my mind, had nearly overset me. I was in need of a kind reception and the sympathy of friendly hearts to soothe me. But, alas! I could scarcely expect these.

I felt much agitated at the immediate prospect of making my appearance among my unknown relations. I could not tell what kind of girls my cousins might be, or whether I was to meet with cordiality from them or the reverse. I already suspected my aunt's sentiments towards me, and feared that her daughters might also regard my society as a burden. It was a painful thought to me, helpless as I was.

I glanced hastily around me when I entered the

house. The lobby was handsome, though somewhat narrow. The staircase fronted the door. There were several doors on each hand. My guide proceeded to one of them, having only paused to put down a small market-basket which she carried on the table in the lobby. She opened it carelessly, making a sign to me to enter, which I did.

"Mrs Dalgleish and the young leddies are baith out," she then said; "but they will soon be in." She shut the door hastily, as if glad to be rid of her task, and I was left by myself.

It was a relief for the first few moments to find that there was no one to receive me. It allowed me time to collect my agitated spirits. I seated myself in one of the arm chairs which scrupulously guarded each side of the fireplace, and endeavoured to recover myself. A few minutes restored me, and I was able to raise my throbbing head from my hands, and look about me.

I had been shown into the dining-room, I found. I looked anxiously round me, to gather, if possible, some impression of my strange relations from the appearance of the room they inhabited. It was a tolerably sized apartment. The walls and woodwork were freshly painted. They were of a bluish white, highly glazed, with a border of light brown surrounding them, finishing with a kind of ornament in the corners, both above and below. This was the fashionable style of house-painting at the time. The furniture, as Mr Dalgleish had informed me at Auch-

termuir, was quite new, and very showy. It was
evidently well cared for: the brightly polished table
was covered with a tight-fitting wax-cloth, another
protected part of the sideboard, and a brown drugget
hid nearly the whole of a glaring but expensive carpet, in which the colour of red predominated. There
were two large staring portraits of Mr and Mrs Dalgleish, in heavy gilt frames, on the wall opposite the
fireplace. Everything in the room was very formally
arranged. There was a large family Bible in a black
cover on one side-table, and a writing-desk to corre-
spond, upon another. A work - table, with a large
green bag attached to it, stood in one of the windows,
and this was the only sign I could observe of female
occupation. A pair of very handsome candelabra
were on the mantel-piece; hand-screens, with groups
of flowers indifferently painted, were between them.
The grate was brilliant with polished brass, and the
fender and fire-irons were equally glittering. The
room had two windows, but the blinds of both were
drawn down, to meet green Venetian ones which covered the lower half of the panes. This rendered it
dull. The blinds were generally kept down, I afterwards found, my aunt being afraid of the light fading
her carpet. The sideboard stood in a recess which it
just fitted, a pair of cellarets stood upon it, and on
either side were cupboards. I am thus particular,
because my aunt, and all her domestic arrangements,
are inextricably connected in my mind. There
was a closeness in the air of the room; but I had

been conscious since I entered Glasgow of a certain
heaviness and want of elasticity in the atmosphere.
The November sun, which that morning had shone
coldly but clearly in the country, was here almost
obscured by fog, and its feeble beams stole into the
room, mottled and misty.

I sat undisturbed for a considerable time.   No
one appeared.   The house was perfectly quiet, except
when the servants, in going about their work, banged
some of the doors, or let some utensil fall in the kitchen.   The distant roar of the great thoroughfare
from which I had lately emerged, was softened into
a gentle murmur.   The street itself was very still,
though occasionally the sound of a passing foot could
be heard on its pavement, or the shrill cry of " caller
haddies " from some fish-girl, as she slowly traversed
it with her basket.   The echo of children's voices, too,
came from the Green, a piece of ground by the river,
intersected with walks and rows of trees, which was
the property of the public.   I had caught a glimpse
of it from the street as we approached the house.

These distant sounds, like the lulling of falling
water, made me melancholy.   The hum of the city
stilled and saddened me.   I felt strange and solitary
among these new scenes.   It was as if I had fallen
from another planet, and found myself in a world with
which I was perfectly unfamiliar, and which neither
knew nor cared for me.   My soul flew back like a
bird to my old country home, and yearned and panted
for its freedom and retirement.   I was sadly in want

of some one (poor young desolate thing that I was)
to be kind to me, and to soothe and reconcile me to
my change of life. This cold reception, this absence
of my aunt and cousins, when they knew the hour I
would arrive, made me feel I was no welcome guest.
" They might have remembered," I thought, " my
recent loss, if not our relationship." My bodily sensations also concurred to depress my mind. I had a bad
nervous headache, and was miserably cold. The
fire was built up with large pieces of coal, and sent
forth little but smoke. I was afraid to stir it, in case
it might be regarded as a liberty; besides it would
have dirtied the hearth and raised dust. So I sat
shivering beside it, with feet which had not yet recovered sensation after the squeezing of Miss Strang,
and with a heavy heart which would have gladly relieved itself by tears, if I had not been momentarily
in expectation of the arrival of my relations.

At length, when a long time had passed, there
came a ring at the street bell, a quick sharp ring, and
my heart began to beat anew, as I immediately expected my aunt and cousins to walk in. Some one
did enter, and there was a good deal of talking with
the servant in the lobby; but she soon appeared to
return to the kitchen, and no one came near me. I
was in anxious expectation for a few moments, and
then relapsed into my former state of melancholy listlessness. Suddenly a slight noise, as of the turning
of the door-handle, attracted my ear, and I looked
hastily round in that direction. The door was slightly

ajar, and a pair of eyes were busily employed in scanning me through the opening; but whenever they encountered mine, the door was roughly shut, with a rude laugh, and I heard a boy's footsteps immediately after running up the staircase.

"Where 's mama — where 's mama, Hannah?" I heard him presently cry over the bannisters to the servant, as if he had been fruitlessly seeking for his mother. He had to shout this several times before he obtained an answer, and each time was louder than the other.

"Your mama 's no in," was at length screamed back from the kitchen in answer.

"And where 's Jemmy, then?" he demanded in the same key. "If ye mean Miss Jemima, Mister Mat——"

"Ye ken weel enough I mean Jemima."

"Weel, Miss Jemima 's no hame frae Miss Blair's yet."

"And where 's Bob—and where 's Snarl? Ye 'll hae locked him up again, I 'll wager? See, if I dinna——"

"Ye needna speak that gait," she answered, still screaming from the recesses, I supposed, of the kitchen. "Mister Bob has ta'en the dog out wi' himsel', and, weel I wat, I wish he wad drown him. Naebody can keep a house clean for you and him."

"Drown yoursel', you muckle—blockhead!" answered the boy, beginning to descend the stairs, evidently taking two steps at a time; and presently he ran along the lobby, pausing for a moment, however, at the back of the dining-room door, to imitate the braying of an ass for my especial benefit. Then, with a smothered laugh, he opened the street door, and banged it after him as he went out.

"Can this be my future pupil?" thought I with much alarm, as for my further behoof he rattled on the panes of glass, as he ran past the windows on his way to the Green.

The house became silent again after his departure. One had long since struck on the clock in the lobby. Still no aunt. I thought once of ringing the bell and requesting the servant to show me to some room where I could take off my things; but somehow feared to do so, in case it might be regarded as a liberty by the smart-looking damsel who had escorted me here. I then endeavoured to warm myself by cautiously walking up and down the room. I lifted a corner of the blind and looked out; but there was nothing to be seen except the house over the way, with its two windows on each side of the door, and its five above, and the vases that ornamented the roof. An old lady sat knitting at one of the lower windows, and a butcher's boy was handing in some meat out of his basket at the door. A young lady, very showily dressed, passed at the same moment over the way, and nodded to me, evidently mistaking me for one of my cousins. I dropped the blind at length, and turned to the room again for amusement. I opened the large Bible which lay upon the side-table, and found that

the blank leaf contained a register of all the births in
the family. There were seven recorded, but my aunt
had lost two of her children in infancy. I sat down
and examined them. It began with a son. There
were first Robert, then Elizabeth and Margaret, John
and Isabella (the two latter were dead), Jemima and
Matthew. I found that my aunt's eldest son must be
three and twenty, and her youngest (the young gentleman whom I had recently heard, I presumed,)
eleven. The young ladies' ages were twenty-one,
nineteen, and fourteen. It gave me some insight concerning the family; for though I knew that I had five
cousins, I was ignorant of their various ages, and how
they stood in point of seniority to each other. When
I had learned all I could obtain from the record, I
went back to my former seat.

I think another half-hour must have passed, and I
was feeling very sad and solitary, when a sound of
footsteps without, and then a ring at the bell, roused
me once more. I listened intently while the door was
being opened; but at first, from the mixture of voices
which broke upon my ear, I could not be certain that
my aunt was there. As those who entered advanced
farther, however, into the lobby, I recognised her
voice putting some queries to the servant, who answered them; and then I heard her inquire if the porter had come with the things. The girl replied in the
negative. My aunt now entered the dining-room,
followed by her two eldest daughters. I rose tremblingly to meet them.

" How are you, Rose?" said my aunt, shaking
hands with me when I had advanced to meet her. A
warmer reception would have overset my unstrung
nerves at the moment, but my aunt's coolness, as formerly, preserved my composure. " This is. your
cousin Eliza (Mr Dalgleish, by the bye, would never
call her anything but Leezy), and—where 's Maggie
—oh! this is your cousin Margaret. What a cold
day this is!"

She advanced without more conversation to the fire,
and held up her feet in succession to the bars. I
shook hands with my cousins. They were tall stoutly
formed girls, and not ill-looking, having high com-
plexions, though somewhat ordinary features. Both
they and my aunt were dressed in very expensive and
fashionable mourning. My plain black stuff gown,
dark cloak, and straw bonnet, must have looked very
ill, I have no doubt, in comparison. I saw they both
examined me from head· to foot, and I am afraid that
I sank very low in their estimation. In Glasgow, at
that period at least, you were very apt, among the
female population, to be valued according to the
dress you were able to wear. Perhaps my cousins,
however, had no objection to feel their own superiority in this respect to their country cousin. It
assured them that they need not fear I should turn
out a rival.

I again sat down mechanically in my chair, for my
limbs still trembled, and they stood near looking at
me.

" And so, Rose," said my aunt, continuing to warm herself, after giving a slight cautious poke to the bars of the grate, " you have had a long journey—you will be tired, maybe. Maggie, take the keys out of my bag, and bring your cousin a glass of wine. We would have been in sooner, but we had some shopping to do, and I wanted to call for old Mrs M'Callum. Where 's Jemima, I wonder ? " This was addressed to her daughters.

" I don't think she 'll be in yet from Miss Blair's," said my eldest cousin, seating herself in the other arm-chair, and continuing to stare at me, while she twisted her somewhat elaborate curls, of a rather bright hue, round her forefingers. " Jemima seldom comes in till after two o'clock."

My second cousin unlocked one of the cupboards, and brought me a glass of wine and a biscuit on a gorgeous silver salver. I took it thankfully.

" You were once in Glasgow before, cousin Rose, were n't you ? " asked my eldest cousin, who had never yet withdrawn her eyes from me except to glance at her own dress, and smooth down its superfluity of trimming. She put the question in a careless good-humoured kind of way, as if, satisfied with herself, she could afford to be conciliatory to me.

" Yes—I was here six years ago ; but you were not in this house then I think," I said, sighing involuntarily as I thought of the change that had taken place to me since that time.

" Oh ! no," said my aunt, turning her back to the

fire, and glancing proudly round her well furnished
room. "We only came to this house a year ago.
When you were here before with your poor father we
lived in Argyle Street: it was a very good house of
the kind, and very genteel—but not to be compared
to this. This is one of the most fashionable places in
the town."

"There's very few of our acquaintances have such
a house," added Miss Dalgleish, triumphantly, "not
even the Mitchells."

"Yes, but the Mitchells are coming to number
ten," said Miss Margaret, speaking for the first time;
"Jeanie Mitchell told me that yesterday; and, by
the bye, Liza, she's got a bonnet just the same as
the one you wore before we went into these mourn-
ings." "Well, I don't care," said her sister, tossing
her head at this intelligence; "mine'll be old-fashioned before I can put it on again, and Mr M'Callum says I look best in black."

"Well, of course you are right to please Mr M'Callum, Eliza," said my aunt, simpering, and glancing
at me; "we must tell Rose about that before long,
for I look forward to her being a great help while
she's here. But now, girls, you must go away and
take off your things, for it's not far from dinner-time.
Maggie, take your cousin to the room Jemima and
she's to sleep in. There's a press there you can put
your things in, Rose; and be sure you lay every
thing past, for Jemima can't bear things lying about
her room."

I rose instantly, as I was bid, and so did my second cousin.

"Come this way," said she, preceding me into the lobby. There her eye lighted on my boxes, which by this time had been brought to the house. She immediately turned back, leaving me standing at the foot of the staircase.

"Mother,—Mama I mean," she said, correcting herself in a manner which showed that the former word came more naturally to her tongue, "where are Rose's boxes to go? There wont be room for them in such a little hole as Jemima's room."

My aunt seemed irritated. "Rose," she said, "I thought I told you not to bring much luggage,—your cousin's things take up so much room that I can't tell what's to be done for yours." She put out her head at the door, and scrutinized my two poor little boxes, most unpretending they were, I am sure, in point of size. "Well, they are not so big after all," she said; "but I don't think Jemima will like them" (she hesitated a moment);—"tell Hannah to take them up to the garret where the lumber is, Maggie—Rose can easily get anything out of them there when she wants it." She then went back to the dining-room. I was glad to hear that there was some corner allotted for them, even though a lumber garret; and I now followed my cousin submissively up stairs.

There was a tolerably wide landing-place above, carpeted handsomely, and various doors ranged round it. She opened one of them which fronted the stair-

case, for a moment, and allowed me a peep of a trap-
stair which led to the garrets.

" Your boxes are to be taken up there," she said,
" but it will be quite convenient, for this is the room
you are to sleep in."   She shut this door, and opened
another near it.   I followed her wearily into the room.
It was a very small apartment,—smaller even than
mine at Auchtermuir; and indeed it deserved only
the name of a closet.   It was neat enough; but then
its size, considering that it was to be shared with another!

No wonder that I was a little dismayed.   There
was a tent-bed, hung with curtains of a grayish stripe,
which filled up about one-half of the room; there was
a chest of drawers opposite the bed, which allowed
but one person to pass between.   A small table with
a diminutive looking-glass stood in the window, and
there were a single wash-stand and one chair.   The
room could hold no more, and was encumbered with
these.   In the wall there was a press.

" This is Jemima's room," said my cousin; " it is
just beside mother's room, and she has always slept
here.   There was no other place to put you in, for
Liza and me always sleep together, and we have just
one spare room.   I would advise you," she continued,
bluntly, " to make up friends with Jemima, for she 's
a spoiled brat, and is n't over pleased to have some
one put in on her."

I did not know what answer to give to this, so of
course said nothing.   I took the opportunity, while

she was engaged peeping into the water-ewer, and looking if the towel she had put out for my use that forenoon was still there, to glance more earnestly at my companion's face. The expression was not a bad one. There was, I thought, a kind of homely sense and good-nature in her countenance, which greatly resembled her father's. She was rather good-looking too. She had a florid complexion, which threatened to become coarse, however, in a few years; a quantity of fair hair, inclining to red; a round chubby face, and a nose decidedly turned up. It was a good face. It did not promise much intellect or refinement, to be sure, and, indeed, was rather vulgar upon the whole, but it was honest and simple. I was a great physiognomist in my own way, and I felt inclined to like my cousin Margaret.

She left the room to see, as she said, about getting up my boxes, leaving the door wide open behind her. In a few minutes I heard her return with the servant carrying my things. They went bumping up the trap staircase, and presently their feet sounded above me in the garrets. When she had seen them placed, I suppose to her satisfaction, and had taken off her own walking-things, putting on a plainer dress than the one she had worn, she returned to me. I had by this time removed my own bonnet and cloak, and, mindful of my aunt's injunctions, had placed them carefully out of sight in the press in the wall. I was sitting patiently waiting for her reappearance, for of course I could not change my walking shoes till I had access

to my trunks. I asked her to be so kind as show me
the way to them, and afterwards I should be able to
find it myself. She was very civil, and led me up
the trap-stair into a small unfurnished garret, where,
besides a quantity of broken chairs and other invalided
furniture, there were various trunks evidently belonging to the domestics of the family. A place had been
cleared at one end for my boxes. My cousin seated
herself in an easy way on one of the other trunks, and
seemed prepared to watch my proceedings. I would
have preferred her absence, but as I had nothing to
conceal, I knelt down immediately and opened the
box which contained the things I was in need of at
the moment. When I lifted the lid, she bent forward, and without the least idea of rudeness I am
certain, lifted some of the articles which lay uppermost and commented upon them.

" Is that your best frock, cousin Rose?" she said,
examining the sleeve of my best mourning dress,
which I had carefully packed uppermost that it might
not crush. " What a coarse bombazeen!"

" Yes, it is my best," I answered quietly.

" Well, I daresay it's very nice—but that sleeve's
quite old-fashioned now. To be sure it was made up in
the country.—Were n't you glad to leave the country,
cousin Rose?"

I stooped low over my trunk, and shook my head.
" It was my home," I said in a low voice.

" Yes, but people do n't care about leaving their
homes—do they? Liza does not care a bit, I know—

but then she's going to be married, and that may
make a difference.—You did not know that, I daresay—it's a secret yet; but it'll soon be out. But
did n't you find the country very dull?—I hate it."

"That is because you have never lived there," I
said; "if you had been born in the country, perhaps you would have liked it as well as I."

"Well, I hardly think it," she answered carelessly;—"there's no fun, I think, like walking along
the streets, and looking in at the shop windows. Do
you know we have a band in summer that plays every
night in the Green.—I am so fond of the music, and
of walking there, for you meet everybody.—But
Mama took us down to the salt water the best part
of last summer, and I was so vexed.—But Mama did
not think it genteel to be here when the Mitchells
and the Morrisons were away.—Liza did not care,
for she had her beau with her.—Were you ever at
the salt water?"

I answered in the negative, and having by this
time got the things I was in search of, I prepared to
lock my box.

"Oh! the douking's fine fun; but one does n't know
what to do the rest of the day—it's so tiresome sitting on the rocks and looking at the water. Are you
ready to go down then?" rising slowly from the seat
she occupied, yawning loudly, and stretching herself.

"Yes. I had better come up here at bed-time and
get what things I may require then."

"Yes; but you must take great care of the candle,

for mother—tuts—mama's very frightened for fire, and she does n't like lights up here."

" Then perhaps I had better take them out now," I said, hesitating.

" Well, maybe."

As she stood still I again bent over my box and unlocked it. I took out my night-things, and anything else that I thought I might need in the morning. We then descended the staircase : a loud ringing at the door bell was audible as we reached the bottom.

" That's papa and Bob," said my cousin. " You'd better put on your shoes as fast as you can, for father never likes to wait for his dinner."

I heard Mr Dalgleish's voice in the lobby just as she finished speaking, talking and laughing loudly with his son.

" You know the way to the dining-room," she continued; " you can come down when you 're ready :" and she went away.

I hurried into the little room, and nearly knocked myself, on entering, against a young girl who was standing by the foot of the bed, occupied in taking off her walking-things. A work-basket, such as girls carry to school, lay on the quilt. It was my cousin Jemima. She turned hastily round, as I drew back involuntarily on seeing her, and looked curiously and almost impertinently at me.

She was the only one of the girls who decidedly resembled her mother. Perhaps this was one reason why my aunt testified so decided a preference for her.

She was very pretty. Her eyes and hair were black, her features good, though somewhat sharp, and her complexion was fine. But her figure was bad, promising to be short, and what is called dumpy,—however, she was only fourteen then. Unfortunately, there was a peevish, fretful expression in her countenance, which spoiled her good looks.

She did not make room for me to pass her. We stood looking at one another for a second or two.

" You 're our cousin, I suppose ?" she said at length rather pertly, and continuing to stare at me.

" And you are my cousin Jemima—are you not ?" I said gently.

" Yes."

I still stood at the door holding my things in my hands. " May I bring in these," I asked, hesitating, for there was no room to pass till she made way, and she seemed in no hurry.

" I suppose so. I see you have got some of your things in my press already." She rather ungraciously made room for me to pass her, which I quickly did.

" And so you are to sleep here it seems," she suddenly said, her cheeks colouring crimson, and her eyes sparkling; " but mind this is my room in the daytime, and I don't like to see people in it. As for the night, if you choose to sleep at the back, you are welcome enough."

I was startled. She spoke in a very angry voice, very fast and sharp, avoiding, however, to look me in the face while she did so ; and when she had

finished, she pursed up her mouth and turned away.
It was as if she said,—" Now, you know what I
think, and I hope you 'll keep your own place."

The rudeness of my cousin Jemima shocked me.
It was a thing I had never encountered in my life
before.

" I am sorry to disturb you," I replied, when I had
recovered from my surprise, " but I shall have done in
a few minutes." And I hastily proceeded to put on
my shoes. The composure of my manner had an
effect upon her. All violent spirits are more or less
subdued by calmness in others. She said nothing
more ; but she looked sulky, as if she had received
a rebuke.

Of course, I felt far from comfortable,—indeed, very
strange and unhappy. I saw that I had come among
a certain order of people, whose ways and expressions
were alike new, and, if the truth must be told, disagreeable.

Constant intercourse with so gentle and refined a
nature as my father's had made me very fastidious,
and caused me to shrink, not so much from vulgar
expressions, as from vulgar actions and habits of
thought. I felt my heart sinking at the prospect
before me ; and though I had been little more than
two hours in the house, I was already busily anticipating the possibility of soon being able to quit it. And
yet that might not be in my power. But that I
would not think of.

I made as much haste as possible, and then left the

room to my young cousin, who instantly shut to the door after me. The dining-room door was partly open, and as the whole family seemed in the habit of raising their voices to a full pitch in conversing, I had, in spite of all my endeavours to avoid it, the benefit of overhearing what I could not but suppose to be remarks upon myself, as I descended the staircase.

What I heard, made me still more uncomfortable.

" I don't deny but she 's well enough," I heard a voice say, which I thought was my eldest female cousin's, " and that those long fair curls of hers are becoming. But she 's too pale and too small every way to suit my taste."

" That 's maybe because you 're so big yourself," said a loud rough voice which belonged to the male sex ; and he laughed at his own wit.

" I 'm no bigger than I should be, Mr Impudence," she retorted. " But, however, Maggie there thinks she 's very like a lady, and that she 's just fitted to be a governess; she speaks such dreadfully fine English."

" Where did she get it, I wonder ?" asked the same hoarse voice. " I thought she had lived all her days at that old out-of-the-way place among the hills. We 'll astonish her here a bit. Mat, lad, what do ye say to your new governess? I hope you mean to be a good miss,—ha, ha, ha."

" I 'll take lessons from no lassie," replied the boy, in a loud angry voice; " and mama may just pack her out o' the house as soon as she likes."

"Whisht—whisht, bairns!" I heard in their father's
voice, " ye maunna affront your cousin, but show her
what town manners is; it's no her faut, poor thing,
that she's no as weel aff as you."

Just at this moment, while I was hesitating upon
the stairs, unwilling to advance, and yet not knowing
where else to go, my aunt came out of a room below.
She saw me; so I was obliged to follow her into the
dining-room, where all the family were assembled,
with the exception of Jemima. They were gathered
round the fireplace. Mr Dalgleish sat in an arm
chair, my two female cousins were opposite to him,
and a vulgarly smart and most conceited-looking
youth stood before the fire upon the rug, whom my
aunt introduced to me as her son Robert. The boy
Matthew was standing beside his brother when I entered; but the moment he observed me, he walked
away sulkily to the window, as if to avoid speaking
to me. The table was covered for dinner.

Mr Dalgleish greeted me with much heartiness,
expressing his hope that I would soon grow as fat as
either Leezy or Maggie on good Glasgow fare. " Bad
beefsteaks to be gotten in the moors, my dear," he
said with a chuckle: "mair muirfowl than stirks.
Ye're in the richt place here—is n't she, Mrs D.—
hem!" My aunt took, however, no notice, as she
was inquiring at one of her daughters for Jemima.

My cousin Robert assented to his father's remarks
by a loud ha! ha! He was a very disagreeable-look-
ing young man I thought. He was somewhat under

the middle size, and, like his sister Jemima, was dark,
while all the rest of the family were fair. But his
looks were far inferior to hers. He had a sallow, un-
healthy complexion : his eyebrows were very bushy
and swart: his forehead narrow and receding; and
he cultivated a perfect mass of hair both on head and
cheeks. His locks stood out straight and greasy on
each side, and when he raised his chin to settle his
neckcloth, which he did frequently from affectation,
he exhibited another thicket of hair underneath. He
was that disgusting thing, a dirty dandy. But his
self-satisfaction was evidently unbounded. He was
one of the class of coxcombs who will stare a modest
girl out of countenance, and then place her blushes to
the account of his own irresistible perfections. He
was dressed in a very showy style, and he wore a
profusion of ornaments, in the shape of gold chains,
seals, breast-pin, and rings, on his person. But I was
not long in the house till I discovered that his taste
was law to the rest; his mother and sisters regarding him as quite an oracle in fashionable matters. It
struck me, however, that his vulgarity was only
equalled by his ugliness. Matthew was just a great
rough schoolboy—no more fit for me to manage, I felt,
than an unbroken colt.

My cousin Jemima now entered, and my aunt, who
had evidently not seen her since she came from school,
asked her a number of questions, showing her partiality in her manner, which was very different when
she addressed either her or her hopeful eldest son,

than when she spoke to the others. The young lady
received her mother's attentions with much indifference
however.

" Was Miss Blair very strict to-day, Jemima ?"
she inquired, going up to her daughter, and smooth-
ing down some creases in her dress.

" Oh ! as cross as two sticks," said the young lady.
" I wish, mama, I was done with the school. I 'm
sure I 'm old enough."

" You wont be there long, darling. But you must
first embroider the globes, and when they 're done,
we 'll get them framed and hung up."

" But it 's so tiresome." She went up peevishly
to the fireplace, without taking further notice of any
one, and sat down beside her brother, who continued
to stare at me, and to talk with his father at intervals,
probably thinking he was making a strong impression
upon the simple country stranger. I had scarcely
opened my lips since I entered the room, and sat rather
apart from the rest. My cousins Eliza and Margaret
were both occupied again in minutely examining me,
and let me sit in silence.

Dinner was now brought in, and we were immediately placed at table. The dinner was very plentiful,
but was somewhat heterogeneous, and the dishes
clumsily arranged. After dinner, Mr Dalgleish
and his son had hot whisky-toddy ; and when
they had finished, went off again to their warerooms.
They did not return till pretty late in the evening—I
should say Mr Dalgleish, for his son did not return

with him. My cousin Margaret informed me that he generally went to a select club of young men, which met almost every night.

After dinner, I was entertained by the two eldest girls, who did nothing in the way of work all evening, with an account of Eliza's engagement. My aunt was absent from the room for a long time, and, in her absence, they got quite chatty and confidential.

" Only think, cousin Rose," said Eliza, " what a fortunate thing for you that you have come here just now—to be at the wedding and all? It will be so gay for you after the dull life you have led all your days in the country. Besides, as mama says, you will be so helpful in the sewing that will have to be done."

This speech of Eliza's at least made me aware what my aunt expected from me. I was glad to know it. Eliza went on at great length talking of her future relations, and of the wedding-dresses she expected to have, evidently supposing I was listening with much interest. But my thoughts had wandered far away from the subject, and her words fell on an unconscious ear.

At eight o'clock, by which time I was feeling very tired, and was longing for the hour of rest to come, although I dreaded sharing Jemima's bed, Mr Dalgleish walked in, accompanied by Eliza's intended, whom he had encountered at the street door. He entered the lobby with one of his loud laughs, and forthwith ushered him into the room, slapping him energetically on the back as he did so.

" Here, Leezy," he cried with another roar, " here 's
a fallow I 've brought to ye.   There, awa owre wi'
ye.—I 'll get nae good o' ye noo that ye 're amang the
women."

Mr M'Callum, Eliza's fiancé, was in my eyes a very
different person from what her very laudatory description would have led me to picture.   He was a man
considerably above thirty, stout in his figure, with a
ruddy good-natured countenance, and hair inclining
already to baldness.   The difference in their ages was
considerable ; but then he was a good match.

Eliza simpered and giggled at her father's speech,
and at the entrance of her betrothed ; and I saw she
turned her eyes on me to read my good opinion of the
gentleman.   He approached her, and looked at me,
who sat near her.   " Oh, it is just my cousin from
the country," said Eliza, carelessly, observing the
look.   He shook hands with me, then with Margaret
and Jemima, and afterwards sat down by his liege
lady.   She affected to feel very much astonished to
see him at that time, and played off a number of
airs and pretty tricks, which young ladies sometimes
think necessary on such occasions.   But she was evidently very glad to have this opportunity of parading
her lover before me.   Mr Dalgleish was in high spirits,
and made many jokes on the situation of the pair ;
and at last, when my aunt re-entered the room, he
asked her to get a " Finnan haddie " or something
to supper, and a bottle of the old ale.

Perhaps my aunt considered it imprudent to allow

me to be on an entire equality with the family; perhaps she thought I would be fatigued, but she soon gave me a private hint that I had better retire to bed. I was thankful to avail myself of the permission; and being directed where to get a candle, I slipt out of the room and went up stairs. I shut the door of the little bedroom, and sat down, thankful that the day was over. It had not been the best commencement. Well, well, I must be patient, I concluded. Providence had led me here, and if I was to be placed elsewhere, he would open the door. I determined to make myself useful, as was expected of me, and to let no false pride stand in the way of being so. Independence before every thing. But I was very lonely and very dejected. I felt that I was alone in the world, a solitary speck on the great ocean of life,—in short, that saddest of all things, a burden to my friends.

I crept carefully to the extreme back of the small tent-bed, to leave plenty of room for my spoiled cousin; and being worn out with the occurrences of the day, I soon fell asleep, long before Mr Dalgleish could have half finished his supper.

CHAPTER IV.

Ah! youthful hopes, that eagle eyed
Did not refuse to face the sun,
Delusive hopes! ye all are gone,
Receding like yon ebbing tide.
Like this, my strand of life is bare,
With weeds and strange unsightly things
Strewed o'er; and coming evening flings
Its lengthening shadows on the air.

AND now commences an epoch of my life on which I
do not like to look back. I have had a melancholy
pleasure in retracing my earlier experiences, but this
period I would willingly pass over. It is painful to
me to think of; but as I am professing to write my
history, I must go on, however unwillingly. It shall
be as briefly as possible. Fortunately the period was
not of long duration.

No change of life could have been greater than now
occurred to me. There was not only change of scene
and interest, but the people around me were entirely
different from all I had been accustomed to. Their
tone of mind was new to me, and I could not sympathize with it. In Mr Dalgleish's family, the power
and consequence which wealth secures was the ruling
idea. In my simple life I had so little opportunity for

spending money that the want of it was not felt, and I was pretty indifferent to its possession. Here it was all in all. Nothing was of so much consequence as money. This was new to me.

Then all I had been taught to reverence and value, religion, literature, the mental riches which great minds pour out from their own fulness upon the world, the wealth of the soul—these, I found, were nothing to them. It bewildered me.

Then my position in the family was a trying one. From the first I was placed in humiliating situations, and made to feel (my aunt thought it a duty she owed to her children) my dependence. And I *was* a dependent. I trust I was grateful for food and shelter, and I did try to recommend myself to my aunt and cousins, though I was never very successful.

I had a long conversation with my aunt the morning after my arrival; and she then made me clearly to understand what position I was to hold in the house. Teaching Matthew was evidently out of the question, and I tacitly acknowledged this; but my services were highly desirable at present I found in assisting to get Eliza's wedding paraphernalia ready. This, with some charge in household matters, my aunt informed me, would occupy me till perhaps something turned up. I thanked her as I would have done a stranger, and endeavoured to be grateful.

I was soon set to my work. There was a spare bedroom on the dining-room floor, and there I was sent to be out of the way of the family and their visiters.

It was a chill dull room at the back of the house, looking out on a long strip of drying-green, with a narrow flower-border running down each side. What a contrast to my old garden! It was a handsomely furnished room; but it was cold and cheerless, and I was allowed no fire.—My aunt was an economist in little matters. I was often obliged to sit with my feet doubled under me upon my chair, to preserve some warmth in them, and to chafe my fingers to restore their circulation. I had been accustomed to a great deal of exercise, and now I seldom had any. My cousins had their own companions, and never took me out with them. Indeed I seldom saw them, except at meal-times, unless there was any service they wished me to do for them, and they came to the room I sat in for the purpose. They were not unkind to me, at least the elder ones; but they knew I was poor, and they did not treat me as their equal. Margaret I continued to like best. She was more sensible and good tempered than Eliza, who was something of a slatternly fine lady, and too much engrossed at present by her approaching marriage to think of any one but herself. My eldest cousin, Robert, I did not like, and shrank from whenever we met. But they were all civil to me, with the exception of Jemima and Matthew. The former was a spoiled girl, and Matthew never ceased resenting the intention of imposing me upon him as governess. My aunt sometimes checked their rudeness; but she evidently did not consider it worth much attention, and would have been astonished, I believe, if I had showed any feeling regarding it. Mr Dalgleish always spoke kindly to me, but I saw him for a few minutes only each day. My aunt seldom allowed herself to say harsh things to me, unless she happened to be peculiarly irritable. She was pleased with the amount of work I performed, and as I made no complaints, did not fancy, I suppose, that I wanted for anything.

Ah! how little did they dream of the sad heart that was silently wasting itself away among them, or the yearning wishes for companionship and sympathy that were doomed never to be satisfied. Day after day did I sit ceaselessly plying my needle in that cold dull bedroom, thinking over the past and earnestly considering the future. Was it always to be thus? I had a craving desire to open my heart to some one, to get partly relieved from the burden of my sensations by communicating them to others; and if my cousins had but shown a slight degree of interest in me, I would gladly have done so; but though they were always ready to talk on their own concerns to a quiet listener like me, they never testified any curiosity regarding mine. My spirits drooped exceedingly. I grew timid and nervous; and at length, from being much alone, got to dislike company and to covet solitude. I began to fear that a situation would never turn up, and that I should sink into a mere sewing automaton for the rest of my life. Sometimes I ventured to inquire of my aunt if she had yet heard of a situation for me, but I was always answered in the negative; and I half suspected that she now turned an unwilling ear to the subject. Some weeks' residence in the house had accustomed her to my presence, and she found me useful. I began to fear she did not wish to part with me.

How I used to long for the return of Sabbath. I had no work upon that day—it was all my own. But I was sadly shocked by the manner of spending it in my aunt's house. My relations paid little attention to religious duties. The young people were entirely engrossed by dress and visiting; my aunt by her family and position in society; and Mr Dalgleish with his business and his old cronies. He was a West Indian merchant, and held, I believe, a high place among mercantile men. He must have been rich, for he was very generous to his wife and daughters, who, however, never dreamt of bestowing their superfluous means in charitable purposes, except perhaps to some ostentatious charity where the act was sure to become public.

Sabbath in Mr Dalgleish's house was much like any other day, except that it afforded better opportunities of exhibiting any new piece of dress. We all went to church regularly, with the exception of Robert, who always disappeared early on that day and did not return till late. Indeed, Mr Dalgleish would sometimes slip away before the bells began to ring for church, and shut himself for the forenoon in his place of business. But it was done privately, and with a view to appearances. At such times it was always to be understood that he was indisposed. Half a century earlier, the citizens of Glasgow were remarkable for their severe and even rigid observance of the Sabbath. Such doings as Mr Dalgleish's and his son's would then have been sought out and exposed. But times were changed, and much laxity had crept in.

The family sat in the Wynd Church (now gone), under the ministry of Dr Porteous. Warrander Balgairney, a kind of character at that time in Glasgow, was beadle there, and having once or twice heard my father preach, he established a kind of acquaintanceship with me. I was grateful then for this rude friendship.

We spent the day thus. Between the morning and afternoon discourses, we returned home and had what my aunt called a chack,—now-a-days it would be named lunch; and at night we had a hot supper in amends for the want of our regular dinner, which invariably consisted, I think, of roast-fowls and potatoes, and at which I was permitted to be present. Mr M'Callum was often a guest at these times. Sabbath evenings were spent by my cousins in listless idleness, lounging over the fire, yawning and making remarks on the acquaintances whom they had met at church. My aunt, however, used to read in the large family Bible which, during the rest of the week, lay unopened on the side-table. Mr Dalgleish, of course, passed the evening with his family; but if none of his friends happened to drop in, he generally slept in his

chair till supper was ready. How the servants employed themselves, I know not; but it was a bad
example that was set to them.

It was a change from the Sabbaths I had formerly
spent, and I often thought with a sigh on the little
simple congregation assembled at Auchtermuir. In
imagination I pictured all the well-known faces in
their old places, the quiet dismissal, and the sober
walk home of many a pious cottar, and his evening
exercises with his family around the peat fire. It was
no fancy picture, for I well knew that it existed. I
wished myself among them. I was beginning already
to feel the deadening effect of the scenes which I wit-
nessed, and feared that at last I might get habituated
to them. It is by little and little that the heart gets
hardened. Still I strove against the evil current of
example as I best could, though by this I exposed
myself to many a sarcasm on my pretensions to superior sanctity. Even the servants taunted me. But
they treated me with contempt because I was poor,
and had no shillings nor old dresses to bestow upon
them,—because I was neither one of themselves (they
might have tolerated me in that case) nor yet privileged to be idle like a lady.

I used to slip away on the Sabbath evenings to the
garret where my boxes lay. It was a very little dis-
mal place, having no ceiling but the naked joists
above, so low that they nearly touched my head; but
it had the charm of solitude. It was a little Bethel
to me.

A small window in the roof, much pieced and dirtied, allowed me a dim light to read. It was sweet to sit and meditate here in quiet—to unite heaven and my old home in my thoughts—and to bear those dear friends I had left behind me there upon my heart before God. Those Sabbath evenings strengthened me for the trials of the coming week. I felt that the future was in God's hand, and I was willing to leave it there. Present duty was mine.

The family had many visiters, but I saw none of them. If any one was invited to tea, my tea was brought to me in the bedroom; but if the family were alone, I was allowed to bring my work into the dining-room, as it saved additional candles. My cousins disliked work, and generally passed the evening in gossip. Eliza sometimes read novels, for circulating libraries had already come into existence. But, however they might be employed, I was generally left to sit in silence.

There were two sisters of Mr Dalgleish's, old maiden ladies, who were often at Charlotte Street, and drank tea there at least once a-week. When they or Mr Archibald M'Callum were there I was permitted to be present, as there was no ceremony required. But I always retired before supper.

These ladies were rather peculiar. Miss Jemima, the elder, was a lively little woman, with much activity both of body and mind. She was always hearing news and retailing them; and as their old servant Katy was as active in collecting intelligence as herself, she was a perfect walking chronicle. She seemed to be ubiquitous, for she knew almost as well as her acquaintances (and they were not few) what occurred in their several houses.   People stood in awe of Miss Jemima—and they had reason.

But there was one most excellent point in her character—her affection for her sister.   When I first met with these ladies, the elder appeared to be a woman of sixty ; Penelope, the younger, might be forty-five. Miss Jemima still, however, considered her sister as a mere girl.   She spoke of her generally as " that lassie Penny," and privately—for they were on their good behaviour before them—it was a subject of much mirth among their nephews and nieces.   But Penny, poor thing, was somewhat weak in her intellect, and her sister had so long cared for her, that she felt as a mother towards her.   She seemed to be jealous on Penny's account, and was apt to get irritated at any want of attention shown to her.   She quoted her wise sayings ; and Penny, like most silly people, did occasionally utter sententious remarks with a profound air.   I have no doubt that Miss Jemima had gradually deceived even herself as to the amount of her sister's capacity, and now regarded her somewhat in the light of an oracle.

Penny bore the marks of imbecility in her countenance.   She had light lustreless eyes, and a vacant expression.   She was also slightly deformed in figure.

These ladies possessed a small independence, and lived in a respectable way with only one servant. It would have been difficult to have discovered three more narrow-minded, wealth-worshipping, inquisitive, tattling, old maids in the kingdom. Their nieces and nephews stood all high in their good graces, but Jemima was the favourite, being her elder aunt's name-daughter.

Jemima made her aunts the confidants of all her grievances, and they petted and indulged her even more than did her mother. She visited them almost daily.

I saw these ladies for the first time a few days after I arrived in Glasgow. They were invited to tea to see some of Eliza's wedding purchases, for they took great interest in sights of that kind. Miss Jemima examined me narrowly when we first met, but I soon ceased to attract her attention, for I was only Mrs Dalgleish's poor niece.

Miss Jemima was a shrewd little woman. While she picked up much tittle-tattle, she also occasionally gleaned some things worth listening to. Her reminiscences of her youth were not devoid of interest. She had rather a happy way of relating a story. I vividly remember one she told that night. Mr M'Callum had dropped in, and they were all seated in a circle round the fire. Tea was over. I was busy at the table with my work, silently listening to the conversation that was going on.

I do not now recollect what it was that suggested the tale, but Miss Jemima at length proposed to tell Mr M'Callum a remarkable occurrence which took place in her young days.

"Ye see, Mr Archibald," she said, hitching her chair nearer to the fire as she spoke, and making herself comfortable before she began, " it 's a very auld story now, for at the time it happened I dinna think I was passing Jemima's age—it 's before maist o' ye here were born.—Ye 've been speakin' the nicht o' folk being buried alive—weel, this leddy that I hae to tell o' was very near it. Ye ken our house in the Stockwell, Mr Archibald—ye were once in it wi' Eliza— weel, it happened there. It wasna our house then, but it belanged to a Mr M'Glashan, who selt it afterwards to my father, and it was in the room I now sleep in that the thing happened."

"Are you no frightened, aunt, to sleep there?" asked Margaret.

"Hout no," replied Miss Jemima, " I never dread sights, though to be sure I have mony a time pictured the body lying stretched oot in my room, and then—but I maun begin wi' the beginning. Ye see, then, about forty years since, or I think it maun be forty-five, this house o' ours was let furnished by Mr M'Glashan to an English colonel—Colonel Myres they ca'd him. I hae seen him mysel', for we lived in Dowie's land at that time, at the corner, pretty high up; and mony a time we bairns, for I had then a brither and a sister aulder than mysel', Mr Archibald, though they 're baith gane noo (and Miss Jemima heaved a sigh), used to watch the grand-looking colonel, wi' his sword at his side, coming up frae the Stockwell—sodgers are aye an attraction to bairns.

Weel, the colonel took this house, and brought his leddy to it. She was a genty delicate-like creature, they said that telt me, and had aye a sorrowfu' kind o' look aboot her face, as if she had some sair heart-trouble; and nae wonder, for if a' stories be true, she had muckle to bear frae her ain gudeman. There was some property that was to come to the colonel if he had an heir, or it was to gang to the bairn,—I dinna mind which it was: but, however, muckle depended on the colonel's having a son. They had been married for some years however, and there seemed nae prospect, and they said he used her very ill in consequence, though it wasna her fault, poor woman, for I have nae doot she would have been glad enough to please him.—I'm sure it was a reflection on God Almighty, but the colonel thought little o' that. Weel, the leddy when she came to the house was in a very dwining way, and she aye got weaker and weaker, (she had nae freends, poor thing, wi' her), till at last she wasna able to leave her ain room, but lay maist pairt in her bed. She had a maid they ca'd Ritson (they were a' English folk), and Ritson just waited alane upon her there. Sometimes the colonel would gang in to see her, and sometimes no; and they said he was just weary till the breath gaed oot o' her body. I am sure I hae sometimes almost grat at the thocht o 't when I was sitting in my room. I little dreamt when I saw him in his braw regimentals gaun doon the street what a black-hearted vagabond he was. Weel, as I was saying, she got aye

weaker and weaker, and they were constantly waiting on for death, and I 've nae doot the colonel rejoicing in his heart, and looking forward to be soon rid
o' her, and to another marriage, (she had married him,
poor woman, against the wishes o' her freends), when
a letter comes down to him on business requiring
him to gang up immediately to London.   Weel, he
couldna wait, and besides what was a deein' wife to
him ? sae he just telt the servants to look sharp after
everything, and to write to him when the thing happened.—But this wasna a', for he gaed to the undertaker, that was Tummas Mortcloth, the father o'
John that now is, and is carrying on his father's auld
business (he was a decent sponsible man, Tummas) ;
and he telt him what was expected, and warned him, as
Tummus was often oot wi' the stretching-brod, for he
had a grand trade, that he might gie a ca' occasionally,
and see how things were getting on. ' And,' says he,
' you 'll no hae to do it lang.'   So he gied him directions aboot the burial, and wha were to be invited,
in case he shouldna be down in time himsel'—Poor
leddy !

   " Weel, the colonel went awa, and though the
leddy aye got weaker and weaker, it was just wonder-
ful how she kept on.   The heart, weak as it was, was
sweir to break.   I'm telt that the servants kept up
a great galravitching during the colonel's absence,
and the cook and the flunky were seldom sober—
(awfu' doings in a sick-house),—but at any rate Ritson watched carefully owre her mistress.   She was a

staid quiet woman, and they said, even the colonel stood in awe o' her at times. But she had nae authority owre the rest, and deed was seldom oot o' her mistress's room.

"Tummas ca'd occasionally by the colonel's orders; but a week and then a fortnight gaed by, and then three weeks, and the leddy was leevin' still. The servants began, they said, to be frichted aboot what the colonel would say, for he was certain to be back in six weeks frae the time he gaed awa; and if he found his wife living, he was like to make a het house o' 't. Weel, just at the end o' the four weeks, as Tummas was one morning passing that way hame wi' the straighting-brod on his shouther, for he had been awa laying oot a corpse, he thocht he wad ca', though the man was beginning to feel affronted to do it, and inquire how the leddy was. The flunky opened the door (and for a wonder he was sober), and when he saw Tummas standing at it in a kind of hesitating way, he says, says he, ' Ye had better come in,' says he, ' for the leddy 's just going.' Weel, he pu'd him in, and set him doon in the kitchen, where the cook and a lassie that did the dirty wark o' the house were baith sitting greeting. However, Tummas was used to seeing sichts o' distress, and he didna think muckle o' their sincerity, I hae heard. Ritson and the doctor were their lane wi' the deeing woman.

" ' Ye 'll no hae lang to wait,' says the flunky, speaking low, just in the same words almost that his maister had used some weeks before. Tummas put the

straighting - brod against the wall, and sat down
doucely to wait till he was needed. But an hour
passed by, and maist pairt o' anither, and the leddy
still was in life. At last Tummas says, says he,
' I 'm fear't I 'll need to gang, for I 've to meet a
gentleman on business at one o'clock. I 'll leave this
here," says he, meaning the brod, ' for it 's a pity to
tak' it awa, since it 's sae sune to be needed, and ye
can let me ken when the event happens ' (Tummas aye
used grand words).   The flunky made nae objections,
and said he would set it oot o' the way ben the house.
And weel I wat, for a' their expectation, it stood in
Penny's room against the wa' three days before it was
needed. But Tummas Mortcloth aye thocht it wad
be wasting time to tak' it hame, when it was like to
be needed where it was every minute. She maun
hae had a strange constitution the leddy.

" Weel, at last the leddy gied up the ghost, and
Tummas was duly summoned. Ritson, — and the
woman was clean dune oot wi' watching sae mony
nichts, and wi' grief for her mistress, for she had been
wi' her mony years, — Ritson, I say, drest the corpse,
and then Tummas took the measurements, and a' was
got ready for the burial, and the letters sent to the
freends, — at least what freends they had in the town
(she had nane, poor woman), — but he had some acquaintances. The flunky wrote to his master ; but it
was expected he would have left London before the
letter could get there, and would arrive at least in
time for the burial. Weel, she was to be buried in

the High kirkyard, and her very grave was dug. I
mind seeing the corner where it was, for it had to be
filled up after, and muckle vexation it gave to John
Howkit, the bethral. 'It was cheating the grave,'
he said. Of course the grave wasna got ready till the
day before the funeral was to take place,—and that
very day the colonel cam' hame. I dinna ken how
he looked whan he heard his wife was dead (it
was the man that telt him); but I can guess gey
and weel how he felt. But his punishment was
awaiting him,—the vagabond that he was. He had
brought a freend wi' him; and it was telt me, that
they were baith very merry that nicht owre their
wine, and that one wouldna hae thocht there was
death in the house.

"Weel, though of course the leddy was chested, wi'
the expectation o' the colonel arriving, the lid hadna
been screwed doon; and next morning, that he might
seem to do a' things decently in the eyes of the world,
I suppose, the colonel went in to take a last look o'
his wife,—his freend was wi' him. She was laid oot
in her braw shroud, and wi' the face-cloth owre her,
in her coffin. A grand coffin it was, I believe, for
Tummas had put on it the best o' muntin', and her
name was on the lid, and her age thirty-five. Ritson
had telt them that, for of course naebody but her or the
colonel kent it. Weel, the colonel stood beside his
wife's coffin. It was placed on a table, I hae heard.
Weel I wat I hae often looked at the place, just be-

tween the bed and the door, sae that when the door was
open, the coffin was right forenent you. The colonel
lifted aff the cloth frae the face, and looked at it. He
had a cruel heart that Colonel Myres. One would
hae thought, now that the poor leddy was gone, he
would hae felt a kind o' pity, no to say remorse, for
the life he had led her for sae mony years, for nae
transgression o' hers, considering, too, that she had
gi'en up a' her ain folk to follow him. But he had
nae sic feeling. He was owre glad to be rid o' her.
He couldna even keep his thoughts to himsel'. 'But,'
says he to his freend, that stood by him, shrugging
up his shouthers as he spoke, and regardless o' the
dead corpse before him that might hae quieted him,
says he, 'we led a very miserable life together,' says
he. 'She was a woman for whom I could have no
affection, and, to tell the truth, for there 's no use in
making a pretence, Weston,' or whatever his freend's
name might be, 'I am much relieved that she 's
gone.' Do ye no wonder that the corpse didna look
up in his face and scaur him as he said it, the hardened villain? I dinna ken what his freend answered.
I hope he didna agree wi' him; but the colonel put
back the crimped cloth, that was a' neatly cut oot by
Tummas's shopwoman, on to the face again, and awa
they went baith oot o' the room,—the colonel never
thinking to see his wife's face again, if he thocht
onything aboot it ava, till the day of judgment.—I
dinna suppose, however, that he believed in such a

day, or he would have been mair particular aboot the reckoning he was to gie in. They left the door open ahint them, for the undertaker's men were in the house, and they were just waiting to come ben to screw on the lid,—it was a mercy it had been left sae lang. Weel, the colonel and his freend gaed ben to the parlour to wait for the arrival of the folk; but they had scarcely got into the room, when there was a loud skreigh through the house, and somebody tumbled outright in the passage, and then there was a hurry-skurrying o' feet, and another scream, and the colonel and the gentleman baith rushed oot to see what the matter was. And, oh! sirs," continued Miss Jemima, raising her hands in the earnestness with which she told the tale, "when they got to the leddy's door again, for the skirls cam' frae there, what did they see? The flunky was lying outside the door in a faint, and Ritson, wi' a face like a sheet, haudin' by the side o' 't, as if she wad fa', and *there—there*— through the open door was the leddy hersel' sitting up in her coffin, and struggling, puir thing, to get her hauns freed, wi' a countenance sae white and ghastly, that naebody that saw it could ever forget it,—and nae wonder. But she was alive for a' that.

"She had been in what they ca' a trance; and deed she micht ne'er hae come oot o 't, they said, but been buried alive as thae folk ye were talking about, if her husband's cruel words owre her very coffin hadna broken the spell. She had heard them a', and every thing else that was spoken beside her, and she

kent she was in her coffin. Poor woman! what a
state her mind must have been in a' the time she lay
there, kenning what was before her. But the Lord
was mercifu', and didna permit it. I suppose she had
come to hersel' just as the colonel left her room, for
the flunky, who passed the door immediately after,
looking just carelessly in as he gaed by, was terrified
to see the dead woman's haun lifted up abune the
coffin, and moving this way (and Miss Jemima waved
her hand backwards and forwards slowly in imita-
tion). His skreigh brought Ritson to the spot, for
she was coming at ony rate to take a last look at her
mistress, and by that time the man had fainted after
seeing her rise up in her coffin. Aweel, she recovered at that time, and lived six years after. But
she and the colonel never met again. Whenever she
was fit to travel, she and Ritson went to England,
where she had some freends, and the colonel had to
allow her a maintenance. But they said she was
never more seen to smile, but just lived on in a
broken-hearted kind o' way.

"As for the colonel, ane can guess gey and weel how
he felt. When he was convinced his wife was living,
they said, he merely uttered a great oath, and turned
about and strode out o' the house. He went awa'
abroad soon after, and I never heard what came o'
him. But it made an unco stir in Glasgow at the
time, and Tummas Mortcloth had to take back the
coffin, gettin' half price for 't, and as for the burial-
bread that was provided, the servants gied it awa' to

their freends. But I hae heard that auld Mrs Shaw, who died soon after, was buried in Mrs Myres' coffin, Tummas, of course, having altered the plate. Weel, bairns, isna that a queer story?" said Miss Jemima, when she had finished.

CHAPTER V.

The roseate hues of morn are fled,
The glow of noon hath passed away;
And youthful dreams, as bright as they,
Are faded all—and some are dead.
And why is this? they were of earth,
And nought of earth can lasting be:
They might be noble, might be free;
But died, because of mortal birth.

Six weeks had now passed away since I had entered
Glasgow.   What a long period they seemed on looking back!   From almost constant confinement and
the uneasiness of my mind, I lost my appetite, and
grew pale and thin.   But no one appeared to notice
the change.   My spirits also drooped more and more.
I grew terrified at the prospect of illness. What
should become of me if this happened?

At length I summoned courage to ask decidedly of
my aunt whether she had yet made any inquiries
after a situation for me.   I received for answer that
she had not, nor did she think it necessary to do so.
She had assured me, as I might remember, at the
first, that I was not fit for one; and she concluded by
advising me to dismiss the subject from my mind, as
she wished me to remain where I was.

My heart sank within me at this answer. I saw clearly that I had now nothing to hope from my aunt's exertions on my behalf, and a kind of despair settled down on my mind.

My aunt, who considered food and shelter such great benefits, had no idea, I am persuaded, but that she was discharging a most exemplary duty to her niece, thrown thus helplessly on her hands. Indeed, I believe that she received much commendation from the circle of her acquaintance for her generosity.

Ah! neither they nor she thought of the loneliness of the orphan girl even among her young relations, the petty slights so irritating to the feelings, the heart-weariness in the strange place, where all was new and uncongenial, that were her daily portion, or the amount of labour that was required of her. I alone knew how much I had to be grateful for, and how much to forgive. I earned my bread, and it was watered with my tears.

I used to ruminate on these things as I sat solitary over my work in that cold handsome spare room, and weep over the days that were gone till my eyes grew so dim as scarcely to enable me to put in my needle. My affections became frozen from want of sympathy in others, and I daily grew more silent and reserved.

I had also a new subject of annoyance. My cousin Robert's behaviour distressed me. This young man insulted me by private attentions. It required all the dignity I could assume to keep him at proper distance. It never seemed to occur to him, however, that I was displeased. His self-love evidently ascribed my coldness to my bashfulness and country breeding ; and the farther I retired the more he pursued. What his object was I know not. But he was constantly on the watch for me on the staircase and passage ; and when my aunt and cousins were out, I dreaded his return to the house for fear he should intrude himself upon me. This also at last made me reluctant to go out, though that was a privilege I rarely enjoyed, for once I had encountered him on the Green, and he had conducted himself with insolent familiarity. Before his mother and sisters he was jealously guarded ; and this made me fear him. I felt painfully my unprotected state, for I could not venture to complain to my aunt of his conduct.

I don't know what I might have sunk to in my aunt's house : perhaps finished in the course of time with being installed in the kitchen, and died in effect to every one who had formerly known me,—perhaps pined away by degrees like Shakspeare's Barbara, though for a different cause ; and at last, after a troublesome though probably short illness, been laid by the side of my infant cousins in the Ramshorn kirkyard, and forgotten for ever, if something had not arisen which infused new life into me, and made me somewhat like Rose Douglas again.

Oh ! sweet Annie Campbell ! you were like a sunbeam breaking in on the melancholy gloom of my

cheerless life! Even the dull back bedroom was illu-
minated by it; and as for my poor heart, it opened a
fresh spring of affection in it which has never dried
up since. Even now, with your neatly crimped cap
and silvery hair, a meek and placid matron, you have
the same look, and the same gentle voice, whose kind
tones sounded so strange but pleasant then to my
ears.

One cause of my despondency had been, that I had
heard nothing from my old home since I had left it.
While I was undergoing the thousand petty annoyances and daily drudgery of my aunt's house, the
knowledge that my memory was still cherished by my
early friends would have been as balm to my weary
spirit. If I could have felt secure in their affection
and remembrance, I would have still been hopeful and
resolute. But seeing no one connected with them,
and hearing nothing, I began at last to feel that fearful vacuum of soul—that terrible listlessness with
which the friendless are occasionally visited. My
heart, which had yearned for some weeks over the
scenes and the persons I had left behind, began now
to droop,—droop, till all its strings were relaxed and
nearly breaking. If this state of things had continued
long, I would have become a mere passive machine—
or died. I did my friends injustice. But I could not
place myself in their position to understand this, and
they were not aware at that time what I endured.

Of course I had heard of the success of the sale at
the manse. Mr Dalgleish's punctilious regard to

business had induced him to make me perfectly con-
versant with all concerning my own affairs. It had
been only tolerably brisk. But everything was disposed of, and now three hundred pounds, being partly
the proceeds of the sale and partly my father's sav-
ings, remained to me after all obligations were discharged. It was a small sum, as Mr Dalgleish, accustomed to wealth, seemed to think; but I was
thankful to possess even that. It stood between me
and want.

There was no talk now on my aunt's part of its
being devoted to the acquiring of those accomplishments which were to provide for my future maintenance. She had changed her mind since the time
she had proposed that. My assistance in the house
was too valuable to allow leisure for such a project.
My cousins, whom I had relieved from many duties
which formerly devolved upon them, did not like to
resume them, now that they had tasted the sweets of
idleness. The piano, in spite of my aunt's promise
regarding it, stood in its green covering, silent and
unopened, in the tawdry showy drawing-room, which,
except on the rare occasion of a dinner-party, or the
more common occurrence of a tea-drinking, was seldom entered, save to be dusted by the servant. Some
of my cousins occasionally made a pretence of repair-
ing thither to practise; but as they generally spent a
greater time before the mirror which occupied the
space between the windows, than in drawing sweet
sounds from the instrument, it could scarcely be con-

sidered as more than a show piece of furniture: And, I think, the extent of my cousins' musical acquirements consisted merely in being able to perform some but indifferently executed reels and strathspeys.

But I must now inform the reader what caused the fortunate reaction in my mind and spirits. It was just the day before Christmas, that, as I was sitting sad and solitary at my work, my aunt and cousins being all out, a ring came to the street door. The family had so many visiters, that I never thought of paying any attention to the circumstance; and of course I expected no one to call for me, so I was greatly surprised when Hannah carelessly opening the bedroom door, put in her head for a moment, and said, " Somebody wanting to see you."

Such an unexpected announcement caused me a universal tremor, and I breathlessly awaited the entrance of the visiter, hoping to see some familiar face, though which I could not guess. There was a light step on the threshold, and then a young lady entered, who was a perfect stranger to me. She advanced timidly into the room. She was very young and gentle-looking; and her face had all the soft roundness and child-like serenity of a cherub's. Her figure had the same character as her face, very youthful and feminine in all its outlines. She was dressed neatly, but with great simplicity. Sweet Annie Campbell, I say once more, it was a happy moment that brought thee into that dreary room!

For one moment I felt disappointed; but the charm

of that gentle quiet presence could not be resisted,
and laying aside my work, which I had held sus-
pended in my hands till her entrance, I advanced to
meet my visiter, both of us slightly embarrassed. I
looked at the fireplace, I remember, and attempted a
kind of apology, and then we both sat down, and my
visiter introduced herself. She was related to my
friends the Misses Weir, and the sister of William
Campbell. I had often thought of his sisters since I
came to Glasgow. She brought me a letter, which
after a minute's conversation she produced, saying
that it had arrived yesterday evening in a parcel by
the carrier, and that she had taken the liberty of
waiting upon me to deliver it, as she knew I was
acquainted with her brother. I knew by the hand-
writing it was from my dear friend Miss Menie, who
I did not doubt had requested Miss Campbell to call
for me; but though longing to know all that I was
certain it would tell me about Auchtermuir, (how I
now blamed myself for my suspicions!) I put it aside
for after-perusal.

We soon grew at our ease, for we were both young,
and both strove to be frank; and I, who had been for
weeks accustomed only to the manners and conversation of my aunt and cousins, was surprised at the
charm possessed by my visiter. She was perfectly
unpretending too, but in the mere tone of her voice,
so sweet and feminine, there was unusual fascination.
She seemed to belong to a different order from my
cousins and their companions. Her language was

correct, and her remarks showed she had been accustomed to intercourse with enlarged and superior intellects. Then during our long conversation, for she stayed a considerable time, there would occasionally slip out some expression, some turn of thought, which showed an advanced and delightful piety for one so young. She was particularly youthful-looking, and such a soft dove-like face, which no storm seemed ever to have ruffled! And yet she had a sick drooping mother, as she told me with tears in her eyes during our talk, upon whom she was in constant attendance.

" My sister Mary is with her to-day," she said; " we take it in turns to look after the house, and to do what is necessary out of doors. We do not like to leave her both at once, though, mama is very patient, and requires little attendance. It was a great trial to her William's leaving us, for he was so attentive, and I am afraid she will miss him very much."

All this was uttered in the same quiet gentle manner; but there was a shade over the fair young face, and a trembling in her voice as she spoke it, which showed her feelings though calm were deep.

" Has Mr Campbell gone to Auchtermuir?" I asked, eager to obtain information about the parish.

" He went there about a week ago," she answered; " perhaps you are not aware," she continued, evidently hesitating whether she ought to enter on the subject with me, but encouraged by my manner, "that William received a call from the people after the presentation from Mr Crawford. They had somehow got aware that he had scruples about accepting without that, so they gave him one. He is not settled yet however, but the presbytery have fixed Thursday first for his ordination. He will afterwards come to Glasgow for a few days to make some arrangements, and to see mama. I shall then probably go with him for a short time, at least mama wishes me to do so; and when I see him settled comfortably, I shall return home. I should not like to be long away from mama, even though it is with William."

Annie Campbell had a peculiar way of speaking of her brother. She was evidently proud as well as fond of him. As she continued in an artless way to speak of the change the presentation to Auchtermuir had made to them at home, acknowledging, however, that the presentation itself was a cause for thankfulness, she constantly betrayed the affection she felt for him. Her cheek coloured, and her soft blue eyes sparkled, when she spoke of him. Ah! if I had a brother such as hers to be proud of, I thought, almost envious of her superior happiness.

[Before we parted we somehow felt like old acquaintances; and we were talking quite unreservedly to one another, except that I made no allusions to my position in my aunt's house; and she had too much delicacy to question me on such a subject; but she could not avoid observing the heap of work before me, and the fireless room, which latter I was grieved at for her sake; for as to myself, I was now tolerably habituated to it. I was afraid to take her into the dining-room.

Among other things I learnt from her that her brother was to remain with his relations at Burnside till the manse could be put in readiness, to superintend which she was going there. She went instead of Mary, she said, for Mary was to be married before long, and did not like to leave mama. But she was to live only a few doors off, she added, and they would still be like the same family of course.—And Mr Grey was such an excellent young man. But for all that, she had to wipe her eyes at the thought of the break-up in the family.

" Mr Grey's mother and mama were like sisters," continued Annie. " And mama is very happy in the prospect of Mary's marriage, for we have known James Grey all our lives, and he is so good and so kind.—I like him next best to William.—And Mary too—but they are just made for one another—you will agree with me when you see them." For she had arranged already, as if it was a matter of course, that we were all to be intimate. Of course my heart did not say no ; and I hoped it might be so, for I had no doubt there was a family likeness through them all, and Annie was very charming.

As she was evidently anxious to learn something about Auchtermuir, I talked to her of the parish ; and delighted her by telling her how acceptable her brother's services had formerly been felt there. I described the manse to her ;·and though I could not avoid shedding tears occasionally, I did not mind doing so before her, she so evidently sympathized with me.

Though I made no mention of my aunt, or of my present unhappy situation, I could not avoid hinting to Miss Campbell how anxious I was to obtain a situation as governess, and to inquire, as she was a native of Glasgow, if she was aware that such a thing would be difficult to find, acknowledging at the same time, that I was possessed of no fashionable accomplishments.

Annie said she would mention the subject to her mother, who had many influential friends in Glasgow, " though they are not gay people," she added with a smile.

" But it may trouble your mama in her present state of health perhaps," I said; if so—pray, don't.

" Oh! but mama is very cheerful; and though she is weak she is generally able to see people, and enjoys conversation. She will be very glad if she can be of service to you, I know, for we have heard of you so often from Miss Menie Weir, that we are quite like old friends. But I must really go now, for I am afraid that mama and Mary will be wondering what has become of me. You will come to see us soon I hope, dear Miss Douglas, for you know I am going from home."

She rose to go. We had sat for more than an hour, but time had flown, at least to me. She gave me a direction to their house, which was in the High Street, and I promised to call soon, with the secret

hope that I might be able. I went with her to the
street door, and saw her out. We parted affectionately, like old acquaintances, shaking hands warmly
with one another.

When I returned to the bedroom to my too long
neglected work, what an indescribable change had
taken place in the room! How cheerful every thing
looked, compared with a short time before! The
room seemed larger, lighter, nay, I thought, even
warmer, than formerly. The change was in my
spirits, not in the room, which was the same as it had
ever been.

As I took up my work, I saw my letter lying on
the table. I had quite forgotten it; and I snatched
it up hastily and broke the seal. I had not been forgotten, as I had jealously suspected. Miss Menie had
only been waiting for an opportunity to save me post-
age—good soul! And *such* news of home, of every
body, and everything, I was pining to hear of!—Mrs
Johnstone, John, old Andrew,—all, in short, that I
wished to know of. My old pensioners were well,
and widow Wilson sent her blessing. John was still
low spirited—but he was at the manse, and that was
comforting. And then they expected me to come to
them in spring, and my journey was already talked
of, and arrangements for its easy accomplishment were
to be made. But this was just a small bit of the letter, and all was kind, motherly, and considerate; and
I had been fretfully murmuring and thinking myself
forgotten. Well, well, I had been wrong—that was

all. Mr Campbell's name was mentioned repeatedly in the letter. She knew I would be glad to hear how happy they were in his society. He was to be ordained and to take possession of the manse immediately, which she was glad of—though it would take him from them—as the manse looked very desolate, and she could not bear now, she said, to look that way on Sabbaths. She recommended me to cultivate the friendship of Mrs Campbell and her daughters. Mrs Campbell was a woman in a thousand; and though she was a poor weak invalid, sinking under a sure though slow disease, she yet loved the society of the young, and might be serviceable to me who was separated from my old friends. I suspect that Miss Menie had heard something from Mrs M'Whirter perhaps, which had prejudiced her against my aunt, for she did not seem to expect that I would remain long with my relations. I was rejoiced at one thing she informed me of, that she had requested a friend in Glasgow to be on the outlook for a situation that might suit me, which if found was instantly to be communicated to me. It cheered me with the hope of perhaps a not distant emancipation from my present situation. There were many kind messages at the close of the letter from the other ladies, and Mr Campbell desired also to be remembered to me. I was very glad to know he had not forgotten me.

I had just got my letter finished, and had placed it with a light heart in my bosom, meaning to treat myself to another perusal that night before I went to bed, when I knew by the bustle and voices in the lobby that my aunt and cousins had returned. And presently my aunt came into the bedroom, for Hannah had told her I had had a visiter in her absence, to discover from me who it was. I soon satisfied her curiosity. But she was evidently very much dissatisfied at the quantity of work accomplished, expecting, as she said, that that skirt of Eliza's would have been finished by this time; adding, that she did not see what was to hinder me working while I talked.

She was obliged to leave me, however, as it was near the dinner hour, and Mr Dalgleish's voice was heard entering the house. In spite of this lecture, and though both Jemima and Matthew were more provoking than usual during the evening, " my bosom's lord sat lightly on his throne." I felt the letter in my bosom, and Annie Campbell's sweet voice and looks were still exercising their power over me. I was already something like my old self; and even Eliza, bound up too much as she generally was in herself to notice changes in others, remarked, that surely Rose's visiter had brought good news, I looked so different from usual. *The cloud was rising.*

Though I had to work very hard that night to make up for the time I had lost, I could think without interruption of the visit I had had, and of the letter I had received. The neglect to which I was consigned by my cousins, even though sitting in the same room, favoured my contemplations, and was now a subject for congratulation. I pictured the family of the Campbells to myself, and from Annie's descriptions was well able to do so, and in imagination was among them, even though Jemima and Matthew were quarrelling, as was their constant custom, by the fire, and my aunt was scolding Hannah for having carelessly burnt a hole in the carpet in the morning, which had remained undiscovered till now. But there was always some fault of the kind to be noticed; and my aunt's reproofs, and Hannah's shrill defence, did at last arouse me from my ruminations: and the dispute ended, I believe, with my being desired to mend the said hole the following morning.

CHAPTER VI.

And old familiar stories,
And household thoughts and cares,
Fond, early recollections
Of mingled hopes and prayers;
These were the ties that bound them
So firm and fast together,
And shed around their path
Bright flowers and summer weather.

Two days after the event described in the last chapter, Jemima fell sick, and of course was kept from school, greatly to the discomfort of every one in the house, with the exception of my aunt. This young girl used to spend a great part of the abundant pocket-money her mother privately furnished her with in purchasing rich cakes and sweetmeats. The consequence was, that she was often ill. But no one dared to insinuate the cause.

During those sick attacks, her temper was most capricious and irritable; so much so, that sometimes even her mother got provoked with her. She required a great deal of attendance both night and day, and was most selfishly regardless of others' fatigue. Formerly her sisters required to nurse her; but now they managed to escape it, by imposing the task upon

me. "What was the use of having Rose in the
house but to do such things? They were always out,
and Rose was in; besides Rose slept with her at
night, and could easily look after her." And so I
was elected Jemima's nurse, and was to be always
ready to wait upon her, and to fly at her bidding
night and day.

It lasted three days, and by that time I was so exhausted by the constant demands upon me, that I was
nearly ready to take her place. If I had been compelled to do so, I sometimes wondered who would have
nursed me. Margaret was the only one who had in
some slight degree assisted me with Jemima, and
seemed to feel for me; perhaps Margaret would sometimes have attended to me. But it was well, without
doubt, that I was able to bear up.

I had to sit up with Jemima the greater part of
three nights. When I occasionally ventured to lie
down, being very fatigued with my attendance upon
her all day, she complained so peevishly of the discomfort of my sharing her bed, that at last I infinitely
preferred sitting up. Her mother, who lay comfortably in her own bed, never inquired how I spent those
nights, and I did not inform her, though my pallid
looks and heavy eyes might. Poor Jemima! she was
a sadly mismanaged creature. Over indulgence had
ruined every generous feature in her character, and,
in truth, at this time she was a burden, not only to
others, but to herself. I bore with her patiently; for
though her caprice and unreasonableness were inex-

haustible, I could not but pity so young a creature already as it were devoted to self.

Working all day at my needle was a light thing in comparison with nursing Jemima, who would cry for an hour at the prospect of a dose of physic, nor be prevailed upon to swallow it, though beset by the flattery and entreaties of both mother and aunts. The old ladies were there in constant attendance during the day, though they rendered no assistance. They would hurry backwards and forwards in a great fuss between the dining-room and bed-room, coaxing and soothing the peevish patient, and looking daggers at me if Jemima fretted and complained while I was performing any office about her. Happily, Jemima became soon convalescent, and, on the fourth day from her seizure, was able to make her appearance down stairs, a little paler than usual, but with neither temper nor manners softened by her illness.

My late visiter had constantly occupied my thoughts since the day she called for me. Jemima's illness had alone prevented me from making an effort to return her visit before this ; but now that she was recovered, I requested permission from my aunt to do so. It was rather ungraciously conceded.

Though I had now been some time in Glasgow, I knew little more of the town than when I first arrived, and always felt bewildered and nervous when on the streets. I was therefore very glad, on setting off the following morning to pay my visit, to encounter Warrander Balgairney, the beadle, near my aunt's door.

As I formerly mentioned, he had scraped acquaintance
with me after discovering (for his curiosity was inde-
fatigable) that I was the daughter of one of his favourite ministers. Our friendship had, however, as yet
only amounted to a word and a nod as I passed him,
when following my cousins into church on Sabbaths.

And here I must pause to say a word or two about
Warrander, for he was too important a person in his
time in Glasgow, and stood too high in his own
esteem, to be lightly passed over. Some who are still
alive there may remember him.

Warrander was a little fat important man, who
pursued many incongruous avocations. He was not
only beadle, but a saulie, or walker at funerals.
He attended public assemblies in the capacity of
waiter, private parties also, and was often employed
in laying out the dead. I am not certain which he
preferred. I should imagine they all came alike to
Warrander.

He had a spice of humour, too, and would often
take liberties with the gentlemen belonging to the
town, who allowed him great license.

Warrander was advancing up the street as if he
were coming from the Green, but he had only been
employed as a messenger to one of the houses farther
down than Mr Dalgleish's. I told him where I was
going, asking him to direct me to the house. Warrander was perfectly familiar both with it and its inmates.

"I ken Mrs Cawmill weel," he said; "she's a

richt good woman, and a kind freend to the puir. Mony a ane—your ain aunty for instance (and he winked slyly), gies less, and says mair aboot it. And she has a fine lad o' a son, and twa bonnie genty young leddies o' dochters. They are weel respectit in Glasgow, the Cawmills. An' ye're gaun there, I'll walk alang wi' ye and show ye the road, for I'm on my road to the Haly Land, as the fulish folk ca't (that's whaur twa three o' the ministers bide), in George's Street, and it's just in the way. Siccan a morning I hae had, and am like to hae! I've been four messages already. The last was to Mr Dauvit Dale's, doon the way there;" (and he jerked his head back in the direction from which we had come, for we had walked on a little way by this time). "He's an awfu' man, Mr Dale, for braggin' o' his early pease. I thocht they wad hae askit me in to see them shutin'."

"What! in December, Warrander?" I said.

"Nae doot. It was just because it was extra-ordinar I expected it. And after I hae dune this errand, I maun awa to Dr Porteous. Honest man, he's growin' unco big i' the bouk, and needs lookin' after. The ministers are gettin' owre proud; and they're lazy, at least the maist feck o' them. Ay, ay, there's a bonny change amang them since the time when honest Mr Laurence Hill (him that was in the Barony) was minister in Kilmarnock, and used to come in to help at the occasions. His wife (and she was a dochter o' the Earl o' Kilmarnock, him that lost his head in that awfu' 45) aye cam' alang

wi' him, and they footed it the haill road, save whan
the minister gied her a carry. He was a big stout
man, as maist o' the family are, and he used to tak'
her on his back nows and thans, honest man, and
whan they came to a convenient wa', he wad just
link her cannily doon on 't and oot wi' his mull, wi'
' Come noo, Charlie,' (he aye ca'd her Charlie, but her
name was Charlotte), ' let 's get a pinch.' And then
whan his back was rested, awa' they wad start again.
Ay, ay, the ministers are sair changed."

With such stories and remarks as these, Warrander
beguiled the way to the Cross and up the crowded
High Street, where he shouldered the people aside
with little ceremony, so as to make ample room for
himself and me, talking all the time at the pitch of
his voice. We passed the ancient gateway of the
college, that college where my father had studied in
his youth, and Warrander seemed surprised when I
acknowledged that this was the first time I had seen
it. I was much interested, and paused to look into
the first court. There were many of the students
going in and out,—some with companions, others
solitary. One of the latter crossed the street directly
in front of us, and hurried away. He was a tall,
pale, meagre lad. His clothes were patched and
threadbare, and evidently country made. He looked a
decided contrast to the knot of gay youngsters who had
issued from the gateway at the same moment as himself.
He was gone perhaps to hide himself in some obscure
den, where, for a trifle a-week, he was allowed a seat

at the hearth and a share of a bed, till the hour for the next class came round. How much humble merit is struggling thus unknown to the world! I had often heard my father speak with deep compassion of the privations poor students were exposed to, especially those whose decent pride made them conceal their poverty from observation. I thought that the lad I had seen might belong to this class. But Warrander again roused my attention, for I was ruminating sadly on those old stories which the apparently poverty-stricken student had recalled to my mind.

"That," said he pointing to a grave-looking gentleman who was descending the opposite side of the High Street, "that's Professor Young. He's an honour that man to the University. They say there's no a book in a' that great college library, and it's been gathering for hunders o' years, that he hasna read. I wonder, though, what they're doing at the college the day, for thir's the holidays. It maun be something by the common. But here's the house, and I houp ye'll find Mrs Cawmill in better health, honest woman."

He left me at the very entry I wanted, and then went on his way. I entered the close he pointed to, which was dark and narrow, and then ascended a staircase till it terminated at the third floor, which contained Mrs Campbell's house: the lowest story of all was occupied by shops. I rang Mrs Campbell's bell, and was in the act of inquiring if I could see the

ladies at that time, when I suddenly stopped, greatly
surprised to recognise in the neat tidy-looking girl
who opened the door, Mary Lowrie, the poor Hamilton girl with whom I had travelled in company in the
caravan, and of whom I had often thought since. I
was glad to meet her here, and to see her with so
cheerful and happy a countenance. She also instantly recognised me; and her eyes filled with tears
while involuntarily she put out her hand and grasped
mine.

"Oh! Mem," she said, her cheeks crimsoning with
pleasure, "I am sae happy to see ye! Mony a time,
when I have been oot errands, I hae lookit aboot the
streets to see if I could meet ye.   But I never thocht
ye wad come here. And oh! Mem, I'm sae happy,
for I hae gotten into sich a good place, that I will be
able to help them that's at hame. And my mother's
better, and my father was able to pay the rent that
was standin', for the five shillings just arrived in time
to mak' it up.   Mony thanks to you, for I'm sure we
were a' strangers to you; but the Lord just put it
into your heart."

She continued to pour forth her thanks.   While I
stood talking with her at the door, for we both forgot
in the pleasure of the meeting that I had come to call
for the family, a young lady came out of a room near,
but hesitated to advance when she saw a stranger
conversing with the servant.

"It's Miss Mary," said the girl.   "Oh! Miss
Mary, this is the young leddy I hae sae often spoke

of, wha was sae kind to me the day that I arrived in Glasgow."

The young lady came forward. She had been standing in the shade of the lobby formerly. I thought, though the girl called her Mary, that it was my former visiter, and advanced to meet her. But though she met my extended hand frankly, she gave no sign of recognition; and from what she said, seemed to think that my call was made simply to inquire for the servant. This, though the resemblance was so very striking, made me suspect that I might be mistaken; and yet, when I looked at her again, I felt bewildered.

"It must have been your sister who called for me," I said, as she was offering to show me into a room; "and yet there is such a likeness." She paused immediately, and turned round.

"How stupid I am!" she said, penetrating my meaning immediately, and smiling pleasantly. "I might have suspected that you were Miss Douglas from Annie's description (she shook hands cordially again with me). Annie and I are often mistaken for each other. But, come this way. Mama and Annie will be so glad to see you, for we have been expecting you to call every day."

I had no time to answer, for, shutting the door she had just opened, she conducted me along the lobby to another. I looked back, and nodded to Mary, who had by this time shut the staircase door, and was slowly disappearing into the kitchen while she looked after us.

"And how strange!" said Miss Campbell in her pleasant cheerful voice, whose tones also strongly resembled her sister's, "that you should turn out to be Mary's friend, though, now that I think of it, we might have suspected that, for Mary said she was sure that the young lady was not a Hamilton person. She told us the story the very night she arrived, and has been constantly on the outlook ever since, when she has been out, in hopes of meeting you again. She is a good, grateful girl, and we are very much pleased with her. But come this way; Mama and Annie are here."

She opened the door of a small neat parlour, and showed me in.

"This is Miss Douglas, Mama," she said. Annie was sitting, when I entered, on a low seat by her mother's couch; but instantly starting up, came to meet me and greet me affectionately. They then led me up to their mother.

It was really singular the resemblance between those two sisters, even when together. Till I got better acquainted with them, and learnt to distinguish the slight difference of expression characteristic of the peculiar disposition of each, and a similar variety in the tones of their voices, I could not tell one from another. It was most embarrassing at times.

They were twins, but Mary was the elder by ten

minutes. The warmest affection existed between them. The longer I was acquainted with these sisters, the more I was struck with the perfect sympathy which reigned between them, in opinions, in taste and in everything. To know the one was to know the other. And how beautiful it was to see this unanimity, this want of selfishness and petty jealousies, which too often make themselves painfully apparent in families! But they had carefully been trained by their pious mother, who herself was a pattern of Christian love and meekness. They were the loveliest examples I ever saw of the work of grace in young hearts,—for heart, time, and means, seemed equally, but unobtrusively, to be devoted to the service of God. Till I knew them, my ideas of Glasgow society were far from high; and no wonder, for I judged by what I saw. But they convinced me there existed a class there far superior to what my aunt and cousins somewhat arrogantly named their set, namely, Christian gentlefolks, with cultivated intellects and refined manners. In this class were included some of the clergy of the town, and several men of eminent learning of that time, all of whom were visiters of the Campbells.

After I knew Mary and Annie Campbell more intimately (and our friendship progressed rapidly), I easily learnt to distinguish them when together. It was more difficult when they were separate, for their sympathy of tastes, and perhaps a wish to amuse themselves by puzzling their friends, led them generally to dress alike. Mary, I found, had a very little the advantage of her sister in point of height: Annie was somewhat plumper than Mary, and her hair was a shade darker. Mary was a little more lively and decided in manner, and Annie, I saw, depended upon her. She had the stronger mind. But they were both cheerfulness itself, and made every one else happy that came in contact with them, though it was a quiet cheerfulness too. No wonder the whole family were so loving and united, for no one seemed to me to be like them. I love to paint their portraits. But I must now return to my entrance into the sitting-room.

Mrs Campbell was lying on a little couch constructed for her peculiar accommodation, which could be easily wheeled to and from her bedroom, which opened from the parlour. She was generally unable to walk, though occasionally she ventured when she had her son's arm to support her. She sometimes suffered severely, but, as the sisters once told me, bursting into tears when they spoke, she endeavoured to conceal it from their knowledge. But at times it could not be hid. However, the suffering was not constant, but had its days of cessation. My visit chanced at one of those easy intervals.

Her couch was extended by one side of the fire-place, and partially surrounded by a large screen to guard her susceptible frame from any draught caused by the opening of the door. A little table, on which were laid a few books, stood within her reach, and a half-knitted stocking (for she supplied many a poor child, I afterwards discovered) lay beside them, which she had put down as I entered. I was struck immediately by her resemblance to her son. He resembled her more than did the sisters, though they had also a certain likeness to their mother, which, however, was only in expression, and therefore varied. Mrs Campbell bore the traces of severe suffering in her countenance. She was very pale and feeble ; and the hand which she kindly extended to me, as I timidly approached, was almost transparent in its thinness and whiteness. But from what a motherly heart did that smile come, which invited me to approach her ! it was so tender, so welcoming, and so sincere. There was a something, even in the first moment of our meeting, which made me intuitively feel the superiority of her nature. I saw she was a woman of a large humanity, and I sat down on Annie's low chair beside her almost as much at ease under the influence of her spirit as if I had known her all my life.

Mrs Campbell was wrapt in shawls, and supported by pillows. Her couch was covered with a clean neat chintz, and the linen of her pillows was as white as snow. Her own dress was delicate in its excessive neatness and propriety. She was attired in a simple wrapping dress, which folded easily round her wasted limbs, but hid their outline. Her kerchief and crimped muslin cap, which closely surrounded her pale countenance, leaving only a band of silvered hair visible above her forehead, were each becoming from their very purity and simplicity. She looked so much the lady, and yet everything, both about herself and the apartment, was plain.

It was a small room which they occupied as parlour, but it was convenient for Mrs Campbell,—adjoining her sleeping-room. The larger sitting-room was seldom used. The parlour was hung with the same pretty light chintz which covered the couch. It contained Mary and Annie's piano, for both the sisters could play and sing, and their mother delighted in music. It was here, indeed, I first heard music as my imagination had pictured it. The family had fine voices (Mrs Campbell, of course, was now unable for the exertion). Their own tastes led them to prefer sacred music; still they never objected, when required, to sing some of Scotland's fine old melodies,—and they sang them, as few do, with a full appreciation of their beauties. What delightful evenings I have spent there, listening, along with Mrs Campbell, and sometimes some old privileged friend (Dr Balfour perhaps, for he was their minister, and I sometimes met him there), to Mary and Annie's voices! They always sang, as they did everything else, in concert, and their voices harmonized delightfully together. Most of the sacred music they sang is, I fear, out of date, for I never seem to hear it now; or perhaps my taste and perception are both enfeebled by years;—and I so loved the singers!

The piano was the only piece of furniture in the room which betokened expense, for it was one of the best of that day. Everything else was plain, but all beautifully neat. A few little slender tables capable of supporting merely a vase of flowers, or something equally light, with long slight stalks and antique feet, black and shining as ebony, were arranged here and there. There were the girls' workboxes for sole ornaments, with the exception of some pieces of old-fashioned china on the lofty carved mantel-shelf, and the large folding screen which protected Mrs Campbell's couch, whose faded embroidery had been wrought by the patient hands of her own mother fifty years before. The windows of the parlour looked into George Street, which was quiet, and the invalid was fortunately not much incommoded by the sounds of its bustling neighbour.

The girls gathered round their mother's couch, and we were soon in the full tide of conversation. I felt great delight (the more so from the long deprivation I had experienced) in being permitted once more to taste the pleasures of intercourse with cultivated and refined intellects, and such were Mrs Campbell's and her daughters'. Mrs Campbell possessed that species of mind which has the power of drawing forth the hidden stores of others. She led one insensibly to talk, and I was surprised at my own ease and fluency during this my first visit. But this did not strike me till after I had left her.

Mary had to tell her mother and sister of the strange coincidence that I should be the unknown friend whom Mary the servant girl had so often spoken about, and

Mrs Campbell's smile was even kinder, if possible, after hearing this.

I spent a delightful hour and a half with them, which flew so rapidly that, but for the sake of the invalid, and because I was still, I knew, in spite of their kindness, a stranger, and ought not to take liberties, I would willingly have remained longer. This consciousness made me sigh when I left them, for I nearly forgot it when talking with them. My life at my aunt's seemed much more distasteful after having seen the Campbells in their home. But it was a cause for congratulation, to feel that there was some congeniality between them and me,—a feeling I had never experienced in Charlotte Street. I was one of them I felt, however inferior.

I talked about Auchtermuir, for I knew it would interest Mrs Campbell, who was now so intimately connected with the parish through her son. Though her eyes were fixed earnestly upon me when I was speaking, she seldom spoke herself, except to ask some new question when I paused. Mary and Annie sat by, deeply interested listeners. I spoke unreservedly to them; and as one must find a vent to what constantly occupies the mind, I found myself in the end, I cannot explain how, detailing the circumstances of my father's death to them, and my own leaving the parish, while Mrs Campbell had somehow got my hand in hers, and Mary and Annie were bending forward and looking tenderly and pitifully into my face, with tears in their blue eyes.

" And Annie has told me, my dear," said Mrs
Campbell, kindly pressing my hand,—a pause having
taken place after this conversation, during which I
was slowly recovering my composure,—" Annie tells
me that you are anxious to get a situation as governess ?"

" Yes, ma'am," I said, looking hastily up.

" You do not think, then," she said, fixing her clear
mild eyes attentively upon me, " of remaining at your
aunt's ?"

I had carefully avoided making any allusions to my
aunt, except general ones, during our conversation,
and did not mean to make any now, so I cast down
my eyes to avoid her penetrating look, and answered
by a simple negative. Mrs Campbell remained silent
for a few moments, and when I looked up I saw she
was in thought.

" I hope I shall be able to assist you, my dear,"
she said gently at length. " I have of course many
friends in Glasgow, as it is my native place, and I
shall set an inquiry on foot immediately. You are
right to desire to be independent. But let us see you
soon again, my dear : we are old friends already—are
we not ?"—and she smiled kindly upon me. To be
fatherless and motherless was to have a powerful claim
in the interest of Mrs Campbell. Her penetration,
and my silence regarding my aunt's family must have
revealed to her, I think, the nature of my position in
Charlotte Street. But she had too much delicacy to
make even a distant allusion to it.

I tried to thank her, but felt the refined kindness of
her manner so much that I could scarcely find words
to do so ; my looks did it however.   I felt that hereafter I should have less to complain of, if I secured
Mrs Campbell's friendship.   I was rising reluctantly
to go (I had already twice resumed my seat at their
earnest entreaty, but now persisted in taking my
leave for fear of injuring the invalid), when Annie,
hastily bending over her mother, whispered something
in her ear, detaining me with one hand while she
did so.   Mrs Campbell put back her daughter's curls,
which fell over her fair face as she stooped down,
with her thin white hand (there was a mother's fond-
ness in the action.—It was a pretty picture, the fresh
youthful figure bending over the feeble wasted invalid), and nodded approvingly.

"Annie says, my dear," she then said, turning
smilingly her eyes to me, " that I must ask you if
you can come and spend an evening with us next
week when my son is to be with us.   It is a long invitation even till next Tuesday, for an uncertain
invalid such as I am, to give ; but we will hope for
the best.   Will you do us all the pleasure of coming,
my dear?   See how earnest Annie looks."

Both Annie and Mary did look invitingly at me.
I coloured with pleasure at the invitation.   I felt how
happy it would make me to be able to accept of it.
But I did not know if I might take the liberty of en-
gaging myself without the consent of my aunt.   So
I hesitated,—not from disinclination, they could not

but see that. At last I accepted it conditionally;—if I did not come, they were to understand it had not been in my power, and that I was disappointed. But we all hoped it would be otherwise.

"And no one need be at the trouble of coming to fetch you home," said Mary, with much consideration, as if she divined that that might be made an excuse for preventing me coming. "We will manage that ourselves. William will go with you."

"Yes," added Annie; "and as it gets so soon dark, and you are not accustomed to the streets, Mary and I shall walk down your way between five and six, and take you with us. You shall find us close by, if you leave at the half-hour."

How considerate all this was! I smiled, and promised; and taking (already) an affectionate farewell of Mrs Campbell, I went away with a light heart, attended by both sisters to the house-door. Then Mary (tidy little housemaid she was) came out of the kitchen to open it, just as if she had been watching to do it all the time, she appeared so suddenly, all smiles and curtsies again, and looking as if she were ready to start off on the first service I might require of her.

"Mary, Miss Douglas is coming back, perhaps, to drink tea on Tuesday evening," said Annie. And Mary's smiles redoubled.

I looked back as I began to descend the staircase, for they had not yet closed the door, on the three affectionate youthful faces which were gazing after me, and thought,—how gratefully of each! I was a dif-

ferent being from what I was when I entered.   Their
natures—the natures of that happy family—had infused
some of their own life into mine.   I felt better able to
contend and to bear,—more courageous, more earnest
to perform the duty at present appointed,—and more
hopeful to overcome.   Before, I was heartless, inert,
ready to sink under what I could not remedy.   And
now my way had all at once wonderfully opened.
Good was already coming from the evil; light was
springing from the darkness ; and I saw the finger of
God in it.

CHAPTER VII.

IT was with some doubt of its being granted that I requested liberty from my aunt to keep my engagement to the Campbells, and she did not consent without some grumbling. She seemed dissatisfied at my making their acquaintance.

It was with a throbbing heart that, after leaving Mr Dalgleish's door on Tuesday evening, I looked earnestly up the street, dimly lighted with oil lamps, to see if I could discern my friends approaching. It was a thick foggy night however, and the mist obscured every thing at the distance of a few yards. As I heard steps advancing in the proper direction, I walked on, and in a minute more found myself shaking hands with Annie Campbell and her brother. It was a pleasant surprise. Mary had remained at home with her mother, and William had accompanied Annie.—In another minute we were walking in the direction of the High Street,—Mr Campbell giving an arm to each of us.

It was very agreeable walking through the streets, which I had never yet traversed, when lighted with two such companions. My spirits were exhilarated with my unwonted liberty, and at the prospect of spending two or three hours with the Campbells. I enjoyed everything I saw—the shops —the crowd—only the fog hindered me seeing the full vista of the Trongate. My friends knew that I was ignorant of the town, consequently everything that was striking and interesting in the streets we passed through they pointed out to me. I was almost sorry when our walk came to a conclusion. They were surprised when they discovered that my aunt's family had not yet thought of showing me the cathedral; and Mr Campbell offered to take me there the first time he paid another visit to Glasgow, if I had not seen it before then. I thanked him gratefully.

" And, William," added Annie, bending forward, " we might take her at the same time to see some of those curious old houses that you first pointed out to Mary and me. Those, you remember, about the Briggate and other places. I know she will like to see them, for she has made us all in love with a picturesque old mansion at Auchtermuir— the Craiglands,—is n't it, Miss Douglas ? "

" Mr Campbell knows it," I said.

" Yes, it is a quaint old place," he said, " and very dreary.—I have many messages to you from Mrs Johnstone, Miss Douglas."

I asked eagerly how she was.

" Very lonely" she tells me,—" however her health is keeping pretty good. But it is a sad solitary place for an old woman like her to live at,—the servants

too seem equally aged. She talks of nothing else
but you."

The tears sprang into my eyes to hear this. "And
Miss Menie," said I after a pause—" and the other
ladies "—

" All well,—and looking forward, I was bid to tell
you, to spring."

" Ah ! I am afraid," I said sorrowfully, shaking my
head, but smiling at the same time, " I am afraid
I will not see them this spring "

But we just then reached Mrs Campbell's entry,
and our conversation was checked. Mary Campbell
opened the door herself.

" I knew it was William's ring," she said, greeting me affectionately, " and have forestalled Mary.—
But how long you have been ! "

" We have only been enlightening Miss Douglas a
little about the antiquity of our town," replied her
brother gaily ; " and proving to her, by ocular de-
monstration, that it was considered a habitable place
a few centuries ago. Miss Douglas, do you remember the ladies we met at Burnside ?"

I knew he meant the Dundases, and smiled at the
remembrance of their surprise when told that he lived
in Glasgow.

When I was brought into the sitting-room, I found
a frank pleasing-looking young man with Mrs Campbell, whom she introduced to me as Mr Grey. It
was Mary's intended husband ; and he seemed worthy
of her, so far as I could judge of expression. Mrs

Campbell received me with even more kindness than formerly, and made me sit by her, congratulating herself that she had had no new attack since she saw me, so that she was able to have us all about her. When her eyes lighted on her son, as he entered the room a few minutes after me, I was struck by the look of happiness which in a moment shed a light over her pale countenance. His customary place seemed to be one near her, for he immediately approached, and, after bending over her, and speaking a few words tenderly to her, he too sat down beside her.

The tea-table was already spread, and was in a few minutes wheeled by Mr Grey close to Mrs Campbell's couch, so that, while we surrounded it, she was not excluded from the party. Her son attended to her. She evidently preferred being waited upon by him. His short absence seemed to have endeared him still more to her heart, and a spirit of quiet thankfulness for the re-union appeared to be diffused over her whole person. She never ceased following him with her looks. Once during the course of the evening did I see her raise her eyes silently upward, as if in devout thanksgiving for the blessings afforded her.

After tea, Mary asked me if I would like music.— Their mother was fond of music, and they generally had some every evening if she was well,—and it was so long since William had accompanied them. They could have proposed no greater pleasure to me, as they saw by my looks; and smiling sweetly, both Mary and Annie went to the piano, calling on their brother to join them. He followed to the instrument, and while accompanying them turned over the leaves of their music book. Mr Grey remained beside Mrs Campbell and me.

"We must have some talk afterwards together, my dear," said Mrs Campbell, kindly glancing from those surrounding the instrument to me; " but we shall first listen to a little music." I was again sitting by her. The sisters soon chose their music and commenced. It was a sacred piece,—and the young voices, gathering power as they proceeded, and inspired by their own strains, soon filled the room with sweet sounds. Mrs Campbell listened with her eyes shut, and tears began erelong to steal down her cheeks under the influence of the music. Mr Grey and I were both deeply interested listeners. But our emotion was far inferior to Mrs Campbell's. It seemed to stir her whole soul—absorb all her faculties.

We had music for upwards of half an hour, and then Mrs Campbell told them that they might cease and amuse themselves as they liked, for she wanted to have a little quiet chat with me. They all, therefore, gathered round the table. Mary and Annie each took up some light work, and they and Mr Grey were speedily in earnest conversation with their brother about his new duties as a parish minister. Mrs Campbell took my hand, and now drew my attention entirely to herself.

" I have been making inquiries, my dear, as I promised you," she said, " about a situation, and have

heard of one.—Nay," she continued, seeing my look
of surprise and satisfaction, " I am not sure that
you may wish to accept of it when you learn the particulars, nor can I exactly recommend it to a young
girl like you, except perhaps in particular circumstances. The emolument is not high, and you will
probably have a good deal of trouble and responsibility."

" I should not care for that," I said, " if—if—"

" If you are treated with proper consideration. Is
not that what you mean to say, my dear?" said Mrs
Campbell, seeing that I paused.

" Yes, ma'am," I answered.

" Well, of that I have no doubt. But the lady,
who is a widow, is somewhat of a hypochondriac, and
is always fancying either herself or her children ill.
So, what with the constant administration of remedies
for imaginary ailments, the fact is, they seldom are
well, and constantly require nursing. She has been
on the outlook for some time for a young person who
could not only carry on the children's education at
home (she does not like schools), but also take a kind
of charge in the house occasionally, when she herself
is confined to the sofa. I have no scruples in mentioning this to you, my dear, about my poor friend;
for it is my duty to see that you do nothing rashly,
or without being fully aware of the kind of situation
that is offered to you. Independent of this foible, she is
a sensible, and, I am sure, a pious woman, and would
treat you kindly."

I paused and reflected. The situation was certainly not very tempting, as Mrs Campbell had described it, to a girl of eighteen. But, then, any independence was better than my present life at my aunt's.

Mrs Campbell waited patiently with her eyes fixed upon my countenance, till I had considered. My prudence in deliberating seemed to please her. It showed that I was not influenced by novelty, or one of those who would embrace anything without reflection, from the mere love of change.

"What is the salary, ma'am?" I asked at length, when my mind had arrived at a conclusion.

"It is small, my dear, considering the nature of the services required. The lady is not rich. It is fifteen pounds."

"Oh! but I did not expect more," I said. "You know I am not accomplished. Besides, I have fifteen pounds a-year of my own, and, with both united, I should have quite a handsome income."

Mrs Campbell smiled. "I see you have decided already as to the situation," she said. "But, my dear,—your aunt."

I saw she naturally expected that I should consult my relations. It was therefore necessary that I should enlighten her somewhat on the nature of my situation in Charlotte Street. But I did it reluctantly, and as briefly as possible. It is a disagreeable thing to be obliged to complain, as it were, of one's own kindred. Still I felt that with Mrs Campbell I was safe, and she, I was happy to see, seemed to give me credit for its being an unwilling task forced upon me by circumstances.

"Then, what course do you mean to pursue, my dear?" she said, when this explanation had been given, and without making any comments upon it.

"Had I not better see the lady," I replied, "before I mention my intentions to my aunt, in case—in case she is not satisfied with me?"

"I think so too." Then, considering a few moments, she said, "I shall send one of the girls to Mrs Ronald to-morrow, to get her to appoint some time for seeing you at her house; and then she can call for you afterwards with the information. Will that do, my dear?"

"Very well indeed. And thank you a thousand times, dear Mrs Campbell."

"Perhaps, my dear," she said, smiling good-naturedly, "you may not be so profuse of your thanks when you come to have some experience of the situation. But you shall see Mrs Ronald and her children before engaging yourself, and you can draw back if you are inclined,—perhaps something more suitable may turn up. Remember, a governess to be conscientious must devote all her energies to the culture of her pupils, and she will often require to sacrifice her own comfort and inclinations. It requires patience and self-denial, besides abilities, to form a good teacher.

"I shall do my best, indeed," I said earnestly. "And, perhaps, dear Mrs Campbell, you will give me a few hints now and then."

"I shall be happy to do so, my dear. But you must also apply to a higher Friend."

There was a pause in our conversation for a little time. Mrs Campbell resumed it. She gave me many kindly advices concerning the life into which I was about to enter, — warning me against its peculiar trials, and endeavouring to set *duty* clearly before me. And she spoke so gently, so motherly, that my heart swelled at her kindness. But her eyes, I observed, often wandered amidst our later talk to the group surrounding the table. And at last, seeing that we both looked towards them, and paused in our conversation, her son smiled, and, stopping in the midst of a reply to some observation of Mr Grey's, he rose, and approaching the couch, asked playfully, if our conference was yet ended, and if the rest of the company might now be admitted into our society. His mother answered him in the same strain. The others followed his example, and we all drew around the fire, Mrs Campbell's couch making part of the circle. The conversation soon became lively and animated. I was the only stranger; but they did not allow me to feel that I was one. Mr Grey and Mary had been so long acquainted, that their attachment, though sufficiently obvious, was yet so calm and regulated, that it was not obtruded upon others. William was affectionate to all. I saw him in a different light altogether in the bosom of his family from that in which he had appeared to me at Auchtermuir. I saw that he had strong social tendencies, and much geniality of disposition. His mother and sisters evidently doted upon him : but they had not spoiled him.

At length the clock in the lobby struck nine, and a sudden pause took place in the conversation. A pleasing solemnity made itself apparent on every face.

"It is our hour for evening worship, my dear," said Mrs Campbell to me,—"can you remain?" I signified my assent. At that moment the door opened, and the two servants entered,—the eldest, a staid middle-aged woman, with the respectable appearance one naturally expected in a servant of such a family. Her neighbour, Mary, brought books which she distributed among the company, placing a large Bible on the table for Mr Campbell's use. He took his seat gravely before it. The servants placed chairs for themselves near the table. Mr Campbell asked a simple but earnest blessing upon the exercise in which we were about to engage, and then gave out a psalm. It was an interesting sight to me to look round upon that family-circle,—to turn from the faded invalid mother to those fair young twin-sisters sitting by one another, their faces quieted to deep seriousness as they bent over their books; and then to the youthful pastor and his friend—both intellectual and pleasing men. I had never seen such a group. Once more the voices of the late singers swelled through the room, but now accompanied by others which, though less skilful, seemed equally earnest. Again the strain after a time melted into silence, and then Mr Campbell's voice was alone audible as he read a chapter of the inspired volume, according to the order of the family reading. When that was finished, we all knelt down, with the exception of the feeble invalid, and in a prayer striking for its simplicity and comprehensiveness, he commended all present to God. I rose from my knees, feeling that the room was a sanctuary, and that it had been according to His promise,—" Where two or three are gathered together in my name, there will I be in the midst of them." I felt God was present amongst us.

Mr Campbell accompanied me home, while Mr Grey lingered a little behind in the house. His marriage with Mary was fixed to take place in the beginning of June, and a house was already secured in the immediate neighbourhood of Mrs Campbell's.

Mary had been reluctant to be separated even for so short a distance from her mother; but the latter was of too pure and unselfish a character to allow her children to sacrifice their interests for her comfort. The marriage, she said, had already been postponed again and again on her account, but she would not allow it to be so any more. It might be God's will to spare her for years in the state of health in which she now was, and were James and Mary to wait that time? It would rather cheer her to see them settled together, and thus a home might be provided for Annie, in case William married before she died. As Mrs Campbell's decisions were always respectfully attended to by her family, no more objections were urged by Mary, while Mr Grey rejoiced that her

scruples were at length overcome. Mrs Campbell's
strong sense and amiable feeling were always to be
depended upon. He knew the state of her health,
and was aware it might be as she had said, and was
quite willing that his wife should devote almost the
same attention to her mother as she had formerly
done. He was truly sensible of Mrs Campbell's ex-
cellencies, and felt as a son towards her.

Mr Campbell, when we parted at Mr Dalgleish's
door, asked me if I should have any letters to send by
him to Auchtermuir. He and Annie were to leave
Glasgow on the day succeeding the next. "If I
should, he would do himself the pleasure of calling
for them to-morrow," he said.

"Oh! pray, don't," burst involuntarily from my
lips.

"Why?" He asked with a look of surprise, which
was sufficiently visible by the lamp over the door,
and which immediately showed me the impropriety of
my words; for how could I explain to him that I
feared it would be considered a liberty for me to receive such a visiter in my aunt's house. I could
receive his sister perhaps in the bedroom, but not him
of course. I tried to laugh it off; but the truth is, I
was nearer crying than laughing, for I saw he looked
disturbed and disappointed. It grieved me to the
heart to think that he should consider me ungrateful
for the kindness of his family, or unwilling to see
him.

"I cannot really explain why, Mr Campbell," I

said hurriedly after a chilling pause, hearing Hannah's slow feet approaching the door, and feeling that now I must say something or never. " But will you believe me when I say, it is not from unwillingness. I am not situated here as I was in Auchtermuir. One of your sisters is to call to-morrow. I shall send my letters by her.

" Well, I *will* believe you," he said, instantly resuming his former manner, and frankly shaking hands with me as the door opened,—" good night, and be sure you remember the letters."

We parted just in time to show Hannah that I had been accompanied home by a gentleman, but to elude the sharp glance she sent after him. I went into the dining-room with a feeling of approaching independence, which was rapidly disenthralling my spirit, and giving a freer movement even to my limbs. None were there but Mr and Mrs Dalgleish. Their two elder daughters had gone out to tea, and were not yet returned. Mr Dalgleish was asleep at one side of the fire, and my aunt sat fidgeting and fretting, with a brow as black as night, at the other. My entrance was followed by a more open and undisguised burst of ill temper than my aunt had ever yet thought it prudent to testify towards me.

" She could not tell why I was so late,"—(ten o'clock had struck as I entered the house). " It was not what she expected from me when she consented to take me into her house,—neither, she *would* say, what she had a right to expect. If she had thought things were to turn out in this way, she would never have made such an arrangement. My cousins were out, and she had had to attend to Jemima herself. Jemima had been ill all the evening, and was but now fallen asleep. It would be better if I would attend to my duties, and not be running after new-fangled friends,"—*et cetera.*

Her *maundering* (as my good old friend Mr Patterson would have called it) had at last, when it reached this climax, the effect of provoking a retort from my long enduring spirit. The thought of all that I had suffered for many weeks from this cold-blooded ungenerous woman, who had made my relationship, and my very helplessness and dependence upon her, motives for tasking me as a slave, and profiting by my services, rushed into my recollection as I stood before her, and would have vent. I met her angry eye with such fortitude, that for a moment she was overawed, and the concluding words faltered upon her tongue.

" They are my only friends here, madam," I replied with emphasis.

" Eh—ay—what !—what is 't my dear ?" I heard in Mr Dalgleish's voice (who had been roused by this scene) as I left the room.

I was grieved, when I had time to reflect, at the burst of temper to which I had yielded. What I had borne patiently so long, I felt I might still have endured, during the short period which I fondly trusted I had now to spend under my aunt's roof. I wished to part with my relations upon good terms. I remembered also that my aunt was my father's sister, and I was sorry to have offended her by my unwonted liberty of speech. But it was done, and I could not recall it.

I had no idea, however, how deeply she was offended at the unusual spirit I had shown, till I descended to prepare breakfast the following morning. I was surprised to find my cousin Margaret at her old employment, for these tasks had formerly devolved upon her, and to have all my offers of assistance snappishly declined.

My aunt seldom seemed aware of my presence when surrounded by her family, so her silence to me during breakfast did not strike me, but I thought she looked flushed and angry. I was anxious to conciliate her, but had no opportunity.

When I had breakfasted I left the room as usual to go to my work, intending to be doubly diligent during the day, as some atonement for my yesterday's freedom, but found to my great astonishment that the bedroom door was locked. I was obliged to return to the dining-room, and I sat down in one of the windows. I now saw that there was a plan concerted to humble me, and to make me feel my dependence upon them. My aunt of course had no suspicion that there was a chance of my being soon emancipated.

In a short time I was left alone. Mr Dalgleish and Robert went off to business as usual, and just as I was summoning courage to approach my aunt to apo-

logize for my late burst of temper, she turned coldly
away, and left the room followed by my cousins.

I sat looking out vacantly through the bars of the
Venetians into the street, half envying the little spar-
rows which were twittering about on the pavement,
and picking up chance crumbs. Hannah removed
the breakfast things, and dusted the room, giving me
occasionally a look which seemed to say—" What are
you sitting there for?" But here I thought it best
to remain.

It seemed as if I was to have a forenoon of complete
idleness, for neither my aunt nor cousins re-entered
the room, and I began to experience something of the
feelings of a criminal. I felt that the family inten-
tionally eschewed my presence, and that I must now
(however little intercourse I had with them at any
time) consider myself in a state of banishment from
their society. It was not kind towards a poor fatherless girl who had sorrows enough already. But that
no one seemed sensible of.

At length I heard my aunt and Eliza come down
stairs. They did not enter the dining-room, where
they must have been aware I was sitting, but walked
straight through the lobby, and into the street. When
they were gone I resolved to offer my services to
attend Jemima, who was still in bed, not from any
liking I had to that office, but simply to show my willingness to be of use. But I got a still more decided
repulse than formerly from Margaret, who was in excessive bad humour at being confined to the house,

when, as she said, but for my impertinence to her mother she might have been out. "And as for not being your friends, Miss Rose," she continued, getting more and more angry as she spoke, "I wonder who else has been.—Pray, what would have become of you if we had not taken you here? But you 're an ungrateful girl, and the sooner your pride 's brought down the better, as Mama says. So please don't stay in this room." And she banged the door to in my face.

I gave her no answer, but walked quietly down stairs again, and sat down in my former place. There were the birds still hopping to and fro, and fluttering before the window, but I could scarcely see them now, for tears were stealing down my face. If I had not had the hope of a change before me, how desolate should I have been! Two days earlier and my spirits would have wholly sunk beneath this treatment. The advantages of the situation mentioned to me by Mrs Campbell became instantly magnified in my eyes, and everything that I had at first considered a drawback connected with it, faded away into perfect insignificance. My very anxiety now to secure it raised fears. The lady perhaps by this time had changed her mind, or she might have had some other person recommended to her. I felt I should be restless and uncomfortable till I knew for certain that Mrs Ronald was willing to see me.

I thought the clock had more than once gone wrong that forenoon, and I went twice to the lobby to ascer-

tain if it had stopped.   I listened anxiously at every
ring, to hear if I could recognise Mary or Annie
Campbell's voice.   I had hastily written two notes (I
had no opportunity for anything longer) that 'morning
in the garret, using my box-lid for a desk,—one to
Miss Menie Weir, the other to Mrs Johnstone.   I had
them ready to give to my friend when she came.

At last to my great joy one of the Campbells passed
the window.   I saw her distinctly through the blind,
though of course she did not observe me.   I flew
hastily to the street door, and opened it for her before
she had time to summon Hannah.   She looked surprised when I suddenly stood before her, as she was
stretching out her hand to ring the bell, but smiled
immediately.

" I do not like to ask you in, dear Annie—Is n't it
Annie?" I said hurriedly,—" for I am in sad disgrace
here to-day.   Could you tell me all that you have to
say here?   Will Mrs Ronald see me?"

" Yes.   But she is anxious it should be to-day, for
she is to be from home to-morrow, and wishes to
get settled.   Is it possible for you to come with me
just now?   Yonder is William at the corner of the
Green waiting for us."

I peeped out as she spoke, and saw Mr Campbell at
the bottom of the street.   I hesitated for a moment.
After all, it was but securing earlier what a few
minutes before I had begun to despair of obtaining.
My aunt could be no worse pleased to-day than to-
morrow, and I had an excellent opportunity at present

of absenting myself. I told Annie I would go; and begging her just to wait for a few minutes, I hurried up stairs, and almost immediately returned with my walking-things on.

"And now, Rose," said Annie, as we turned down towards the Green where her brother had strolled, weary of waiting for us, "before we reach William I must tell you about Mrs Ronald. She seems perfectly willing to engage you on Mama's recommendation, if she is pleased with your appearance—so I have no doubt but she will. Mama is very anxious that this situation should turn out a tolerable one, as she will have been the means of placing you in it,—in other circumstances than yours she would not have proposed it to you. We were quite aware, before I called for you at first, that you had not a comfortable home at your aunt's.—Miss Menie Weir had learnt this, I think, through a lady at Auchtermuir, who heard of it in some round-about way, through your aunt's own servants, who, it seems, speak openly on the subject of your position in the house. Servants' gossip is not much to be relied on,—but what you said to Mama confirmed what Miss Menie had heard. Miss Menie wrote a very earnest anxious letter to Mama on the subject, begging her to make every inquiry after a situation for you. It is this that has reconciled Mama to what she feels is underhand dealing in regard to your aunt, who ought otherwise to have been first consulted. She thinks you should accept the situation, though it is not very eligible, as it will be a certain independence in the meantime, while you may be looking out for something better. But here is William. William and I will walk with you to Mrs Ronald's, and leave you there.—You could not call at our house afterwards and let us know how it is settled,—could you?"

I said I should, and just at that moment we overtook Mr Campbell. I felt a little embarrassed at first meeting him; but his frank cordial address immediately re-assured me. I gave him my letters, and explained why they were not longer.

" William was afraid, I suppose," said Annie laughing, " that I should not take proper care of them; for whenever he found that I was coming here, after seeing Mrs Ronald, he offered to meet me, and I found him at the foot of her stair." Her brother, contrary to his usual custom, made no answer to this playful remark; and I felt, though I could give no reason for it, the blood rising in my cheeks. What connexion, indeed, had Mr Campbell's movements with me that they should excite any emotion in my mind?

They took me to Mrs Ronald's. Her house was in Craig's Close, on the south side of Argyle Street, so we had not a long walk together. My heart began to palpitate sadly as we drew near the house; and Annie, who noticed my agitation, came closer to my side, and said with a smile,—

" I see you are very anxious, Rose. But don't be alarmed. Mrs Ronald is a very easy unpretending person, and I know she will like you immediately.

You have just enough of quickness in your face as to assure her that you will be a good teacher, and as much gentleness as will set her mind at rest as to your kindness to her children. What! tears in your eyes! Keep a good heart, dear. It will all be settled in ten minutes."

"Oh! Annie," I answered in a low tone, for Mr Campbell was walking by my other side; "you do not know what it is to feel alone in the world,—to have no one to counsel and direct you,—but to be left entirely to your own guidance in a matter of this kind.

"But you are not alone in the world," said Annie gently, but reproachfully. "Are not Mama and William, and Mary and I, all your friends? And think how many are interested in you at Auchtermuir."

"It is quite true," I said; "and I am very ungrateful to forget it. Though my own relations have shown me little kindness, God has raised me up other friends to fill their place. I feel quite courageous now, Annie."

"That is right," she answered cheerfully. "But here is the entry. William and I will walk home, and you will follow us, Rose—wont you?—when you have finished your business. Two stairs up on the right hand, and the name is on the bell.—Good-bye, dear."

"Good-bye." And nodding cheerfully to both with a view to hide the uneasiness I really felt, I hurried into the entry. I stole a look behind as I was about to ascend the stairs, and there they were both still looking after me, and talking earnestly together. When they saw me look towards them, Mr Campbell waved his hand, and Annie nodded encouragingly, and then they turned away.

Courage now! said I to myself, as I slowly ascended the staircase, to meet probably my future employer. Courage now! and remember you are only about to enter on what for months you have anticipated. If it is not sanctioned by your aunt, it is by your own deliberate judgment, and the judgment of that friend whom you have known so long, and of those recent ones to whose kindness you are so much indebted. But still my feet moved slower and slower, and my heart beat faster and faster, as every step in the staircase brought me nearer to Mrs Ronald's door. At length I stood before it, and read the name Ronald, engraved on a brass-plate upon it. I rung the bell so timidly, that the servant-girl seemed uncertain whether it had rung, and peeped out merely as if to satisfy herself. She did not observe me at first, as she looked towards the stairs, and I stood in the opposite corner, and was about hastily to close the door when I stepped forward, and inquired if I could see Mrs Ronald.

She looked surprised, but immediately answered in the affirmative. She asked me to walk in, and then closing the door, led me through a long darkish lobby, which was only lighted by a false light, as it is called, above the staircase door. A peevish wailing, as from

a young child, came from some room near, and a
woman's tones, evidently coaxing the child to quietness. "Hush now, lovy—hush now. Take it to
please Mama, and you will get a bit of barley-sugar
to put away the taste. It will cure Tommy's sore
head."

"No, no, no!" shrieked the little patient, each time
more determinedly than before. "Tommy's head
better—Tommy no take nasty medicine."

"Hold him, Jenny," I heard the other voice say,
as if worn out by the child's resistance. "Hold him,
and we will put it over his throat."

And it seemed as if they proceeded to this, for an
indistinct noise, between screaming and struggling,
and the gurgling of a person compelled *nolens volens*
to swallow something, reached my ears, as the girl
showed me into a parlour. I involuntarily made a
grimace, as if I myself tasted the potion. The door
was shut behind me, the girl having first inquired my
name, and fortunately it kept out all noise.

The parlour was handsome and well furnished. It
looked out on Argyle Street, a continuation of the
busy Trongate. And as I had some time to wait before the lady of the house made her appearance, I
amused myself as well as my anxiety would allow
me, by watching the passing crowd; at last I hastily
started back as I beheld my aunt and Eliza walking
just opposite. They did not see me of course, as they
had no suspicion to guide their eyes to the particular
window in which I sat; but I felt almost like a crimi-

nal, who dreads detection, when I observed them.
They entered one of the shops over the way, and I
thought it prudent at present not to run the risk of
exposing myself to their notice by remaining in the
window.

In about ten minutes from the time I entered, the
door opened and Mrs Ronald made her appearance,
excusing the delay on account of the illness of her
youngest child. I did not need to introduce myself,
as I had given my name to the servant; and it was
fortunate for me that I did not, as my presence of
mind had almost deserted me in the new position in
which I stood, uncertain whether my appearance
might please the lady to whom I wished to recommend myself. But a few minutes restored my composure and dispelled my fears, as they enabled me to
judge something of the character of the person with
whom I had to do.

Mrs Ronald seemed a woman not far from forty
years of age, but perhaps was not so old, for it is difficult to judge of the real age of a person of her complexion. She was fair and freckled, and an air of
languor, either resulting from ill health or indolence,
was diffused over her whole person. Neither mind
nor body appeared to me capable of much exertion.
She looked quiet and gentle. Perhaps the most
striking expression in her countenance was a look of
anxiety, which was never absent from it; and which
probably resulted from her constant apprehensions
about her own health and that of her children. This

also was perhaps the reason of her habit of sighing, which she did frequently, whether conversing or silent. She looked like one who had likely been over-indulged in youth, at a time too when her character more required bracing and hardening. One could not help liking her appearance, though your regard was not mingled with respect, but took the form of compassion. No violent emotion seemed ever to have disturbed the calm even current of her existence. Her very affection for her children (I afterwards thought) appeared to have more of the nature of instinct in it than of the thoughtful active tenderness of a mother; and though the death of her husband had doubtless cast a cloud over her, still I do not think she had depth of character sufficient to make it either severe or lasting. I do not believe she ever felt anger in her life. Fretful she might be occasionally if her children were ill, or her servants neglectful, but a downright genuine hearty passion I cannot think she ever experienced. And yet, though weak-minded and indolent, she was a woman who really acted from principle, as far as her lights went, and endeavoured to bring up her children in the fear of God. I am anticipating so far, for of course I could not judge of this till I had become an inmate in Mrs Ronald's family; but all the rest I could easily picture from her countenance and manner.

There could not have been a greater dissimilarity between any two beings than between my aunt and

the lady, who, dressed well but not very tidily, in
widow's weeds, advanced with a languid step and air
into the room. I rose to meet her, glancing anxiously
at her, to read, if possible, her character in her countenance. She shook hands with me, and then invited
me in a plaintive voice, which harmonized with her
features, to be seated again. Fear could not exist in
her presence. Annie spoke truly when she said, that
there was nothing in Mrs Ronald to alarm me. I
felt at my ease in a few moments, though my anxiety
remained till I found that she was willing to engage
my services.

Mrs Ronald I saw threw various furtive glances at
me for the first few minutes; but her scrutiny seemed
to satisfy her, for she drew a deep sigh, like one whose
mind is relieved of something which has been oppress-
ing it. She then smiled, and settled herself more
comfortably on the sofa.

" Well, my dear," she said, " I know what you
have come about—and I think (here she took another earnest look at me) that you will suit me, if my
situation will answer you.—I have heard already all
about the teaching from Mrs Campbell, who, I know,
would not deceive me, so we need not trouble ourselves
to speak about that.—And I hear too that you have
been accustomed to housekeeping: I wished to see
you, that I might judge myself if you would be kind
to the children,—and I think," she added, stealing
another anxious glance at my face, " that you have a
kindly look, and would not be too severe on them, if

at a time they could n't say their lessons.—Would
you now?"

"If I can satisfy you in other respects as well as I
am sure I shall do in that, my dear madam," I said,
"you will have no cause to complain of me."

"Then it is all settled," said she, "and I am sure
it is a relief to get it off one's mind. It has been har-
assing me night and day for weeks.—And you understand all about the terms too, don't you? Well,
we need not speak about that either then. You will
have no objections to sleep with one of the children—
will you? Helen sleeps very sound."

"Not in the least," I said.

Mrs Ronald looked pleased at this. "I think,"
she said complacently, "we will sort very well together.—And—and you have no objections to go with
us to the same church on Sabbath? We have always
sat under Dr Balfour. It 's on account of the children you see, that they may be made to behave themselves."

I had none to that neither.

"And—and—you'll not be displeased if I say
that I hope you have not very many acquaintances to
come about the house.—You see, my dear, I am not
very strong."

"Besides my relations," I said, "I know but one
family in Glasgow—Mrs Campbell's"—

"Oh! as to the Campbells," Mrs Ronald said,
"they can 't come too often—I only wish I saw them
oftener,—and it would be hard to keep your own

relations from coming about you. (I felt that she
would have little cause to complain of their inroads.)
What I mean are the kind of acquaintances girls
sometimes pick up and keep running about them.—
You are a pretty girl, you see, my dear—now, you
understand what I mean. But if you are a stranger
here, of course there is not the same chance. Well,
my dear," with a sigh," is there anything you would
like to mention yourself?"

"Only this," I said, gently but decidedly; "that
I may occasionally have the privilege of visiting my
friends; I should not seek it often, but I would like
to be at liberty to do so when I wished."

"Certainly, my dear—certainly," replied Mrs
Ronald. "Is that all?"

"Yes, I think there is nothing else," I said, after
a moment's pause.

"Then," said Mrs Ronald, raising herself from the
sofa with an effort, and fumbling in her pocket for her
keys, "we will look upon it all as settled. But you
must take a glass of wine to seal our bargain. It's
the New-year time too." And languidly crossing the
room to a cupboard, she unlocked it, and pouring out
two glasses of wine, she brought one of them along
with some cake to me, and took the other herself.

"Here's your good health, my dear," she said,
"and I hope we will please one another." I returned
the compliment.

"Shall I not see the children?" I asked.

"O yes,—if you like, my dear," she answered,

glancing helplessly towards the bell which hung by the fireplace, and making another effort to rise from her seat.

" Pray, allow me," I said, starting up to prevent her. " Do not disturb yourself; I shall ring the bell."

I accordingly rang it, and returned beside her.

" Thank you, my dear," she said, very much pleased. " I see we shall do well together, for you are an obliging girl. I am not very able for exertion myself—a poor weak invalid. Kathrine, bring in the bairns. You needn't bring Tommy, but all the rest."

The girl received her message, and shut the door. In a minute or two it again opened, and three little pale delicate creatures shyly entered the room. The second oldest was a boy, the other two little girls.

" Come away, my dears," said their mother, anxious to show them off to the best advantage before the stranger. " Come you here, Helen, as you 're the eldest, and should set an example to the rest. This young lady is to be your governess, and you must be very good, and do all that she says."

I received the little slender hand in mine, and meeting the timid wondering look she cast up into my face with an encouraging smile which dissipated her fears, the other children, who had lingered behind her at the door, were emboldened also to approach, and at their mother's command shook hands with me.

" Shall you like to learn lessons, my dears ?" I said kindly.

"Are you to teach us?" anxiously inquired the eldest, who had made room for her brother and sister to approach me, and was now leaning against her mother's knee, with her eyes (and they were very intelligent ones) fixed upon my face.

"Yes, my dear, I hope so," I said.

"Then, I think I shall like it," she answered. Her mother smiled and patted her head.

"You'll not scold us?" said the boy, who was the most delicate-looking of the three, with all the air of making a bargain with me; "you'll not scold us as they used to do at the school?"

The children, I found, had been under a harsh teacher formerly, who did not make allowances for the drawbacks of weakly constitutions and timorous natures. He had employed severity when kindness would have been more successful. This was the reason which had led Mrs Ronald to decide on taking a governess into her family.

I promised I should not, unless they deserved it. And at this, they looked grave for a moment, and then broke into a smile, which ended in a laugh. It was pleasant to see those little delicate things laughing,—it seemed so unusual an emotion with them.

I rose to go ; but sat down again, remembering that nothing had been yet arranged as to when my duties were to commence. Mrs Ronald, I found, was anxious that I should enter on my new situation immediately.

" The children have been so ill attended to of late," she said, " that it would really be a great convenience if you could come without loss of time. I am not fit to look after them properly myself, and it doesn't do to let them be always with the servants, for they learn tricks with them. They are getting behind too in their learning; for since my poor Jamie here came back all black and blue from the school, I have never had the heart to send them to it again." And the poor mother's eyes filled with tears at the recollection of the schoolmaster's harshness, while she drew her hand caressingly over her little boy's head.

" Poor little thing !" I said, looking with pity on the delicate child; " he seems as if he needed gentleness and care rather than severity."

" Yes; he 's not very strong," said the mother, who, however, seemed a little mortified by my remark; for she added, " But for all that, they have good constitutions, though they may be rather little for their age. Helen, here, is eight." She did not look it.

At last it was settled, that as it was perfectly convenient for me (truly it was), I should take up my residence in Mrs Ronald's family on the day succeeding the next, which seemed to delight the children very much. Mrs Ronald appeared to have no misgivings on account of my being a total stranger to her. " Mrs Campbell's recommendation was quite enough for her," she said. " She had no need to make further inquiries.

I at last took leave of Mrs Ronald and her children, after she had shown me the room I was to occupy, which she insisted upon doing. It was a very comfortable one, proving by its neatness that, however indolent the mistress might be, the maids did not neglect their work. Mrs Ronald seemed in easy circumstances, to judge by her house. Little Helen laughed again when she heard that she was to sleep with me in the spare room. I felt that I should like the children. I have always loved children. And those little pale faces were already recommending themselves strongly to my interest and tenderness. If I could but have influence enough with their mother to induce her to try the effect of plenty of fresh air and wholesome food hereafter, I should, I was sure, be as serviceable to their bodies as their minds.

I descended Mrs Ronald's stair with a light, joyful heart; and carefully avoiding to look towards the shop into which I had seen my aunt and Eliza enter, in case they might still be there, though it was not likely, I walked hastily on in the direction of Mrs Campbell's house.

The Campbells rejoiced to hear that Mrs Ronald and I had come to an agreement. Mrs Campbell spoke to me with much tenderness on the subject, and Mary and Annie congratulated themselves that now we should be able to see one another often. Their brother was present; but while I was talking to his mother and sisters, he had a book in his hand, and was apparently engaged in reading. But he laid it suddenly aside when I announced that I must hurry home, as I feared I had trespassed already, and looked as if prepared to accompany me. I would have declined giving him the trouble, but he persisted in his intention. As Annie was to start with him the following morning, I bade her an affectionate farewell. She entreated me, in a whisper in the lobby, to come as often as Mrs Ronald could spare me, to see her Mama and Mary. I did not need to be asked to do so. I promised, however. Poor Annie's eyes, I could see, were red with weeping. She was to return home in three weeks; but her mother's feeble state made that time appear very long.

Mr Campbell accompanied me to the corner of Charlotte Street. I begged him to leave me there. He then made the same request as Annie, that I would be a frequent visiter at his mother's, and looked much gratified when I repeated the same promise. How kind it was thus to shift, as it were, the obligation from me to themselves!

When I was standing conversing with him, who, to my great embarrassment, should come up and pass us, but my aunt and Eliza! I observed them, for the first time, as they swept by. My aunt looked straight before her, with a cold stately air; but Eliza showed a strong inclination to giggle, at having surprised me in this unexpected manner. They walked on without looking back. Mr Campbell, who did not know them, appeared struck at the change in my looks, for

which he could not account. I told him who the
ladies were, and he immediately turned and looked
after them; but they were near their own door by
this time. We now shook hands and parted. I followed my relations with restored composure, having
the comfortable consciousness that I had now succeeded in freeing myself from a yoke that was bearing down both body and soul, and rather thankful
that their encountering me, as they did, had broke
the ice in regard to the explanation I must immediately have with my aunt.

CHAPTER VIII.

THE same avoidance of me by the family continued during the rest of the day. Mr Dalgleish, however, was evidently uncomfortable under it. I felt it painfully. Sometimes I was grieved by it, and sometimes indignant. Surely my hasty words did not deserve this continued harshness. I knew that I should soon escape from it; but I was sorry to part from them thus.

This treatment nerved me so far, however, for the disagreeable task before me, though I considerably dreaded the effect upon my aunt of the intelligence I had to communicate. I had no opportunity of informing her of my intentions this day, for she was engaged all the evening with company who came to tea. I determined, however, to do so in the morning.

I spent a sleepless night in consequence of the prospect before me. After breakfast, I was about to request an interview with my aunt, when she herself addressed me for the first time since the luckless moment of my offending her. She desired me, in an authoritative tone, to go to the bedroom, and she would follow me there instantly. I obeyed her. I suppose she felt that I had now been long enough idle, and was now sufficiently humbled.

I was scarcely a minute in the room when she came to me. I saw by her look, when she entered, that there was a severe reproof in store for me.

But why recall that interview? Suffice it to say, that it was a painful scene. I was accused of ingratitude,—insolence. My aunt upbraided me with her generosity, and with my evil return for it. She called for my cousins into the room, and in the most cutting and contemptuous terms, informed them of what I had communicated; and, finally, she prophesied that I would come to destitution, and threw up all charge of me in future. I bore it patiently at first; but I grieve to say, that erelong a scene of violent altercation took place. My heart swelled indignantly at the coarse unwomanly treatment I received, and I uttered retorts which, however just, had better have been spared. At last they left me.

And then a revulsion of feeling speedily took place. The disgust and indignation which had nerved my little passionate heart during the late scene gradually softened down, and I burst into tears. I was humbled in my own eyes. Where had been the charity which " beareth all things ? " Where the Christian meekness which is " not easily provoked ? " I could not deceive my own heart. However the world might justify me, I knew that the all - seeing God must have detected revenge and bitterness, and an unforgiving spirit in my heart, while outwardly I had been all calmness and composure. Had I really been deceiving myself? Was my religion that of the meek and lowly Jesus?

Bitter was my self-condemnation at the very time that my aunt and cousins were probably supposing I was triumphing. If either had then re-entered the room, I am certain I would have humbled myself before them. But not a creature came near me. I went for refuge and privacy, at length, to the garret, and, with bitter tears and deep repentance, acknowledged my sin before God. That alone relieved me. And I fully resolved, God enabling me, to make atonement to my relations for my pride and unforgiving spirit, by a studiously kind and gentle demeanour during the short time that I was now to be with them. As things turned out, however, I had not much opportunity for testifying this.

I put up all my stray articles in my boxes to be ready for the morrow. My trunks had never been unpacked since I left Auchtermuir; so that did not occupy much time. I wished to make a few purchases before going to my new situation (I had made none since I came to Glasgow), and I put on my walking-things, and went out for the purpose. I bought the articles I wanted in a shop in the Trongate.

I was strongly tempted, now that I was out, to go up to Mrs Campbell's and inquire for her and Mary, since William and Annie were gone. They were three hours by this time, I knew, on their journey. So strong was the temptation that I could not resist

it: so I turned my steps up the High Street, instead
of passing down the Gallowgate towards home. I
was now quite familiar with this street. When Mary
Lowrie opened Mrs Campbell's door at my ring, I
was alarmed by the expression of distress in her face.
She smiled, however, when she saw me, but instinc-
tively held up her forefinger to enjoin silence, glancing backward in the direction of Mrs Campbell's
room.

"What is wrong, Mary?" I asked breathlessly, as
I softly stept within.

"Oh! Mem," said Mary in a faltering voice, which
was cautiously lowered, "the mistress has had a sair
time o't since Mr Campbell and Miss Annie gaed awa'.
They werena gane mair than half an hour when the
turn cam' on her. Waes me! how she suffered, and
how my heart bled for puir Miss Mary left her lane-
sel'!" And Mary lifted the corner of her apron to
her eyes, and wept outright—but still silently.

"But is it over?—Is she suffering still?" I asked,
much distressed at this intelligence.

"Oh, no!—Thank God it's owre!" replied Mary,
endeavouring to compose herself. "The doctor gied
her some draps, and she has faun into a sound sleep
this wee while. We are sae feared to disturb her that
we hae tied up the tongue o' the door-bell, and I hae
to keep an eye on the wire, in case onybody rings.
My neebor Merran is watching beside her the noo,
for she has been lang in the family, and kens the
nature o' the mistress's trouble. Miss Mary's lying

doon on her bed to rest hersel'—but she will be glad to see you, I 'm sure."

" Which is her room, Mary?" I asked.

The girl pointed it out to me, and then hurried back to her kitchen, that she might be at hand to watch the bell. I opened Mary's door softly and stole in. One half of the shutters was closed to darken the room. Poor Mary lay on her bed, pale and exhausted with witnessing her mother's suffering. Her eyes were heavy with weeping, and her fair hair lay loose and disordered on the pillow. She looked up anxiously when I entered, as if she feared that it might be a summons to her mother.

" Oh! Rose, how kind—how very kind!" she exclaimed as she recognised me. " You could not have come at a better time, for I am all alone, and dear Mama has been so ill.

I knelt down beside her bed, and soothed and wept with her.

" William and Annie were not long gone when she was seized with such terrible spasms,—I never before saw her so ill. Fortunately she was in bed, for she does not rise early. It is over now, and she is asleep under the influence of laudanum. I left Marion with her, and came here to rest, for my poor head is very bad."

She was evidently suffering very much. I bathed her forehead with cold water, and made her lie quiet. I sat down beside her—she seemed soothed and comforted by my presence. I remained nearly an hour with her, during which all was quiet in the house, and then I stole out of the room to inquire after Mrs Campbell.

I knew that her bedroom was off the sitting-room, so I went there. The door of the bedroom was ajar, and I ventured to peep in. The room was partially darkened, and the curtains were drawn around the bed, so that the invalid was hid from my observation. The servant who was left in attendance upon her was seated in the easy-chair, by the side of the bed nearest to the door, so that I soon succeeded in attracting her attention. She rose immediately, and followed me into the other room. She looked surprised when she recognised me, evidently supposing I was her young mistress.

" My mistress is still sleeping," she said in answer to my inquiries, " and her breathing is calm and quiet. I think her pain is quite gone. How is Miss Mary, ma'am?"

" She is suffering from a severe headache," I answered.

" Nae wonder," said the servant, shaking her head earnestly ; " for how that dear young lassie stood and strove to ease her mother's suffering during that wearifu' twa hours, when my ain nerves, sae much mair used to seein' sichts o' distress than hers, could scarcely bear it, is no to be telt.—She's a blessed creature—and sae are they a' ; and weel should I ken them, for I hae been wi' them since they were bits o' bairns. I houp, Mem, ye 'll no be obleeged to leave

her.—I wad gang and see to her mysel', but I 'm
fear't to leave my mistress."

" Do not be afraid," I said, " I shall not leave
her."

" God bless you!—I maun awa into the room again.
Wad ye just step into the kitchen, and tell Hamilton
Mary to warm a drap soup for her. I ken she took
nae breakfast, on account o' her brother and sister
leavin'."

I promised I would, and she stole noiselessly back
into her mistress's chamber.

Mary Lowrie was sitting with some needlework in
the bright little kitchen, so placed that she could raise
her eye occasionally to the bell, without requiring to
shift her position. She was glad to hear that her mistress still continued to sleep, and cheerfully prepared
the soup. When it was ready, she covered a small
tray neatly with a napkin, and I carried it to the
bedroom.

Mary was not much inclined for the soup, but she
forced herself to take it to please me. It revived her
however, though the intelligence that her mother still
calmly slept was her best restorative. She would now
have risen, but I prevailed on her to lie still a little
longer. By this time I was considering what I should
do. Mary still looked ill—my presence seemed to
comfort and cheer her. Could I leave her alone?—
newly deprived of her sister as she was,—her mother
ill, and with a heart filled with anxiety concerning
her! How kind those friends had shown themselves

to me! Was it not my duty now to endeavour to make some return for it, even at the risk of more deeply offending my aunt?—I felt it was.

"Mary dear," I said, after I had answered all her inquiries about her mother, and watched her take her soup, "I cannot think of leaving you in this state. If you have no objections, I shall write a note to my aunt, telling her that I shall not be home to-night, and send it down by Mary Lowrie. I can watch the bell while she is away.

Mary was all gratitude and thankfulness. My proposal seemed to relieve her mind of a heavy burden. I left her then to write the note, which I did in most respectful terms. I mentioned the state of things in Mrs Campbell's house; and briefly saying that I felt I could not leave it while both Mrs and Miss Campbell continued so poorly, warned her that I should not return to Charlotte Street that night, but would call next day for my boxes, and to bid them good-bye. Having sealed my note, I gave it to Mary Lowrie, urging her to use all despatch, as I should have to take her post in the kitchen till she returned, and Miss Campbell would be alone.

Mary hurried away, and I was left in the kitchen to watch the bell. It was a pleasant place to sit in, for though small it was beautifully nice. I confess to a partiality for kitchens—when they are clean "redd-up," the floor whitely sanded, the fire bright and clear reflected in every polished tin upon the wall—no parlour comfort can equal them. It was in the ingle-nook of the kitchen at Auchtermuir that, when I was a child, I loved to sit and pore over my story book, with no other light than what came from the fire, where a tiny bit of "candle-coal" was economically placed every evening to serve (as it admirably did) in lieu of a lamp. The women-servants then span, and sometimes they sang old ditties while occupied with their wheels, while John sat beside us knitting great woollen hose for his own wearing. Those were some of the happiest evenings of my life. Mr Patterson supplied me liberally with story books— Jack the Giant-killer—Ali Baba—Sinbad the Sailor, and a host of others, are all commingled with my recollections of the manse-kitchen at Auchtermuir.

Mary Lowrie was not long in returning. I now returned to my friend Mary, having first ascertained by listening at her door that her mother's slumbers still continued. Mary was able to rise before long. She and I established ourselves in the parlour, where we could hear every sound in Mrs Campbell's bedroom, relieving the faithful old servant, who was despatched to her kitchen. She soon returned, however, with a tray, on which she had placed some dinner. Mary could eat nothing, but pressed me to do so. We afterwards each took up some work, and conversed together in such very low tones as could not rouse the invalid.

Mrs Campbell did not awake till the evening. She then made no complaint of pain ; but she was still confused and heavy under the influence of the opiates she had been made to swallow, and seemed scarcely conscious of who was attending her.

About seven o'clock, Mr Grey and the doctor simultaneously made their appearance: the former had heard nothing of Mrs Campbell's seizure till a short time before. While Mary accompanied the medical man into her mother's room, I described to him the manner of the attack, and the present state of the invalid. He was glad to see me there, and still more so when I told him that I meant to remain with Mary all night.

When the doctor re-entered the sitting-room, in answer to Mr Grey's anxious inquiries, he said, that he thought Mrs Campbell had considerably rallied since he had left her in the forenoon, and indeed was getting on as favourably as he could possibly expect: he seemed to dread, however, a return of the spasms. The doctor then went away, promising to pay an early visit next morning. Mr Grey sat some time longer with us.

I slept with Mary that night in her mother's room. Mrs Campbell had no further attack. She slept occasionally, and upon the whole her night was a tolerable one.

We rose early, and Mary got her mother's tea ready. Mrs Campbell revived very much when she had taken it, and smiled kindly on us all. She now recognised me, but was too weak to converse. Her room was just made tidy, when the doctor came according to his promise. He thought his patient much better this morning, and could joke with me on coming out of her room. I determined not to go to Mrs Ronald's till the evening—so I remained during the forenoon with Mary—Mrs Campbell continuing to improve.

After Mary and I had dined, I was compelled to leave her, as I wished to have an opportunity of wishing Mr Dalgleish, who had always shown himself friendly towards me, good-bye. The only chance I had of seeing him was after dinner, before he returned to business. I did not disturb the invalid by taking leave of her. Mary and I parted with mutual regret. We had become better acquainted with each other in a few hours, than in other circumstances we might have got in weeks. Our minds were now greatly relieved about her mother. I knew that Mary would not be wholly alone, for Mr Grey was sure to be there in the evening. I promised to come and see them as soon as Mrs Ronald could spare me. Marian, the servant, was very much grieved when she found that I was leaving her young mistress solitary; but I convinced her of the necessity. Mary Lowrie engaged to let me know at Mrs Ronald's at night how Mrs Campbell continued.

When I reached Charlotte Street, I found, as I expected, that the family were at dinner. I had brought a porter with me from the Cross to carry my luggage. I asked Hannah if I might take the man up stairs for my things. She supposed so, she said, for she had " nae time for ony sic wark hersel'." She might have added—inclination. A sharp voice (it was my aunt's) from the dining-room, the door of which was partly open, now demanded what noise was that in the lobby. My aunt must have heard my voice, and been quite aware whose it was. Hannah was obliged to return to the room.

I made the man clean his shoes well on the mat, and then quietly follow me up stairs to the garret. He carried down my boxes to the lobby—then fastening both securely with his rope, he hoisted them from the table upon his shoulders, and was ready to start. I gave him Mrs Ronald's direction, and paid him, desiring him to tell that lady that I would shortly follow him. I saw him out of the house, and then with an agitated heart prepared to enter the dining-room from which Hannah had now removed the dinner.

All had left their places at table but Mr Dalgleish and Robert, who were taking their usual tumbler of toddy, and were gathered round the fire. No one rose or moved in any way when I entered, which made my situation more embarrassing. All sat still, and all were silent, though my three female cousins coloured violently, and looked to one another.

I said to my aunt, who listened to me with a very cold expression of countenance, that I hoped she had received my note yesterday. She merely answered " Yes," in a formal manner. I then went on to say, my voice gathering strength as I proceeded, that owing to the very weak state in which Mrs Campbell

had continued during the night and part of the forenoon, I could not leave Miss Campbell till now,—
that I trusted this had not offended her, which, if it
had, I would very much regret (here my aunt broke
into an incredulous smile),—and that I had now come
in to bid them all good-bye, as Mrs Ronald expected
me.

There was a general movement, I saw, among the
circle of my cousins, though none of them spoke. No
one invited me to take a seat. I stood with my back
to the table, fronting my aunt. Mr Dalgleish and
Robert were therefore behind me, and concealed from
my sight. My aunt looked at none of them. She
fixed her eyes severely upon me. Her expression
grew even more ungracious than at first; and a red
spot, the sure sign of concentrated displeasure, as I
.by this time well knew, glowed on either of her
cheeks. She paused for a few seconds, as if to give
greater weight to what she had to say, and then spoke
in a sharp voice.

"There is no need of making any apologies," she
said. "I little thought, when I settled to bring you
here, that things were to turn out as they have done.
But since you prefer other people to your own relations, who have done so much for you, all I have to
say is, that you are perfectly welcome.—I wash my
hands of you, that's all.—You seem so well fitted to
guide yourself, that it would be a pity not to leave
you to do it." And my aunt pushed back her chair,
and began to smooth down the folds of her black silk

dress in such a hasty manner, as clearly showed the pique and agitation of her mind.   My cousins tittered. Both Mr Dalgleish and his son were silent.

"I am very sorry," I said in a different spirit than actuated me the previous day, which, if it had still possessed me, would have now led me keenly to retaliate upon my aunt, and with justice,—" I am very sorry that my conduct should have displeased you.   God knows I have endeavoured to perform my duty in this family.   There may have been much misconception upon both sides, perhaps ——"

" There has been no misconception, as you call it, upon mine," said my aunt, hastily interrupting me. " But if people will act without common sense, they must just take the consequences.   You have made your own bed, and you must just lie down upon it. Wait till six months are over, and my word but your pride will be brought down a peg."

" You are really mistaken," I said earnestly, anxious to remove her unfounded ideas.   " I am not proud in the sense you mean.   I only wish to be independent, and to earn my own bread.   You yourself must recollect, and Mr Dalgleish too," I added slightly turning towards him, " that it was arranged before you left Auchtermuir, that my stay here was to be limited to the time of my being able to procure a situation.   Was I wrong to endeavour to obtain one? —or is it strange that I should prefer teaching—an employment more congenial to the education which my father gave me, and to my own tastes—than constant sewing or household work. You have a large family of your own. I am not needed here. Surely, Ma'am, you must acknowledge that I am right." But my aunt was inexorable.

" Let us have no more words," she said at length. " I, for my part, hope you may get on well "— (the wish did not seem a very sincere one, to judge by the tone of the voice which expressed it)—" though, I must say, I can hardly expect it after the conduct you have manifested. Ingratitude," she added, with the authority of one entitled to read another a moral lesson, " is one of the worst of all vices. But to show that I have no unforgiving spirit, none of us have any objections to shake hands with you, and bid you good-bye." And she rose formally, upon which her daughters followed her example.

I was now thankful to let the matter rest as it was, for I saw that she was either determined to appear to misunderstand me, or really did so ; and I knew that it was useless to endeavour to remove the impression in either case. Therefore it was as a culprit to whom forgiveness is extended, that I went through the ceremony of leave-taking.

When I had bidden her and my female cousins farewell, I turned to Mr Dalgleish, and with real sincerity thanked him for his friendliness towards me since we had first met. The honest man wriggled in his chair, and seemed somewhat uncomfortable, while reminded in this open manner of his kindness. " Ay, yes, my dear—ay—I wish ye weel ; and sae do we

a'—nae doot o 't.   Dinna we, Mrs D. ?" (Mrs D. dis-
dained to reply).   " But—ay—gude-bye, my dear."
And he shook hands with me in a hasty tremulous
manner, which showed his great fear of offending
the domestic powers by testifying any undue share of
heartiness and vigour in going through the ceremony.

My cousin Robert now only remained ; for Matthew,
faithful in his resentment to the last, had vacated
the room, and to him I now glanced with secret re-
luctance.   But his conceit of late had not prevented his
suspecting that he did not please me.   His pride was
mortified by one whom he considered much his inferior, and from whom he had fully expected nothing
but simplicity and strong admiration.   He therefore
neither rose nor extended his hand, but bestowed
upon me merely a sulky nod, which well expressed
his feelings.

I was now left to make my exit unaccompanied by
any of the family.   Though I left them voluntarily,
it was as if they thrust me forth.   But they were
welcome to the feeling, since it seemed to soothe their
resentment.   There was a lingering touch of sadness
in my heart as I left the room.   However little consideration I had received at my relations' hands, still
I felt they were the only kindred I had, and I was
leaving them in displeasure.   There was a kind of
awe too on my spirit.   After this period, I was in
reality to begin to act for myself.   I drew my breath
deeply for a moment or two, and silently commended
myself to God.   Hannah was not in the lobby ; so I

walked quietly through it, opened the door, and passed out into the street.

I felt it necessary to have my spirits a little calmed down before presenting myself at Mrs Ronald's : so I went down the street to the Green. It was a little after four o'clock, and getting duskish, though still light enough to enable me to stroll about for some time. As there had never been either affection or esteem between me and my relations (I did, indeed, think kindly of Mr Dalgleish), my feelings of regret were not severe. I was young and hopeful too. And was I not once more a free woman ? I soon felt as if I could run, could leap, could fly at my release from bondage. If I had been conscious of leaving even one sorrowful heart behind me, I should have been downcast too. But I knew that there was a sense of relief on both sides. Occasionally a little tremor would steal over me in regard to my future fate ; but hope and cheerfulness were in the ascendant.

I had had little exercise for many weeks, so I took a rough walk before going to Mrs Ronald's. I crossed the bridge at the foot of the Stockwell, walked up the main street of the Gorbals, penetrated a little way the road which is a continuation of it, turning neither to the right hand nor to the left for fear I should lose myself, and returned the same way. The twilight, however, was deepening, and the lamps were lighted as I walked back.

I would have willingly paused for some time on the

bridge,—for the dark-flowing river beneath, the rows
of lights in some places reflected upon the water, the
huge frame of the old glass-work looming like some
monster in the distance, the hum of the town, and the
moving figures of the passengers, had a powerful effect
upon my imagination. I felt like the one solitary
being in the busy scene ; all others were hurrying
on, some on business, some in pursuit of pleasure—
and how many in sorrow or in guilt?—and would
gladly have hung over the parapet, and forgetting all
around, have dreamt of Mirza and the bridge, and the
dark ocean which received those who fell. But as
my aunt would have said, it was not respectable, and
might have drawn attention to me, so I sighed, and
walked on like the rest.

It wanted but a quarter to six on the Tron church
when I emerged from the Stockwell, and cast a backward glance on the steeple as I proceeded along Argyle
Street to my destination. In a few minutes more I
was ascending the stair which led to Mrs Ronald's
abode. The exercise I had taken had braced and in-
vigorated me. I felt confident in my own resources
for the new life that was opening to me.

Mrs Ronald's lobby looked more cheerful by night,
for it was then lighted by a lamp, — the daylight
there was a mere pretence. She and the children
came immediately out of the sitting-room to receive
me, for the little things were all dressed in their best
frocks for the occasion, and they had been sitting in
state for the last hour expecting my arrival, and were

beginning to weary. My reception was very cheering. Mrs Ronald moved as languidly and talked as much of her ailments as before, and sighed frequently; but she was evidently very glad to see me, and anxious to show herself hospitable. I had been so little accustomed to be considered in my aunt's, that I almost felt her attentions embarrassing.

The children looked a little shy at first, and hung behind their mother; but when I knelt down and kissed and spoke to them, they began to be quite merry and happy again. The youngest held by his mother's hand. I had not seen him before. He was a pet of a child, though delicate-like (no wonder) as the rest. He was three years old. He had lovely blue eyes, which he raised tremblingly to scrutinize me, a little coral mouth, the fairest skin in the world, and flaxen hair, which hung in wavy curls around his white forehead.

" What a darling!" I could not help saying admiringly, and raising him in my arms. His cheeks coloured crimson as I did so, and he looked anxiously from me to his mother. I saw that he would cry if I detained him a minute longer, so I set him speedily on his legs again, when he hid his face in his mother's gown, peeping out at me, however, from among its folds.

Before I was shown into the parlour, where the tea-table was spread with great glory and magnificence to honour my arrival (Mrs Ronald was evidently not accustomed to governesses, for unlike most ladies, she treated hers with distinction), I must be taken into my bedroom to put off my things, and Kathriné, one of the maids, being desired to bring a candle, I was accompanied there not by Mrs Ronald only, but by the whole bevy of children, who seemed resolved not to leave me. My trunks were already in the room—I was informed that the chest of drawers there was to be appropriated to my use and little Helen's—so my clothes had a chance of getting un-packed at last.

When I was ready, they all conducted me to the parlour, and Kathrine was summoned to bring tea. I knew the best plan to adopt here, so I quietly entered upon my duties immediately. I insisted that Mrs Ronald should not move nor disturb her-self. I placed an elbow-chair for her at the side of the table nearest to the fire, brought seats for the children, gaily lifted them upon them to their great delight, and then proceeded to make tea, helping every one, and attending to myself last. Mrs Ronald let me manage every thing as I chose, but she said occasion-ally, " Thank you, my dear," almost energetically. We all enjoyed ourselves very much. The children were excessively amused to see me performing their Mama's office ; but they were too delicate to be noisy. Mrs Ronald smiled and talked, as she sat at her ease and drank her tea. When the tea-equipage was removed, I amused the little things, and did not let them trouble their mother, who sat by the fire and knitted,—a quiet employment which suited her admirably. Little

Tommy at last overcame his shyness, and was prevailed upon to sit on my knee, and I told them stories, and repeated old nursery rhymes to them, till it was time for prayers.

My first evening had proved a most successful one with both mother and children.

CHAPTER IX.

And children blossomed round them there,
Like simple flowers, as sweet and fair—
That in the forest dwell.

WHEN I awoke next morning, I could scarcely tell where I was; but the sight of little Helen's sleeping face beside me soon restored my recollection. She did not awake till I was drest, and then when I bent over her, she put her arms round my neck and kissed me. I was chatting pleasantly with her, with a view of gaining a little more insight into the character of the child, when the maid came to fetch her.

"I think I might spare you the trouble," I said to the girl, "you must have a great deal to do with the rest of the children in the morning. Fetch her clothes, and I will dress Miss Helen here, and she will not run the risk of catching cold in the lobby." The girl was very glad to do so.

" And will you dress me, Miss Douglas, and every day too?" Helen eagerly inquired, as if she scarcely believed that I was serious.

" Shall you like it?" I said.

"Oh! very much."

"Then get up," I said, "for here come the clothes;" and Kathrine re-entered with them, and then hurried away to prepare the children's breakfast.

Little Helen was soon washed and drest, and then without hint from me, for I was anxious to observe the training the children had had, she knelt simply and quietly by the bedside and repeated her morning prayer. My heart was gladdened to see this. There is the fear of God here, I thought—it will be easy teaching these children.

"And where is the porridge, Helen?" I asked, when we were ready to leave the room. She took me into the nursery, where the three children and the servant slept. It was a close small room containing two beds. Those were still unmade, the hearth was dirty, and the children were clamorous for their breakfast. Kathrine was absent about it. In spite of their peevishness, they came instantly around me, and were delighted to see Helen, whom they had missed since they rose. I thought the children were breathing an improper atmosphere, and was anxious to remove them from it and air the room, but I was afraid I might displease the servant by interfering with her vocation. She came hurrying in at this moment, bearing a smoking tray covered with the children's porridge-plates and a jug of milk.

"Here's the parritch at last," she said good-naturedly, "but ye'll no be fit to sup them for a while yet, for they're just bilin'. If they wad but gie ye eneuch o' meat at aince, ye wadna be aye cry, cryin' this way

for your meals, as if ye were hunger't, and deavin'
folk."

"Perhaps the best way will be," I said, with a view
to gain what I wanted, "to take the children for a
few minutes into the parlour. I suppose the fire is
lighted there by this time, and then you can raise the
window here to cool the porridge."

"And sae it would, Mem," she answered, readily
consenting; "but naebody can lift a window whaur
these bairns are, for they are aye takin' caulds or
something."

"Come away then, my dears," I said, "only for
a few minutes, and by that time your porridge will be
cool, and fit for you to sup."

The children were not of refractory natures; and
though they looked wistfully at the porridge plates,
still they accompanied me without resistance. I carried Tommy, and was glad to hear behind us the
sound of the opening window. I amused the children
for a few minutes in the parlour, and then Kathrine came for them, and we all went back to the
nursery. The sickly closeness of the air was gone.
A little table was set out in the middle of the room
with their breakfast, and the girl placed chairs round
it for the little ones, taking the youngest, however, on
her own knee to feed him.

I saw that though this girl had a quick bustling
nature, she was kind to the children. From her remarks during breakfast, I also noticed that she was
sensible of the faults in the system pursued by Mrs

Ronald in her family, and that I might rather reckon
on her assistance than opposition, if I ventured gradually to introduce a few innovations on the old customs.
I stood beside the table till the children had finished,
helping them, and talking occasionally with her. She
seemed pleased with my frankness, telling me, without scruple, that she had not been much taken up with
the idea of a governess coming, for she had expected
that I would be " high and proud, and above speaking to a servant."

I answered that her notion was quite an unfounded
one. I was above speaking to no one but those who
conducted themselves ill.

" I 'm sure," said Kathrine, scarcely attending to
my answer in her own desire to speak, and continuing to feed her little charge, who kept his blue eyes
fixed upon my face,—" I 'm sure I 'm glad that ye 're
come noo: for what wi' the mistress no being strong,
and my ither wark, the bairns, puir things, are no
half weel eneuch lookit after; and if they had just a
wee thocht mair air and meat, and less dosing, they
wad dae fine."

" Do they go out little ?" I asked.

" Far owre little, even in summer. Just now, it 's
sometimes owre damp, and sometimes owre cauld, and
sometimes ae thing, and sometimes anither, sae that
a week will aften gang by, and no see them owre the
door-stane,—nae wonder that they dae get caulds
when they are oot. But I canna persuade the mistress that it 's a' the faut o' keepin' them sae close

mewed up in the hoose. Gudesake! when I mind
the time I was a bairn mysel', how I used to herd my
uncle's kye amang the braes, and cared for naething
but my plaid, and a broom bush to keep me frae the
rain,—and whan had I caulds or headaches? I could
hae suppit four o' thae platefu's ony mornin'."

"How pleasant it must be to be a herd!" said
Helen, who had been greedily drinking in every
word of our talk. "Did you gather flowers in
summer, Kathrine?"

"Never you mind, Miss Nelly," replied the girl
smartly, "but sup up your parritch, and let me get
the room cleaned—it 's high time it was dune."

I thought it was only prudent to drop the conversation. The girl seemed inclined to reflect on her
mistress, and I hardly considered it right to listen to
it myself, or allow the children to hear it. So after
she had given utterance to a few similar remarks as
the foregoing, such as the folly of administering physic to cure trifling complaints, and slops instead of
solid food, in all which I certainly did secretly agree
with her, I silenced her by unobservedly drawing her
attention to Helen's earnest eyes and listening attitude. The girl glanced at her.

"Ay, she 's a quick ane," she said.—"Come, sir,"
setting down on the floor the little boy, who had
now concluded his breakfast, and carefully wiping his
mouth on her checked apron before kissing him,
" ye 've got yours owre your throat at ony rate ;—stand
still my bonnie man till I brush your head ;—there 's

no ane o' them to match ye (she looked at him with great pride). Be aff wi' ye a' noo, for I hear your mither opening her door, and that 's a sign we 'll hae worship sune." And hastily applying the brush to the rest, she left me to take them from the room.

Mrs Ronald made her appearance a few minutes after I returned with the children into the sitting-room. She had not seen them this morning till now. Her manner lacked energy so much, that her greeting to me seemed as warm as to them. The little things evidently knew their mother's ways, and did not speak to her, or run about her, as children in general are inclined to do.

We had prayers without delay, and then breakfast, which I prepared, relieving Mrs Ronald of all trouble, as I had previously done. I saw that it would soon become a matter of course my taking charge of every-thing. Mrs Ronald had such strong faith in Mrs Campbell's recommendation, that a period of proba-tion was evidently not deemed necessary to satisfy her of my trust-worthiness. She already gave me the keys of her cupboards, and on my offering to re-turn them, after getting out what articles were wanted, told me to put them in my pocket, that they might be at hand when anything else was required.

She complained much during breakfast of a pain in her shoulder, which she thought might turn out to be inflammation, and was rather low spirited in conse-quence; but yet she made a pretty tolerable meal

considering. She liked to sit and dawdle over her breakfast, so we were long in coming to a conclusion.   The
children, poor things, behaved very quietly and well,
not crowding round the table and greedily watching
for stray bits, as many youngsters consider themselves
privileged to do.   When we had finished, I asked
their mother if I might give a bit of bread and
butter to each, as a reward for their good behaviour.
She looked anxious and uncertain.   She was so afraid
of disordering their stomachs—and they had had their
breakfasts so lately.   I pleaded, however, for a little
bit, and she at last consented, only, I saw, to get rid
of the trouble of refusing.   I did not give them much
in case it might alarm her; but the children managed
the bread, so as to show that the porridge had not
entirely satisfied their appetites.   How they did enjoy it !

Next morning, I did not ask her consent, but gave
it them as a matter of course; and as she soon began
to have a kind of blind reliance upon my judgment,
she let me do as I liked.   I went on, therefore, beginning with a quarter, getting then to half a slice,
and, finally, ending with a large thick slice, which
might have satisfied Kathrine herself under the broom-
bush.   It was not too much for their appetites.   It
was the first time, I suspect, in their lives, owing to
their mother's dread of illness, that they had ever felt
fully satisfied; and as the change was gradual, there
were no injurious consequences.   Kathrine assured

me, in confidence, at the end of the week, " that she had never seen the bairns sae thriving-like, or sae manageable, since she came amang them."

On examination, I found the children far behind in their education. Of course they had lost a great deal during the weeks they had been kept at home. I inspected their books, and found they were mostly all too advanced for their powers. I therefore turned them mercilessly back, giving their mother my reasons for doing so.

And now I began to feel happy. With my little pupils clustered round me—docile little things they were too—certain that I had no severe monitress in their mother to deal with, and being on the best terms with both servants (and let me tell all governesses that is a great point gained), I had nothing left to wish, for several days. I enjoyed the peace and quietness of my new life extremely. It was as if I had anchored in a calm haven after a long and stormy voyage. But as there is no such thing as perfect contentment in this life, I began at the end of that time a little to weary,—that is, to feel a want.

Our days were spent in this manner. I rose at seven. To rise earlier would have been useless in the dark mornings. I drest Helen, and always assisted Kathrine in giving the children their breakfasts, for the girl had a great deal to do at times. She and I, by the way, soon understood each other. She was a clever shrewd girl; and as she saw that I earnestly wished to benefit the children she was attached to, she was not too proud to be advised. The nursery was never so airless as at first, and it was more tidy.

Mrs Ronald rose late. We had prayers at nine, and breakfast followed immediately. She then generally dawdled into the kitchen to give her servant orders about the dinner, or rather to receive suggestions from her. When they had agreed, Jenny went off to market, and her mistress would return to the sitting-room, and sit down by the fire with her unfailing knitting.

In the meantime, I had begun with the children's lessons, seated round the table, for we had no regular school-room,—Mrs Ronald liking to have our company in the parlour. We commenced with religious lessons, and here I found that the little things had been tolerably attended to. I gave them very easy tasks, and varied their lessons, so that they got interested in them.

At twelve o'clock we had a walk. I had a little difficulty at first in persuading Mrs Ronald to consent to this. Colds and sore throats she was certain would be the consequence of exposing the children to the air at this season of the year. But after being confined three days to the house, I did at length accomplish it, by *almost* convincing her that in a clear frosty day, such as that one was, when there was not the slightest damp in the air, the children would be benefited by the exercise. Kathrine, with beaming eyes, wrapt them carefully up, and I pro-

mised to keep them out only a very short time. Poor
Mrs Ronald looked wistfully after them, as Kathrine
and I led them away; but when I brought them back
from the Green in a short time, happy and rosy, her
countenance cleared up. She contended no more on
the subject, but yielded peaceably.

We had several days of hard frost, and the children
went out on each; and as their shoes were changed
the moment they returned, they caught no cold,—
their better feeding, too, strengthened them to resist
it. As I had incurred the responsibility, I was a
little apprehensive till I saw how well they stood the
change. We dined at one to suit the children, and
then to our lessons again. Before long we fell into
the habit of going out twice a-day, when the weather
permitted. Helen had a sewing-lesson when we returned, and then our labours for the day were finished.

Mrs Ronald seldom went out. To sit at the window and view the passing crowd, sometimes recognis-
ing an acquaintance in it, was sufficient excitement
for her. Occasionally a visiter would drop in: but,
as she seldom made calls herself, few people visited
her, none indeed but those who were kindly disposed
like the Campbells, and could bear patiently with her
infirmities. The family had no near relations in
the town. And really numerous forenoon visiters do
interfere very much with one's plans and comfort.

What can be more tantalizing and irritating to
the mistress of a family, possessed perhaps but of a
limited income, and with many duties pressing upon

her, than to be detained from the performance of those by a succession of gossipping visiters? There is something wrong in this. A state of society which may suit the idle and rich is most unfavourable for those who have themselves to put their hand to the wheel. But what remedy is there for this? None that I can think of, unless people would adopt reception-days, and close their doors at all other times, except to those friends they choose to admit; and that all ladies who are troubled with too much leisure be admonished to get rid of it, by visiting the abodes of the poor and the afflicted. I think it would be well if the clergymen of our day, when rebuking the follies and vices of society, would occasionally enlarge, for the benefit of their fair hearers, on those words of the great apostle—" And withal they learn to be idle, wandering about from house to house; and not only idle, but tattlers also, and busybodies, speaking things which they ought not."

The children and I had the benefit of any company Mrs Ronald had, for we always sat together. I thought at first that I should not like this arrangement, as it might materially interfere with my freedom in instructing; but I soon grew accustomed to it, and thought no more of Mrs Ronald's presence than of the arm-chair she occupied. I could not help feeling affection for her; but it was merely the affection one bestows on something that depends and reposes confidence on you. I could not like her as a companion. And it was this defect in her that made me erelong feel, as I have already hinted, that my new situation had its own drawbacks.

The life that Mrs Ronald led would have been insufferable to any one of a different nature from hers. She was no manager, and the servants arranged most things their own way, (it was much to their credit that they did not take advantage of her), but she liked a little quiet gossipping with her inferiors. She and Jenny were cronies. Jenny made the marketing, and was the family purveyor in all things; so she had often small chit-chat picked up in the shops, or at the butcher's stand, to retail to her mistress when she returned home. I could always observe that Mrs Ronald got fidgety, if Jenny delayed her return longer than usual; and she was sure to pay a visit of some length to the kitchen when she heard her arrive. If it was to settle accounts, they took a long time to do it.

The natural consequence was, that the servants could not respect their mistress, and took liberties with her at times, which she had not spirit to repress. But they served her faithfully nevertheless, and nursed her carefully in her sometimes real, but oftener fancied ailments.

In the evening Mrs Ronald depended upon me for amusement, and this was a sad infliction. Occupied by my cares for the children during the day (and I did not spare myself, for I loved the little things), I naturally looked to the evening hours for some relaxation. I should have liked to read then — to

have taken up a book now, and now to have taken
up my work, just as I felt inclined. But Mrs Ronald
never read anything but her Bible morning and night;
and the evening was the time, as she informed me,
when she liked to have a quiet chat. Knowing this,
and seeing her sitting silently opposite to me, (for we
occupied different sides of the fireplace, hers being the
side farthest removed from the draught of the door),
while the children played about the room till it was
time for prayers, I could not, from pure compassion,
pursue my own way independent of her. With a sigh
I would relinquish my own amusement, and exert myself for hers.

Once a bright idea seized me, which I thought
would reconcile all difficulties : I offered to spend the
evenings in reading aloud to her. But Mrs Ronald
had no inclination for that: she would rather chat
with me about Auchtermuir and my aunt's family;
for she was very inquisitive about my personal history,
and would even exert herself to question me on these
subjects, with a happy disregard to anything like re-
luctance exhibited in my manner and answers. She
had not observation enough to discover this, honest,
well-meaning, though weak woman; but seemed to
think that I must like as well to gossip about my
friends and private concerns as she did.

Many traits in the character of the late Mr Ronald
became thus familiar to me, besides incidents in his
history. She spoke in a low monotonous tone of
voice, the constant uniformity of which was trying to

the patience of a quick nature like mine. While she went on in this manner, relating her reminiscences of her departed husband, dropping her words like so many stitches in the stocking she knitted, I could not help sometimes secretly wondering, as I raised my eyes from my work, and silently surveyed her, what had been the attraction which had led the deceased Mr Ronald to unite his destiny with hers. She could never have been a beauty, even in her most attractive days; and her intellectual powers could not have been greater then than now. It fairly puzzled me. But one does see such strange marriages!

I learned at a later period, that Mr Ronald had engaged himself to her when somewhat young and inconsiderate,—that Mrs Ronald was also young and sweet-tempered (often the description of mere mental weakness), and that she was comely, and had two thousand pounds, which Mr Ronald wanted to assist him in business. The same authority informed me, that they had lived a tolerably happy life, as things go.—Mr Ronald managed the house, and bore very well with the helplessness of his wife, being active and good-natured himself. They had a child every year and a half—so that Mrs Ronald was always nursing when she was not an invalid—and she lay upon the sofa three months when she was *enceinte*. She was a treasure to the family doctor, and the best customer at the druggist's.—*They* felt her value.

But at length poor Mr Ronald was suddenly seized with a malignant fever, and to the consternation of all the household, who had never seen him ill before (Mrs Ronald having hitherto engrossed all the maladies, allowing no one to be ill but herself), he died in a very few days, leaving his wife a truly helpless widow, with four young children. Fortunately she did not require to make the struggle some have to undergo for a maintenance. For that her powers would have been altogether inadequate. She and the children were comfortably left ; and their affairs were happily in the hands of an honest man of business, who acted for her without consulting her, except occasionally as a matter of form.

She was a good woman, and in spite of her weakness had a sense of her responsibilities in regard to her children. She carefully attended to their religious instruction. But it would have been as well if she had felt less anxiety about their bodies, and trusted them a little more to Nature,—the great Mother. She had gradually got into such a habit of physicking herself, that she could not help using the same *precautionary* measures towards her children. They were not naturally robust, and she enfeebled their constitutions still more by this foolish apprehension. Then she had somehow got it into her head that children's appetites should be restrained, and that their meals should be very light, and never include animal food. Vigorous children thrive sometimes on any nourishment; but those little children were delicate things, puny and stunted in their growth, with looks which pleaded for nutritious diet and frequent feeding : but this never struck their mother.

Such was the system pursued with them till I entered the family; and then by quiet exertion, by detailing my own experience among the poor at Auchtermuir, and (excuse me reader) by the influence which my stronger nature had over Mrs Ronald's weaker one, I gradually succeeded in introducing a different mode of treatment, which was erelong followed by the happiest results.

It was remarkable that none of the children's temperaments resembled their mother's, unless it might be the youngest's. For a boy, he was certainly unusually passive and gentle. They were quick, lively children, though seldom noisy. In those dull evenings, it was interesting to me to watch them at play. Helen was a sweet child; she kept all the others in good humour. Jamie and little Jessie were apt to get petted if they had not all their own way, so Helen, though the eldest, had often to sacrifice her own inclinations to theirs: her nature was a yielding one.

When I first became her governess, there was a well of deep affection in her young heart, whose depths had never been stirred. Though Helen loved and obeyed her mother, the latter had not a mind to draw out and appropriate her child's sympathies. She was not fitted to understand Helen. The child clung to me from the first. Learning became easy and pleasant to her. As her difficulties were smoothed for her, and she had no punishment now to dread, her progress was rapid and delightful. I was at times astonished at the quickness and thought evinced in her

remarks. She became passionately fond of books. I
have often observed her, while her brothers and sisters
were amusing themselves with games, coiled up in a
corner of the room with a book in her hand, utterly
insensible to what was passing, — one might speak
to her, but she heard you not. I was always sure at
those times that it was either Robinson Crusoe, or a
small book of natural history embellished with plates,
which occupied her. Dear little Helen: she was my
first pupil, and I loved her much. She had all the
germs of a valuable woman in her nature. Hers was
a spring-time of much promise.

I was delighted with the quiet of the Sabbaths
in my new home. Mrs Ronald had been strictly
brought up, and now practised her father's good old
rules in her own household. To her maids she made
it literally a day of rest. The house was locked
up during divine service, except in time of illness,
and we all went to church. We regularly went
through a portion of the Shorter Catechism in the
evening. The catechism was divided into two parts,
and we had these on alternate Sabbaths. Poor Mrs
Ronald was generally very sleepy on these nights.
The unusual exercise of walking to church and listening to two sermons was too much for her lethargic
nature. It was a sore struggle she had sometimes to
preserve appearances before her assembled household,
and not to set us an evil example by dropping asleep
amidst our exercises. The later portion of the
Sabbath evening was my own, for Mrs Ronald was

then never inclined for conversation, and I could read in peace. The three eldest children liked the Sabbath evenings, for I told them stories out of the Bible. But it was a sad day to little Tommy, who slept in church and got cross when roused; moreover, all his playthings were locked past. His only resource was to sit on Kathrine's knee in the kitchen, while she sang psalm-tunes to lull him.

While I was busy with my pupils and the various duties of my new situation, Mrs Campbell was slowly recovering. At first, Mrs Ronald sent kindly several times to inquire for her. But after a few days had passed, I asked permission to go myself to the High Street in the evening; which was willingly granted. It was a pleasant surprise to Mary, who did not expect that I would get so soon to see them. She was very glad to hear I was happy in my situation. I was somewhat grieved by her appearance— she looked pale and worn-out; but she would not acknowledge that she felt ill. She took me into her mother's room for a few minutes. Mrs Campbell looked decidedly better than when I last had seen her. But she was not fit for much conversation; so I only mentioned briefly how I was getting on, as she was anxious to know, and soon left her.

I saw Marion, the servant, before I came away, and she told me that Mary had had no exercise since her mother's seizure, which accounted for her looks. But she had complained to Mr Grey (Marion had), and he was coming next day to take her out with him, while she watched the invalid. Mary smiled, for this was told me in her presence, and said that Marion was growing quite despotic. She was always tormenting herself about her (Mary's) looks, "and never thinking," she added, patting the faithful old servant on the shoulder, "that she has much more fatigue than I have."

"Fatigue!—hout, fye! I wonder to hear ye speakin', Miss Mary. What fatigue hae I, I wad like to ken? An auld body like me has naething else to dae but to look after ithers. But ye are young, and ye maun tak' tent o' yoursel'. It's no canny to see a young creature wi' sae white a face."

"Why don't you lecture Miss Douglas?" said Mary. "Isn't she pale too?"

"She would thole amends," replied Marion, turning her eyes from her young mistress to me, and nodding with great good nature; "but she has a wee glint mair colour in her face than she had when she was last here. It's no muckle, but it's the promise o' mair.—Bairns! bairns! if ye had seen as mony fair young faces pine away and vanish as I hae done, ye wad cherish health when you hae 't." She seemed to be looking back into the past. Her serious manner affected us. But she shook it off, and bidding Mary "gae back to the room, and no be gettin' her death o' cauld in the lobby this frosty nicht," she ushered me to the door herself, carefully feeling my *haps* as she did so, and lecturing me on the propriety of warm clothing.

Mary soon paid me a hasty visit at Mrs Ronald's. She found me seated in the midst of my little pupils, happy and busy. She told me Marion had made good her point of getting her to walk every day, by appealing to her mother. She had therefore come to see me. They had now heard from Auchtermuir. Annie was delighted with the manse, even at this bare season. All the neighbours were very kind; but she hoped soon to be home. She had seen Mrs Johnstone, and had many conversations with John, in spite of his gruffness (Annie's gentleness could disarm any one). But she had one sad piece of intelligence for me. Widow Wilson was dead. Neither Annie nor William knew their mother had been so very ill. Mary thought it would only distress them unnecessarily; and in the letter she had written to Annie, she had carefully avoided alarming her. Now, indeed, there was no occasion to say anything about it, as it was probable, that by the time they saw her again, she would be restored to her usual state. Mr Campbell was to see his sister safe home.

Mary had time to tell me all this before Mrs Ronald made her appearance. She was in the kitchen when Miss Campbell called, and had to go to her room to change her cap, which was not always fit to receive company in; and this detained her some minutes. She was very much pleased to see Mary, and to hear that Mrs Campbell was getting stronger. But she was most profusely complimentary regarding me— almost embarrassingly so. She bade Mary again and

again convey her thanks to her mother for having recommended me to her.   The children were getting on
so well, and were so happy with me, and she herself
had so little trouble now about anything.

Mrs Ronald said nothing but what she really felt,
I believe.   The little scene was got up, I knew, as a
kind of recompense to me, and because she liked the
Campbells, who were my friends.   But I should have
preferred its taking place in my absence, and not in
the hearing of the children.   However, it was of no
great consequence.   I was a little too fastidious
perhaps.

I made a point of calling on my aunt the second
Saturday after entering on my situation.   She had
not invited me to do so; but I considered it right to
pay her this attention.   She was my dear father's
only sister, though she had perhaps been wanting in
kindness to me.

I was received coldly.   Her two eldest daughters
were at home, and they were also stiff and ungracious.   No inquiries were made about my situation,
and how I liked it.   But though they did not conde-
scend to show any interest in my affairs, they vouch-
safed me, before I left, a few particulars concerning
themselves.   Eliza's marriage was fixed, and was to
take place in about three weeks.

My cousin Eliza had certainly been fortunate as to
mere worldly things.   Her future spouse had not only
an excellent business of his own, being a partner in
the house of Morrison and M'Callum, West India

merchants, but his father was wealthy, and had no other child alive. No wonder then that Eliza Dalgleish had paid so much attention to old Mrs M'Callum the previous winter, when she was laid up with cold; had so denied herself to sit by a deaf old lady's bedside for hours, and scream herself hoarse in telling her the news. If ill-natured people thought that she aimed at the son through the mother, what did it signify? Eliza had accomplished her object, if it was that; the old people judged her a pattern of every kindly virtue, and her very detractors would be glad enough to visit her, in her handsome house in Millar Street.

Eliza could not now speak without lisping, or move without affectation. I was amused watching her during my half hour's visit. What would she be as a wife, when her splendour so elated her as a bride? My aunt herself was evidently swelling with vanity and self-importance. Though I was informed of the approaching marriage (indeed they could not have been silent on that subject for the world), there was not the most distant intimation given of a wish on their part that I should be present at it.

I at last took my leave, without any one hinting about returning my visit. No doubt they considered that to have a niece or cousin a governess in the same town with themselves was bad enough, without seeking her out in her situation. Neither was there a word said about my renewing my visit. My aunt seemed resolved to let me do as I liked,—she was quite indif-

ferent about me. Margaret's mind was occupied with
her sister's marriage. I thought her manner, however, a little softened towards me before I came
away. Hannah was ready with a gibe in the lobby,
but it was less caustic than formerly, as if absence
had somewhat disarmed her. I was glad to feel so
independent of them all. I had got a disagreeable
duty over when I had made the call; and I returned
to the home that Providence had allotted to me, doubly
sensible of the blessings of its peace and kindly
simplicity.

When Mrs Ronald heard of my cousin's approaching marriage, which she did that very night, at our
usual hour for such gossipings, for I knew it was just
the thing she would like to know, she seemed to take
it for granted that my presence must of necessity be
required at the ceremony. She was much grieved
and disappointed, therefore, when I assured her of the
contrary; and I had some difficulty in convincing her
that there was no chance of one of my cousins coming
yet with an invitation. It spoiled our whole evening,
for she was never done condoling with herself on being
thus deprived of a full detail of the ceremony. Some
women have an absolute craving after those things.
It took a visit to the kitchen, and admitting Jenny
into her confidence, before her mind got quieted on the
strange fact, that I was not expected to be present at
my first cousin's marriage. I suspect that Jenny,
from her frequent visits out of doors, knew the world
better than her mistress, and was not so much sur-

prised that so grand a lady as the future Mrs Archibald M'Callum should overlook her cousin the governess on such a high occasion.

When I first entered Mrs Ronald's family, I could not help thinking (though only for a time) that she was not unlikely to enter Hymen's bands a second time herself. She would, no doubt, have been an easy prey to any man who might have thought her income worth the penalty of encumbering himself with a weak helpless wife and four children.

The most frequent, indeed almost the only, visiter we had, was a grey-haired preacher, who lived somewhere in the town. He was a great favourite, I soon discovered, with Mrs Ronald, and I do believe he might have married her if he liked. I wonder he did not, for he was poor and solitary, and he might thus have secured a comfortable home. He had been disappointed in getting a living, and was now turned of fifty. He had an income barely of the same number of pounds a-year to support him. He sometimes eked it out a little by officiating for ministers who wanted to go from home, and were willing to pay him for performing their duty. Still, Mrs Ronald told me, he had a difficulty in making both ends meet.

He used to drink tea with us every week. Tuesday was his regular night, and those were my most comfortable evenings. Mrs Ronald was always sufficiently amused by Mr Lochead's conversation. They suited each other admirably. He knew a great deal of small gossip, and his voice was pitched low. He sat opposite to her by the fire, for I vacated my seat in his favour. He used to bend forward in his chair while he conversed, his legs crossed, and his hands clasping his knee, with his eyes thoughtfully fixed upon the embers. This was his favourite attitude. He was very formal and precise, and quite of the old school both in dress and manners.

He always uttered a most interminable grace before tea, I remember. The first time the tea got cold, but I knew better afterwards, and never poured it out till after he had finished the benediction.

Mrs Ronald was very kind to him, and sometimes pressed him to partake of her good things, as if she meant to propitiate him through his stomach. I believe she liked the man. Be that as it may, there was no courtship on his side. He partook liberally of her tea and toast, and cookies and jelly; and he talked to her afterwards for two hours generally on religious subjects in old-fashioned phraseology, which had a smack of quaint old authors about it, but he never advanced a step farther.

He always conducted family worship before he left. One thing struck me in connexion with Mr Lochead: the servants could not endure him (perhaps they suspected their mistress's partiality as well as I), and the children evidently did not like him. I noticed that on Mr Lochead's nights, as we called the Tuesday evenings, the children would steal away to Kathrine, though on other nights they preferred to play in the dining-room. Children understand when they are liked. Mr Lochead was a disappointed man, and an old bachelor; and like most such he was selfish, and liked his ease, which children are apt to interfere with. This was the secret, I suspect, of his unpopularity with them.

CHAPTER X.

Again the spring came round,
The sun shone blithely down;
The ivy on the ancient wall
Shook off its tinge of brown.

In three weeks time, as I expected, the news of
my cousin's marriage reached Craig's Court. The
M'Callums and the Dalgleishes were people of too
great consideration in Glasgow for a connexion to
take place between the families and not create a sensation.

Miss Eliza Dalgleish's dresses had all been exhibited and commented upon in Miss Pinners' show-
room. Half of the ladies in the town had been
there to see them; the old ones were amazed at her
extravagance, while the young ones envied her luck.
Those who were of her acquaintance congratulated
themselves, that some portion of this splendour might
be reflected upon themselves: those who were not
were severely censorious on her red hair and fine pretensions, and criticised her taste. This is just human
nature—feminine nature, at least. I cry you mercy,
my dear sisters.

Mr Dalgleish had not been slow in relaxing his purse-strings; and the mercers and other trades-people had reaped a bountiful harvest. The whole town rang with the splendour of the marriage pre-parations. No wonder, therefore, that Jenny was able, by her visits to the shops and to the pump-well down the street a little way, to bring in so much in-telligence on the subject. Her mistress was almost satisfied, though (as I warned her) no invitation came for me. She expected it every day, and, of course, every day was disappointed, for I was entirely over-looked. My aunt and cousins had other matters to occupy them at present.

The marriage did take place at last, and Jenny was our informer, and could even tell us who were present, and how most of the company were drest. Dr Porteous, the bride's minister, had performed the ceremony, and Warrander Balgairney had been one · of the waiters.

Mrs Ronald amused me. She resented things on my account, which gave me myself no concern what-ever. Resented is perhaps too strong a word to apply to her feelings; but she was indignant so far as her nature would allow her. When the marriage was over, and she was convinced that there was no mistake about it, she turned her attention to the cake. She was in hourly expectation of a packet arriving for me, and Kathrine never entered the room without her raising her head from her knitting, and inquiring if such a thing had not come and been left lying about in the kitchen by some oversight. Kathrine's patience failed at last, after having had the same question put to her for half a dozen times.

" No, it 's no come," she said briskly, as she swept up the ashes from the hearth ; " and what 's mair, ye needna expect it.   Proud dirt that are owre grand to notice their ain relations, what wad they be sendin' cake here for ? "   I beg the reader to understand, that whatever the servants suspected of my position with my relations was communicated by their mistress and not by me.

I thought that Mrs Ronald would have shown herself displeased with Kathrine for speaking her mind so freely, and glanced towards her when the latter left the room after disburdening herself of this remark. But no ; Mrs Ronald sat as placidly in her arm-chair as usual, and was just then engaged in hunting after a stitch, which, on account of her lazy way of handling her wires, she had dropped in her stocking. When she had secured it, she rose and went " ben" to the kitchen to interrogate Jenny on the subject, in whom she placed more confidence than in Kathrine.

But her anxiety was thrown away, for the cake never arrived; and as she could not credit such neglect, and had besides a high opinion of my merits, she decided at last, that the parcel must have been intrusted to the care of some dishonest servant, who had appropriated the contents to her own use : an opinion of which Kathrine did not scruple to profess her utter disbelief, and at which even Jenny shook her head doubtfully. They were much more interested in the matter than I was.

But the subject could not last for ever; and in about a week's time I heard no more about it, though Mrs Ronald often expressed her wonder that my aunt and cousins did not visit me, and could not make up her mind whether I ought to wait upon Mrs Archibald M'Callum before some explanation had been made. This furnished conversation for our evenings. I let her *maunder* on without troubling myself at all about the subject. As I was quite indifferent to Mrs Archibald M'Callum's grandeur, and had never felt any esteem for her,—it depended entirely on *her* feelings what terms we were to be on. Relations as we were, I would not enter her house without an invitation.

I was more interested in the return of Annie Campbell from the country, which happened about the same time as the marriage, in the middle of February. The first intimation I got of it was by Mr Campbell's walking into the room one forenoon while I was giving the children their lessons, and Mrs Ronald was dozing like the cat by the fire. She had a little rheumatism in her head, and she had wrapt so many things round it, that she fell asleep from pure inability to hear a sound. His entrance did not disturb her. I saw a smile cross his face as he looked at her. I did not wonder at it,—her attitude was so peculiarly comfortable and unstudied like. He did not wish me to rouse her; but when I said, that I thought I ought, he only stopped me till he had presented me with a little bunch of snowdrops, which he had held till now unobserved in his left hand.

They were from my own garden—Auchtermuir snowdrops from the early bed sheltered by the hedge. Mr Campbell said he had been watching them for a week past, that he might have the pleasure of bringing them to me.

I don't know how I thanked him. But I know that I forgot to waken Mrs Ronald, and ran out of the room to kiss and cry over the lovely white blossoms in my chamber, with a mixture of sweet and sorrowful feelings I did not then seek to analyze. When I had placed them carefully in water, and out of Tommy's reach and sight, for he sometimes paid my room a visit, I returned, not without embarrassment for having betrayed so much emotion, to the sitting-room.

I found that Mrs Ronald had woke up in my absence. Mr Campbell and Helen had managed to rouse her between them; and poor Mrs Ronald was looking very stupid and nervous in consequence of the surprise. But she was acquainted with Mr Campbell, and fortunately was not aware what a strange appearance her manifold wrappings gave to her head. I heard him telling her when I entered, that they had been glad to see their mother so well, and to find her as cheerful as ever after such an attack as she had had. Here I caught a grateful glance of his eye. I asked him, when had they arrived? He

told me, last night; and added, that he was charged
with a commission from his mother and sisters, partly
to Mrs Ronald and partly to me. It was to request
that I would spend the evening with them in honour
of Annie's return, if Mrs Ronald could spare me.

Mrs Ronald had not the heart to refuse anything:
she was ready and willing. Moreover, it was rather
lucky that on this very evening she expected a visit
from her old monthly nurse, with whom she still kept
up an acquaintance; and they had all her four con-
finements to talk over. Indeed, I was better out of
the way. Mr Campbell was assured that there was
nothing to prevent me coming; and my looks, as well
as my lips, told him that there was no objection on
my part. He played a little with the children, and
set them a laughing by insisting that I should also
give him a lesson, which tickled them for the rest of
the day, for they believed he was in earnest. He
then left us.

None of us, I believe, were quite in a mood for
lessons for some time afterwards. I was inclined to
reverie, and I suspect had been in one for some minutes, when little Helen startled me out of it by
whispering in my ear: " What lovely flowers those
were, Miss Douglas! Don't you love the gentleman
for bringing them ?—I do."

I was very glad to see Annie again: and she was
as light-hearted as a bird to feel herself at home once
more. She was on the watch for me at six o'clock,
and ran down a bit of the stair to meet me; and then

she had so many things to tell me, that I thought
I should never get my bonnet and cloak off; and
Mary was at last obliged to seek us to bring us in
to tea.

We were just the same party, in all respects, as
had formerly drank tea together here,—Mr Grey and I
being the only visiters.   I had often seen Mrs Campbell since her sudden illness, but not upon her couch.
She had left her room for the first time the previous
day, and had stood the change well.

I spent a very happy evening, principally occupied
in listening to news of Auchtermuir.   Annie had a
letter for me from Miss Menie Weir, which contained many advices concerning my conduct as a
governess, and hopes that, if it were possible, I would
visit them in the ensuing summer.   Mr Campbell
saw me safe home at night to Mrs Ronald's.   He
required to return to his parish the following day,
but told me that it was his intention to ride down
every ten days or so to visit his mother.   I promised
to have a long letter ready for him to carry to Miss
Menie by the time he returned.   He had already
made himself acquainted with all my old pensioners.
I was even astonished at the minuteness of his information concerning them, considering how short a
time had passed since he had been placed in the
parish.   I almost felt as if it were a personal service,
and required my thanks : but I checked myself.

I was afraid that Helen might waken up that night
and see me hanging over the snowdrops ; and yet if

she did, what would it matter? But there are some emotions which we cannot bear others to witness, not even a child like Helen. I jealously guarded those snowdrops. I would not have parted with one of them for the world. I changed the water in which they were, placed daily to keep them fresh; and when at last they grew dry and withered, they were taken out of the glass, wrapped carefully in silk paper, and hidden in my bosom. Ah! Were they not flowers from my own home? Mr Campbell brought me others each time he came, but still I wore the first in my bosom.

The weeks wore quickly on. Spring was advancing. I paid occasional ceremonious visits to Charlotte Street. Sometimes I missed my aunt and Margaret, for now they were constantly at Eliza's. When I did see them, I was received with indifference. My aunt's irritation against me was now almost forgotten in the increasing prosperity of her family. Once something was said by her about my drinking tea with them some evening, but it was never followed up by a direct invitation. I have little doubt she was glad enough now that I had saved her trouble by looking after myself. They could talk of nothing but Eliza, her house, her dress, and her parties, for the M'Callums were already entertaining their friends. It made me thoughtful after I had left them, and led me to muse on the engrossing nature of riches. That prayer of Agur's,—" Give me neither poverty nor

riches," seemed to me to contain the essence of true
wisdom.

Once when I was there Eliza came in. It was
about three months after her marriage, and the first
time I had seen her since.   She was now no longer
the young lady, who is generally considered an in-
significant person, and must yield the *pas* to others.
She was metamorphosed into a stately dignified matron, covered with as much finery as her milliner
and mantuamaker could manage to adorn her with
at one time, or her husband's purse purchase.   She
came swimming in at the door, greeting her mother
and sister somewhat slightingly, as if she was conscious that Miller Street was a step in importance a
little before Charlotte Street.   Her furbelows and
trimmings reduced one in a moment to insignificance.

Her mother could not make enough of her. It was
" my darling," and " my dear Eliza," at every word ;
and there were so many anxious inquiries about Mr
M'Callum, that I thought once of asking if he were
ill.   But I found that they only arose from the interest my aunt took in her son-in-law.   Mrs M'Callum
received all these attentions very coolly,—indeed, just
as a matter of course, and as what she was entitled to,
—and was excessively communicative (for my behoof
doubtless) about her house, her servants, and the style
in which she lived, in return.

Her aunts happened to walk in while she and I
were there, and such an affection they testified for

their dignified niece! I thought they never would be done embracing and admiring of her. Margaret came in only for a cool shake of the hand, though they were sisters. Mrs M'Callum seemed flattered by her aunts' *empressement*. They all gathered round the idol, so I thought it as well to come away. Mrs M'Callum took leave of me by extending her forefinger, and lisped out that she would be glad to see me any day in Miller Street. I thanked her, but I did not say that I would come. I had never seen Mr Dalgleish since the day on which his house ceased to be my home. I had once caught a glimpse of Robert on the street, but fortunately we never met face to face.

My little pupils and I all this time progressed happily. They were advancing in their studies, and were all attached to me. I strove to preserve constantly fresh in my mind a deep sense of my responsibility as their teacher. I was aided in this by the friendly counsel and warnings of Mrs Campbell, from whose house I was never long absent. She was of much service to me in this respect. I felt that God had given me those children in charge, and that I was either educating them for or not for Him. I therefore made them the subject of earnest prayer. I strove to check the little wayward tempers of the younger children, and to lead them to be affectionate and gentle to each other, and certainly they did improve. Helen was all I could wish. I had no trouble with her. She was so sensitive, that a look was sufficient to punish her at any time; and if she thought that I was displeased with her, she would fling her arms round my neck and burst into tears. No one could help loving such a child. I did most fervently. I pitied her mother that she could not comprehend the treasure she possessed in Helen.

The children had also improved greatly in health during the months that I had been with them. They had had slight illnesses occasionally, but as I was their nurse, they soon got over them; for I warded off the doctor, (who was of the old school, and drugged his patients unmercifully,) and coaxed Mrs Ronald into forgetfulness of the druggist's shop. The children enjoyed a healthy spring. They now had plenty of wholesome nourishing food, plenty of fresh air when the weather permitted them to take exercise on the Green, and abundant daily ablutions of soap and water. I had made an early convert of Kathrine to my views. She was a sensible girl; and feeling now that there was some kind of management in the house, she seconded me admirably. She also listened to my admonitions concerning her want of respect for her mistress, and amended wonderfully. For my part, I was always careful to treat Mrs Ronald with the observance due to the mother of my pupils, and the mistress of the household. She was so contented with my behaviour, and she led so easy a life, that she conceived as strong an affection for me as she was capable of feeling for any one. She could not do without me now she said. I was happy myself in having inspired this affection, and in being necessary for her comfort. It made me feel more at *home* in her house. I still felt the evenings to be a bondage, all but the Tuesdays and Sabbaths. I spent almost every Tuesday evening at the Campbells, and blessed Mr Lochead for enabling me to do so. I always, however, made tea for Mrs Ronald and him before leaving, that she might have no unusual trouble.

Mr Campbell generally rode down to see his mother as often as he had said. He always staid one night, and sometimes two. He obtained Mrs Ronald's consent to show me the Cathedral, and everything that was worthy of attention in the city. There are many natives of Glasgow who are perfectly ignorant of the old architectural relics which still linger in the nooks and recesses of the town. Mr Campbell had the taste of an antiquary, not as regards ancient manuscripts and "nick-nackets" (I rather think he was indifferent to these), but he loved to search out those fast-decaying specimens of early greatness, no matter where they were situated. My feelings were congenial to his in this respect. He was proud of his birthplace, and was versed in all its early history.

The time for Mary's marriage drew on. It was fixed for the first of June. To have had it in May would have driven Marion, the old servant, distracted, for it would have brought ill luck, according to her belief. Nothing occurred to postpone it. Her mother was tolerably well, and able to be present. I was there, for I had a full holiday. There were no

strangers,—two of Mr Grey's married sisters, and
their husbands, being only invited.   Dr Balfour,
whom I had now met often, married them, and William gave his sister away.   Mary looked very pretty,
but pale.   She trembled very much ; but I saw that
she endeavoured to command her feelings, on account
of her mother.   Annie's tears would not be restrained
however.   She evidently felt that she was losing her
sister,—they could be no more the companions they
had been,—and so overpowering was her agitation,
that she had to leave the room more than once to give
vent to it.   Mary had a sore struggle in parting from
her mother ; and I once expected that she would
have been fairly overcome.   But she mastered the
emotion.   She kissed Annie and me tenderly ; but she
hurried away from the former, as if she feared to trust
herself with her.

It was a sad day altogether.   I would have liked to
have got away, that I might have had a good cry by
myself.   But I had to exert myself, and appear cheerful, that I might keep up Mrs Campbell's and Annie's
spirits.   I was greatly aided in this by Mr Campbell,
who kept close by his mother's couch the rest of the
day.   Mr Grey's friends and Dr Balfour had taken
their leave almost immediately after the bride and
bridegroom had left us.   I am sure I don't know how
we got through the day.   But we did get through it at
last, and Annie and I put Mrs Campbell to bed before
we parted at night.   I believe that Marion and Mary
Lowrie had been shedding tears all the afternoon in

the kitchen, for their eyes bore all the traces of them when they appeared at worship-time. Mr Campbell told me, on our way to my abode, that he himself had had great difficulty in preserving anything like cheerfulness before his mother through the day, and that he had observed I was in the same predicament. So I am afraid that none of us imposed upon the others. Mary was gone, and all felt the value of what had been taken from the household.

But when Mary was once fairly established in her own little dwelling, when we had seen how well she looked in her pretty simple drawing-room, and at the head of her own table; especially when we saw how proud James Grey looked of his little wife, and how well pleased all his friends were, no one could wish her back. Annie and her mother of course missed her often, but she daily spent hours with them, and her husband and she were there almost every second evening. The houses, too, were so near each other, that Annie could run in to Mary's for five minutes, and never be missed.

How happy Mary looked (her bashfulness as a bride giving her a greater charm) the first time her brother dined at her table! Her only drawback was, that her mother and Annie could not be there also. She took me that same evening through her house, and showed me how convenient it was, detailing all her plans with the pride of a young housekeeper. It was a very nice roomy house, not too large, but just the thing for a young couple; and

it was very neatly, though plainly, furnished. Mr
Grey had a good business, though he was a young
man, and not long established. He was bred to the
law. Mary herself would inherit three thousand
pounds at her mother's death. But both had the
desire to live quietly, and without ostentation. " We
shall have the more to assist others with, Rose,"
added Mary, when speaking of this. Mr Grey and
his wife seemed to have a fair prospect of happiness
together, as they were both sincerely pious, and had
commenced their married life with prudence and so-
briety. Upon the whole, it was a happy arrangement for all parties; for the marriage once over, I
thought that Mrs Campbell's mind was more at rest
concerning her daughters. I suspect that she was
secretly conscious by this time of an increasing debi-
lity in her system.

For some weeks Mrs Ronald had been talking, in
our evening *tête-à-tête*, of perhaps taking the children
down, for a month or so, to the sea-side. She seemed
very undecided on the subject for some time, as it was
not easy for her to make up her mind to anything
where the responsibility lay entirely with herself.

She liked plans to be recommended to her, and
then she would settle. The children heard her often
dwelling upon the subject, and were most anxious to
go. The idea of playing on the shore, and gathering shells, was quite exciting. A few foreign shells
lay as ornaments upon the mantel-piece, and they
thought that the shells at Largs or Rothesay (for it

was to one of those places Mrs Ronald decided to go, if she went at all) would resemble them, and that they would also hear the sound of the sea in them. Nothing would persuade them that it was not the distant murmur of the ocean they heard in the shells. Jenny had told them so, they said, and Jenny had been born at the sea up the Gairloch, a great bit farther down than the great castle of Dumbarton.

At last Mrs Ronald's mind was made up in this manner. The servants, of course, were well acquainted with the domestics in the family who occupied the second floor of the house, the one immediately beneath ours. This family were going to the sea-side, and, as Jenny said, " were quite astonished that anybody could be so ungenteel as think of remaining in town all summer."

Now, Mrs Ronald, for some reason or other, had a little spice of jealousy in her heart about this particular family. She thought (I quote her own words) that they considered themselves above her, because she lived in a higher flat,—another stair up. Though a well-meaning inoffensive woman, who lived in peace with her neighbours, she had still her little piques and resentments at times with them all, but particularly with this family. There was some old dispute, I believe, about the washing down of the common stair, the " camstoning " of it, as it was called in Glasgow, in which Mrs Ronald conceived herself aggrieved, and in regard to which she did not think that Mrs Baird had used her well. To be twitted with want of gentility by such a person was not to be endured, especially considering who Mrs Ronald's father had been, and who Mrs. Baird's father was; so, after a great many desultory remarks of the same kind, and consultations with Jenny in the kitchen, who was decidedly on the side of the "saut-water" expedition, Mrs Ronald finally made up her mind upon taking us all to the sea-side, and "there was no doubt," she thought, "but that the children would be the better of the bathing."

Then came the settling as to the place. But it was at last fixed, that if Mrs Bannatyne's lodgings in Rothesay were unlet, we should go to that island. I was empowered that very evening to write the letter of inquiry to Mrs Bannatyne, and to inform her, that if she could accommodate us, we might be expected to arrive sometime about the beginning of the following month.

The steam-boats that now hourly ply on the fair bosom of the Clyde, bearing crowds of passengers on their decks to their villas and lodgings, scattered liberally on the various shores, were not then in being. Small vessels called packets sailed from Greenock to Rothesay, and other places frequented by the Glasgow citizens, for the accommodation of the public. If the wind was favourable, those packets could cross to Rothesay in little more than two hours, but sometimes the same number of days might elapse before the little vessel could reach its destination and land its sea-sick and worn-out passengers. The voyage therefore was sometimes a serious matter, especially where there were children.

And now, till the answer arrived, poor Mrs Ronald was in a perpetual fidget. She could not rest, nor let any body else rest a minute. It was such warm weather too, that I wonder she did not throw herself into a fever from anxiety of mind. The exertion of going from home was so great, that the bare anticipation of it, now that the first impulse was gone which had led her to decide upon it, was quite overpowering. What would the reality be? The children were in great spirits. They began the first night it was decided to pack up all their playthings to be in readiness, and had been alternately packing and unpacking ever since.

At last the answer came, and Mrs Ronald heaved a deep sigh when she read it—Mrs Bannatyne's lodgings were at her service. And now began the packing in right earnest; the buying in of stores to take with us; the rummaging out of old mouldy boxes from under servants' beds, and from dark closets, to hold them, most of these proving quite unserviceable when examined; the deciding what amount of napery would be requisite, and whether it would be necessary to take knifes and forks, as well as silver spoons with us, no one being able to say whether Mrs Bannatyne undertook to furnish those useful articles. Mrs Ronald had none of the actual labour of preparation, the servants and I taking it all upon ourselves, but she looked as miserable, and sighed as frequently, as if

the whole burden were upon her own shoulders. She
could not remain still, but kept wandering from room
to room like an unhappy ghost, sitting down to rest
herself occasionally, and looking with a dejected air
at the bustle taking place around her. She sometimes ventured a suggestion, as if to maintain her
character foı usefulness; but her suggestions were
seldom much to the purpose.

"Gude sake! Mem," said Kathrine, (who, as the
reader knows, had not much forbearance with her, one
day when this happened,) "Canna ye gae wa' ben
the hoose, and rest yoursel' on the sofa?—ye 're just in
folks' way here, and we dinna need your help."

"Kathrine," I said in a low admonitory tone. The
girl coloured up, and softened her voice immediately.

"I mean, Mem," she added quickly, "that ye are
just fatiguing yoursel', and we dinna wish that—let
Miss Douglas and me fecht awa—we 're fit for 't, and
you arena."

"Well, I think you 're right, Kathrine, my woman,"
answered her placable mistress, and she rose from her
seat and went back to the sitting-room, leaving us to
proceed with our packing without interruption. I did
not wonder that Kathrine was fretted, for at the moment Mrs Ronald ventured the suggestion she was
earnestly employed in endeavouring to accomplish an
impossibility, namely the insertion of a parcel into a
place too small to hold it. The day was very hot too,
and Kathrine was tired, and Mrs Ronald's languid
sleepy tones were most irritating to flesh and blood.

At length the time arrived for our departure. I was sorry to leave Glasgow for so long, on account of my friends the Campbells, who of course were compelled to remain there during the whole summer. But I was pining after fresh air and country scenes. The hot dusty town was so unlike the wild moorland walks and quiet woodland paths I had been accustomed to in former summers. The children were also drooping, and needed change of air. I knew that the four weeks would soon fly past, and then I would be with those dear friends again. I had declined Miss Menie Weir's invitation. It was impossible to leave Mrs Ronald and the children at present; I could not tell how I might manage in future.

Two days before we left town, I asked Mrs Ronald's permission to call in Charlotte Street. I had not been there for some weeks, and considered it right to pay my aunt the attention of inquiring for her, before we went to Rothesay. I had to ring several times before I was heard, and then Kirsty, the cook, opened the door instead of Hannah. She had always been more civil to me than the latter, who liked and disliked to suit her mistress; and after telling me that all the family were from home, with the exception of Mr Dalgleish and Robert, was earnest that I should come in and rest: but I declined doing so. I asked where the family had gone to, and was informed that both they and the M'Callums were at Rothesay, our own destination, where they had taken lodgings for two months. I thanked Kirsty, and came away.

I could not help thinking my aunt very indifferent to the fate of her niece, her only brother's only child, when she could thus leave town without caring to know whether I was or was not to remain in my situation (she knew my engagement was quarterly), and had the certain prospect of a home to shelter me. She might have sent me a note, I thought, or one of the girls might have called. It created within me a sudden and strong desire to economize my little income, that on any unlooked for contingency I might not be thrown altogether destitute. I felt that I was truly left to fight the great battle of life unsupported. The half year's interest of my three hundred pounds had been faithfully remitted to me in May by Mr Dalgleish. The sum was seven pounds ten shillings, and I had about the half of it still remaining. I determined if possible to make the fifteen pounds, which was the interest of my money, serve for my dress and my small charities, and to lay by my salary.

Our mode of travelling to Greenock to meet the packet was this. Mrs Ronald hired a caravan from a man in Glasgow, which conveyed us and our luggage to Greenock. We locked up the house, leaving the keys with a trustworthy person in case of fire. The caravan was a common plan of conveyance at that time for families to the seaside. There was a coach which ran between Glasgow and Greenock, but there were so many of us, and we had so much luggage, that the caravan was both cheaper and more convenient.

It was a tiresome journey to us all, for though the children set out with high spirits, they soon got fatigued and impatient, thinking we were rather going from the sea than towards it, because they had not yet got a sight of it. Mrs Ronald too was filled with dire apprehensions concerning the place we would get to sleep in at Greenock, and could not be convinced that we had not left some of our bundles and boxes behind us in the lobby,—undoubtedly that one which contained all the candles and soap intended for the four weeks' consumption. She knew the prices of those articles at such places as Rothesay, she never ceased repeating.

" Wull I unlock the boxes, Mem, to satisfy ye ? " screamed Kathrine, who was seated at the other end of the cart with Tommy on her knee. " Gudesake ! Jenny, tak aff the rapes, and let the mistress see wi' her ain een. They' re in that wee black trunk wi' the brass nails on 't."

I could have laughed, though I was as tired of Mrs Ronald's complaints as the rest, but I prudently restrained myself. When the box was finally unlocked, after a great deal of trouble, Kathrine was found to be wrong. A quantity of broken lump-sugar, done up in paper not of the strongest, came suddenly tumbling out, owing to an unlucky jolt of the cart over a stone at that moment, and was scattered liberally among the children's feet. But that was not all. Mrs Ronald had privately with her own hands stowed into that very box sundry bottles of medicines, intended, in case of emergencies, to be at hand during our residence at the sea-side, and these followed the sugar, and were broken in pieces. They were not odoriferous,—indeed very much the contrary; but happily their contents were absorbed by the straw, or dripped through the crevices of the cart, nobody suffering any damage by them, save in their olfactory organs. I earnestly requested that no further search might be made after the missing candles and soap till we had reached Greenock. But the current of Mrs Ronald's thoughts was changed, and now she could think of nothing but the broken bottles. Her lamentations were piteous to hear. She seemed certain that we were to be seized with every disease under the sun (by the bye she occasionally studied Buchan), and without proper remedies at hand. I was thankful when we reached Greenock.

We got pretty comfortable quarters at an inn there, which our driver recommended to us, and I succeeded in getting both Mrs Ronald and the children early to bed, after fully satisfying her mind that the candles and soap had accompanied us. Next day was fine. We got on board the packet without any accident, and without leaving either child or parcel behind us.

It is a charming sail down the Frith of Clyde, but unfortunately the water was rather rough, under the influence of a strong breeze, and I could enjoy little of the ever-opening views, as, with the exception of Mrs Ronald and Jenny, we were all sick. The former, instead of being cared for as usual, was obliged to exert herself for others. I do believe she was nearly angry with me for being ill. I don't know what we should have done but for a kind-hearted fellow-passenger, who helped Jenny to look after the children. Happily we had not a long voyage, the breeze which made the little vessel pitch so was in the most favourable direction for us, and in less than three hours' time from our embarkation at Greenock we were landed at Rothesay pier,—all more or less in an exhausted state however. Our landlady was on the pier waiting the arrival of the packet, which she thought might likely have us on board.

Sea-side lodgings in those days were somewhat cramped places. We were pretty closely packed. We had a bed in the sitting-room, and there was a folding-down sofa there too, which was made useful. The servants had a queer nook to sleep in. But by the following morning we got wonderfully reconciled to all our discomforts. The sight of the sun dancing on a broad expanse of heaving water—boats shooting here and there upon it—" far ships lifting their sails of white like joyful hands"—the firm pure sand glittering to the eye, sprinkled here and there with rocks covered with sea-weed — the unusual spectacle of bathers hurrying from the shore into the sea—and above all, the fresh bracing breeze which met one at every turn—all these enlivened the spirits, and made us satisfied with everything. Even Mrs Ronald enjoyed herself, and moved with something like animation along the shore.

The children were wild with delight. And though they could not find any shells equal to the ones at home, still they were quite satisfied with what they did pick up. They and I were seldom in doors. Our lessons were very brief. We had a month of delightful weather, and the children and I were quite rosy by the time we returned home. What appetites we had! The bottles were well broke; for the sea-air was the best medicine we all could have. We led a very idle, wandering, gipsy kind of life, servants and all, and we even got Mrs Ronald dragged out before we left as far as to Ascog, and had our dinner on the shore. Mrs Ronald was astonished at herself.

That lovely Rothesay bay! How long it is now since I have seen it! But I cannot forget it. I hear that the shore is now all specked with villas, and that the town has become a large place. But the view must be still the same. It was the first time I had seen the sea when I accompanied Mrs Ronald and her children there; and the delight intoxicated my senses for a while. We bathed the children, Kathrine and I. At first they were frightened, but they soon grew to like it, and we had a scene of fun and frolic every morning while performing it.

We were not long at Rothesay when the children and I encountered my relations. It was impossible to avoid meeting. It was no welcome recognition on either side. They seemed surprised to see me, and looked with some contempt on my little charges, who were only plainly drest. They gave me no invitation to call for them, and I kept out of their way as much as possible afterwards. But I was doomed, a few days after this, to give my assistance to Jemima and Margaret in rather a whimsical way. The former did not thank me for it afterwards, I daresay, though she was glad enough of my help at the time.

One fine evening the children and I had taken a walk by the hill-road to Ascog, and were returning, when who should we meet in a hollow but my two cousins,—Jemima mounted on a stout pony (for she had taken it into her head to learn to ride), and Margaret walking. They were in a sad dilemma when we reached them. The pony had a will of its own, and its old home lying in an opposite direction from the town, it seemed determined to proceed thither in spite of the opposition of its rider, and the timid attempts which Margaret occasionally made to turn it by the bridle. They had been struggling in this manner for half-an-hour before we came up, and no one had appeared to help them, for the road was lonely. Jemima's courage had fairly failed her at last, and, as the pony continued wilfully to advance in the wrong direction, was divided between crying and scolding Margaret for her ineffectual attempts. The moment they caught sight of me, I was earnestly entreated by both to give my assistance.

I had been well accustomed to horses at Auchter-muir; so, desiring my little pupils to stand still, I advanced cautiously towards the struggling pony, and succeeded in seizing the reins, and turning its head

towards the town. But Jemima, through fear, was
now perfectly unable to manage it; and I soon saw,
that if I quitted the bridle, matters would just be as
they had been before. So, at Jemima's urgent entreaty, for she was humble enough at present, I
led the pony back to Rothesay,—Margaret condescending to look after the children,—for I made that
the condition of lending my assistance.

Not a word was spoken by any of us on the road.
I walked foremost, pulling the reluctant steed by the
bridle, and Margaret came up a short way behind
with the children. Jemima was probably ashamed
to be indebted to me, but dared not relinquish my aid.
A pretty figure we must have cut entering the town.
I led the pony to their lodgings. My aunt was
seated at the window, and I saw her start with
amazement when she caught sight of us. But now
that I had got my task accomplished, I made no
delay. Hastily relinquishing the reins to a lad in
waiting, I caught hold of my little pupils' hands, and
bidding Margaret good-night, I hastened home with
them, without looking behind. I never saw Jemima
again on the pony. The next time I met her, she
coloured and pretended not to see me.

My aunt and the M'Callums had the best lodgings
in the town. They kept themselves very much aloof
from the plainer Glasgow families who were there,
and were no favourites in the place. Mrs M'Callum
walked about the shore, astonishing the natives with
the splendour of her dress and the grandeur of her air.

The gentlemen were only occasionally able to leave the cares of business, and pay their families a visit. I don't think Robert was down at all, for in a small watering-place like Rothesay one knows exactly who comes and goes. I once met Mr Dalgleish on the shore, and received a very kindly greeting from him, as none of the family were within eye-shot.

The children and I left Rothesay at the end of the four weeks with great regret. Mrs Ronald and the servants, however, were beginning to weary to get back to town. The former missed Mr Lochead's society, and the latter that of their cronies. They had had enough of the sea-side. I was reconciled to go, because I should again see the Campbells. I had had a letter from Annie soon after we left, and they were then in their usual way. William had not been down again, but they expected him soon.

We were once more fortunate in weather and wind, and reached Greenock on our homeward route without sickness or delay. The same caravan that had conveyed us there was now in attendance to transport us home. We got into it immediately, and reached Glasgow that same night.

There was much to do of course the following day. Mrs Ronald wisely kept her bed during the forenoon, so she was in no one's way, and we got everything unpacked; and the carpets, which had all been taken up before leaving home, were laid down, and the rooms made comfortable before the evening. When the children were quiet in bed, and Mrs Ronald en-

gaged in a gossip with the trust-worthy neighbour,
who was the wife of a grocer close by, settling with her
for her outlay and trouble in providing for our return,
I stole away to pay a hurried visit to the Campbells.
They had heard that we were expected home, so
they were not surprised to see me. Mrs Campbell
was looking but poorly, and had been confined for
some days wholly to bed, but she was cheerful as
usual. Annie seemed to me as if she would be the
better of a trip to the sea-side herself. I heard that
Mary and her husband were both well. I had not
time to pay Mary a visit that night.

I promised to drink tea with them on Tuesday
night, if Mr Lochead made his appearance. Annie
thought I should probably see William then, as it was
about his usual time for coming. I blushed, and she
smiled, I could tell why.

I visited Marion and Mary Lowrie in the kitchen,
and was kindly welcomed back by both. The former
highly approved of the complexion I had brought
from Rothesay, and said I looked " vera weel indeed," and that she wished she could just get Miss
Annie to the same place whaur I had been.

CHAPTER XI.

The summer passed and autumn came,
With berries red and brown;
And foaming from the mountain-side,
The stream came rushing down.

MR LOCHEAD having made his appearance at his usually early hour on Tuesday evening, I was able, after caring for his and Mrs Ronald's comforts, to drink tea myself with the Campbells. And there I met Mary and her husband, whom I had not seen (except at a distance in church on Sabbath) since we had come from the sea-side. William had arrived too just a few hours before me, and as usual he brought me flowers, for he expected that I would be back from Rothesay by this time. His sisters smilingly upbraided him with his forgetfulness of them; so I wished to share my treasures with them, but they would not permit me. Dear Mrs Campbell was not on her couch to-night; but her door was kept open, as she liked to hear our voices she said, and one or other of us was constantly beside her: and we had music too, which she was able to enjoy. As some of us had not met for a number of weeks, we had much to tell, and were more than usually happy, at least I was.

About this time poor Mrs Ronald met with a serious affliction. Her only brother, who, I think, was manager of a bank, or some such thing, either in St Andrews or Dundee, (I cannot recollect which at this distance of time,) died suddenly, and left his family in rather straitened circumstances. Mr Craig had been a genial cheerful man, fond of company, and very hospitable, and had lived up to his income. He had always kept from getting into debt; that was all that could be said of his prudence. As he was only fifty-five when a stroke of apoplexy carried him off, perhaps he looked forward to a long life, and to commence saving. But I suspect he was one of those easy, good-tempered, but selfish characters, who live but to enjoy themselves, and never think of the future at all.

One thing he deserved commendation for; he had educated his family well, at least those who were grown up. The eldest was nineteen, a daughter. There were seven others, both boys and girls. Fortunately Mr Craig had not encroached on his patrimony, which, like his sister's, was two thousand pounds. This was all that the family had now to depend upon; and as there were three boys, whose ages varied from five to fourteen, to educate, it was rather a dull prospect for them. The two elder daughters were alone fully educated, and they had enjoyed the advantages of Edinburgh schools,—of

course they could teach the younger ones. Mrs Craig
was a sensible woman, who had done what she could
to restrain her husband, though to little purpose, and
she made retrenchments immediately. An old friend
of their father's took the eldest of the boys into his
office, and promised to look after him, but that was
only a slight relief. Mrs Craig thought of taking
boarders, and her friends undertook to exert themselves on her behalf. But two months passed by
after her husband's death, and they had not yet succeeded in hearing of one.

Jane, Mrs Ronald's eldest niece, wrote occasionally
to her aunt. From her letters we learned all those
particulars. I say *we*, because Mrs Ronald had got
into the way of consulting me on every thing. I
thought that Miss Craig must be a sensible girl from
the manner in which she expressed herself when
writing of their future prospects. She seemed anxious to relieve her mother of the burden of her maintenance, and said that she and her sister thought of
taking up a school in their native town, but feared
they might not get pupils, as there was a very good
establishment there of the kind already. It appeared
to be a relief to her to unburden her mind by writing
to her aunt, for she had not yet mentioned her plans
to her mother, waiting till they should have somewhat
ripened.

Mrs Ronald was sorely disturbed by these commu-
nications. She had by this time got pretty well over
the shock of her brother's death; but her niece's let-

ters kept her spirits in a state of constant despondency. As for giving advice, she was perfectly helpless: still she could not rest till it was settled what the family were to do. She was always lamenting over the style in which her brother had lived, and the privations his children would now feel; and to do her justice, I believe she often thought of how she could benefit them. She once proposed to make a journey for the purpose of seeing them, and having a talk over matters; but it was too formidable a thing for her to undertake, and she abandoned the idea.

Those letters of Miss Craig's made me very thoughtful. For some time I could not see my way clearly; but at last I unburdened my mind to my friends the Campbells, and they approved of what I could not but think it was my duty to do. This was no other than to resign my situation in Mrs Ronald's family in favour of one of her nieces, and to look out for another for myself. It was very painful to me to come to this resolution, for I was strongly attached to the children. I knew the idea had never suggested itself to Mrs Ronald's mind, and that I should have no easy task to reconcile her to it; for though she was interested in her brother's family, they were almost strangers to her, and she was accustomed and attached to me. But that did not make it the less incumbent upon me to recommend the plan to her. If there had been any defect in the education of the Misses Craig, I might have hesitated, on account of my pupils' interests; but Jane Craig's letters spoke highly for her attainments.

Many a sleepless night did this subject cost me, and many a tear did I shed over little Helen; but I felt that it must be done. I put myself in the position of Mrs Ronald's relations, and I saw it was what they would naturally expect—nay, did expect—from the tone of Miss Craig's letters, though too delicately alluded to, to suit Mrs Ronald's powers of comprehension. I could not bear to be an obstacle in their path. My spirits were affected by my ruminations. I could not preserve my former cheerfulness. The children and servants noticed how dull I was, but could not comprehend the reason. Even Mrs Ronald became at last sensible of the change, and inquired if I were ill. She did this one night when we were sitting alone together, after the children had gone to bed. She had made some remarks, to which I had returned no answer; and as I had fallen into her habit of sighing very often of late, she immediately decided that I must be ill, and looked very much concerned.

I had not yet given her the slightest hint of what had been occupying my thoughts, thinking that, till my own mind was quite made up, it was best not to annoy her by introducing the subject. But now that I was satisfied as to what my duty was, I felt that the sooner the matter was discussed the better. Therefore, after relieving her apprehensions of my indisposition, I set myself seriously to make a convert of Mrs Ronald to my views. I commenced cautiously, for I knew she could endure little excitement. I began, therefore, with lamenting the change which had taken place in her brother's family, spoke of the difference there must be in their mode of living, and in their expectations, to all of which Mrs Ronald responded with deep sighs and gloomy shakes of the head (she had evidently prepared herself for a comfortable gossip, little dreaming of what was in store) ; then I praised the young lady, whose letters I had read, her common sense and clear-headedness ; said she must have got an excellent education, and be well fitted for instructing others ; and, finally, seeing that Mrs Ronald was pleased with my remarks about her niece, I insinuated, that though she perhaps might not succeed in the plan she had lately proposed, she might be able to procure a governess's situation.

Mrs Ronald listened to me with much satisfaction, having no suspicion of my drift, and said that she would mention it to her niece when she answered her letter, which she had been talking of answering for the last week. But when I grew more explicit, and told her what situation I had been thinking of for her niece, her distress and bewilderment were extreme. I thought she was really going to be ill, and almost regretted I had been so precipitate. She was quite reproachful about the willingness I showed to leave her ; spoke of the comfort and quiet she had enjoyed since I came to the house, the progress the children had made, and now to talk of leaving her ! She did not doubt her nieces would get on very well where they were, or they might get other situations which would suit them as well as hers. She at last

ended with a fit of crying, and I sat and joined her
heartily.

I saw that it would not do to press the matter farther at present, and, indeed, poor Mrs Ronald's mind
had got such an unexpected shock, that she kept her
bed all next day. But the ice was broken, and I
was quite aware that when the idea became more
familiar to her mind, she would probably get reconciled to it. I had observed, on former occasions, that
by constantly dwelling upon any subject, she came at
the last to relish and approve of it. But it always
took some time.

I was myself rather glad to defer the question, as
she earnestly requested. I was in no hurry to leave
my pupils. I felt relieved that I had made the proposal, and willingly allowed a week or two to pass
without making any further allusion to it.

Mrs Ronald, in the meantime, I could see was fidgety and uneasy. When alone with me she carefully avoided mentioning her relations' names; and if
any more letters arrived she did not show them to me.
She spent even more time than formerly in the kitchen, and I have no doubt but Jenny was quite con-
versant with the whole affair. I noticed too that she
grew a little jealous of my going out in the evenings,
as if she suspected I was situation-hunting, and that
she looked narrowly at my countenance when I returned. My friends the Campbells were certainly
exerting themselves on my behalf; but they agreed
with me that I must make out the year at Mrs

Ronald's (Mrs Campbell saw no need for haste), and there still wanted three months of that time. Of course, if Mrs Ronald continued resolutely opposed to the scheme, it was settled that I should remain quietly in my situation,—to act otherwise would be disinterested folly. But I thought I knew her character too well to believe she would keep so. I was aware that she was consulting Mr Lochead on the subject, and her decision depended very much on his opinion.

My conscience being relieved, and having at all events three months to spend with my pupils, I was resolved not to allow myself to be too much cast down, though sometimes, when teaching or playing with them, the thought of being obliged to leave them did make me feel acutely. I saw that Helen, with her usual quickness, noticed something was wrong, but as she could not discover what it was, she only doubled her usual testimonies of affection. She caressed me oftener, sometimes looking pitifully into my face if I was sad, and then clasping her arms round my neck and kissing me. This tenderness and sympathy on the part of the child made me feel the prospect of parting from her all the more keenly. I do believe, in spite of my desire to be unselfish, that I secretly hoped Mrs Ronald might continue in the same mind as at first.

It was an anxious exciting time for me that, for more reasons than one. There were hopes in my breast, that I scarcely dared to whisper to myself, in case I might be deceived, far less to confide them to others.   The future was enveloped in mist and obscurity, but still a bright ray would often steal across the void, and fill it with beautiful images and rainbow tints.   But they were *so* evanescent.   I tried to keep from thought as much as possible.

My aunt's family arrived at home a few weeks after us.   I called for them about this time, a piece of civility which I performed merely from an undefined idea of the duty of doing so, not because it gave satisfaction to either side.   I said nothing about the probability of my having to leave my present situation, in case my aunt might suspect that I wanted to return to my old quarters.   I knew differently, and that under her roof I should never more seek a shelter, homeless though I might be; but it would not have been easy to convince her of this.

Jemima had now left Miss Blair's school for good and all, and though she was so young, I learned that she had persuaded her mother to bring her out during the ensuing winter—that is, to take her along with Margaret to the public assemblies.   My aunt and cousins had attended these for the last year or two, though, owing to my father's death, they had been forced to absent themselves from them during the past winter.   Jemima was at home when I called on this occasion.   She had all the airs of a grown-up woman, though she was only fifteen.   She received me very haughtily indeed, and while I conversed with her mother, affected to be so occupied with some beads she was stringing, that she could not speak.   Mar-

garet was not there. Eliza was not many months
from her confinement, and she now generally resided
with her.

It was sad at this time for me to observe how that
good and valued friend of mine, Mrs Campbell, was
gradually failing. I thought I could see a change
upon her almost every week. Her own daughters
were not so sensible of it as I, who saw her seldomer.
Marion, her old servant, however was well aware of
it, I am sure, from some remarks she made to me one
evening when she was lighting me to the door. I
could not disguise from myself the secret apprehension, that probably she might not live over the winter.
At every visit I paid to them now, I brought away a
heavy heart. I felt keenly for Annie. I remembered
my own clinging to hope during my father's illness,
and unwillingness to believe the worst. I saw she
was low-spirited at times, and that she would occasionally gaze anxiously at her mother when she
thought she was unobserved. She seemed afraid of
having her fears confirmed, for she carefully avoided
asking my opinion. Mary was more unrestrained,
and spoke earnestly to me about the new symptoms of
weakness her mother was exhibiting. I could not
deny that I had myself observed them. Mary said
repeatedly that she wished Annie could have some
one with her constantly, and then she paused and
looked at me wistfully, as if she wished to say more,
but did not know how to do it. I did wish that I
could have aided Annie in nursing Mrs Campbell, but

there were reasons then, even were I free from my engagement to Mrs Ronald, which made me reluctant to offer my services. I could not explain these to William Campbell's sisters: so when Mary spoke and looked thus, I coloured and was silent. I hoped that Mary did not think I was unwilling. I do not think she did, for her manner to me was still as sweet and kind as ever.

William still came and went, and I saw him constantly. I could easily perceive he was not fully aware of his mother's state. Perhaps I was the most quick-sighted of the whole, on account of having so lately watched the dying. Mrs Campbell was very cheerful though weak. The spasms to which she had been subject for years were less violent when they occurred, but they returned more frequently. She still took as lively an interest in all around her, and in every scheme for good, as before. Some time after this, nearer to her death, she informed us that from the period of that violent attack which I described some chapters back, she had felt sensible of a gradual decay of all her powers, and knew that death was at hand. But her life had been a long preparation for death, and she looked calmly towards it.

It was a melancholy time to me, and so occupied was I by my apprehensions concerning Mrs Campbell, that, at last, when Mrs Ronald, somewhere about the middle of November, informed me that she had consulted with her friends about what we had spoken of, and as they were unanimous in advising her to adopt my advice, she had now made up her mind to do it, I felt less than I once expected to do. I certainly did cry bitterly over my little sleeping pupil at night. But I was not taken by surprise, for I had seen that Mrs Ronald had been gradually veering round to approve of my suggestion for the last three weeks. She had occasionally dropt hints which showed me this. Mr Lochead had been her principal adviser, and being both shrewd and worldly-wise (no wonder considering his struggling life), he had counselled her rather to bestow board and salary on her own flesh and blood than upon a stranger. He warned her, that if she did not adopt this plan of relieving her sister-in-law's burden, she would probably be expected to contribute something towards the support of the family. And no doubt Mr Lochead's advice was both prudent and sagacious. This alarmed Mrs Ronald, and though with some regret, she allowed herself to be convinced.

And now where was I to wend my weary homeless feet? Not to my aunt's; oh! no. How was I with my limited resources to procure another situation? My present engagement would close in less than two months. Did I regret, however, that I had recommended to Mrs Ronald the course which she had now adopted? No. I felt I had only acted justly, and that if it had again to be done, I should offer the same advice. Those children though—how painful it would be to part from them! I could scarcely command myself in their presence for some days.

Where was I to apply to?—that was the question now. I turned plan after plan over in my mind. To write to Miss Menie Weir, and request her to influence her Glasgow friend again on my behalf, was the only feasible one that occurred to me. The Campbells had enough of anxieties at present about their mother for me to mention the subject to them. Besides I did not like to tell them it was now settled I should leave Mrs Ronald's, in case they might propose I should take up my residence with Annie. That would have pleased me well, what indeed my heart was yearning for, and what they I knew earnestly wished; but I thought there was an obstacle to it. I therefore kept my sorrows and cares for the future hid from them. Mrs Ronald had no influence I knew, and could not assist me. She might have offered me the shelter of her roof till I procured a situation; but obligations of that kind were distasteful to me.

I sometimes thought of now accepting the often re-newed invitation of the ladies at Burnside; but to remove to such a distance from my dying friend I could not bear; besides there was a stumbling-block in the way there too. I was afraid of ill-natured sur-mises if I went to that part of the country at present. I should also be completely out of the way for hearing of any situation. So I did in the end what I ought to have done from the beginning, cast myself upon Providence, and left the future to His care. Ah! if we would always do so while diligently using the means he has placed in our power, how many cares and anxieties might be saved us ! This was peculiarly exemplified in my case.

And now, reader, I approach the most momentous period of my life. Such an event as that I am about to mention is the most important one that can occur to any woman, for the whole complexion of her after-existence depends upon it. It was peculiarly momentous to me, for the future was a bleak and formidable prospect just at that time, and doubts and fears oppressed my heart.

I had sometimes lately dreamt of happiness,—of a return to scenes and to a life which were very dear to me; but yet, I as often feared I was deceiving myself, and that I was mistaking mere brotherly feeling for a deeper and warmer affection. I was afraid I had bestowed my own affections where they might never receive a return; and I became jealously sensitive that my secret might be discovered. William Campbell was so superior, so excellent, that I often blamed myself for foolish vanity in fancying that his regard for me was more than common,—and yet—. It was my uncertainty about this that made me reluctant to share Annie's cares and become an inmate of his mother's house, which otherwise I should anxiously have wished. But all was for the best.

One night, about a fortnight after Mrs Ronald had announced her intention to me, I had gone up to the High Street to inquire for Mrs Campbell. I was in low spirits. My troubles were pressing hard upon me, and I had had great difficulty all that day in casting

them where I wished to do. I remember vividly my
feelings as I walked along the streets—how I longed
for some light to break in on the future, or a friend to
whom I could speak of some of my perplexities!
As I said before, owing to my peculiar feelings,
I had not mentioned to the Campbells that it was
at last fixed I should leave my situation at Mrs
Ronald's. I felt a craving for a friend. I was very
dispirited indeed.

When I entered the Campbells' parlour, I was surprised to find William there, for it was not his usual
time for coming. His mother was confined to bed,
as she had constantly been for some time, and
Annie was with her. He was standing leaning
against the mantel-piece, with his eyes thoughtfully
fixed upon the fire. He started when he saw me,
and seemed flurried and agitated when he spoke. I
was the same, for I was taken by surprise, and could
only utter something about his visit being unexpected.
Before he could make any answer, Annie, who had
heard my voice, made her appearance, and I went in
to the bedroom to see her mother. I sat for a little
time with Mrs Campbell; but I required to be early
home that night, for Mrs Ronald was alone, and it
had been merely my anxiety about the invalid that
had brought me out. I wanted besides to breathe the
fresh air, and was in hopes that exercise might lighten
the burden on my spirits. I told Annie I required to
go home, when she pressed me to remain after we returned to the parlour. Mr Campbell did not second

her invitation, but left the room to get his hat and
greatcoat to accompany me. As he had only arrived
a short time before, I meant to beg him to let me go
alone; but my voice was so low and faltering to-night
that I could not get my words out. So we went down
stairs and along the street together, as we had often
done before.

Ah! that was a momentous walk to me, and to
him also. Had I been deceiving myself?—No. Before I reached Mrs Ronald's, and we took a considerable time to do so in spite of my hurry to be gone at
first, I found that I had indeed been so fortunate as
to secure the affections of a warm and generous heart.
What he said, and what I answered, I cannot tell now
particularly; but I learnt that this explanation would
much sooner have been made if he had not been
labouring under the same doubts and fears as myself. But he had left Auchtermuir that day determined to have these doubts settled either one way
or the other, and when I made my appearance so
unexpectedly at his mother's, was revolving in his
mind how to obtain an opportunity of seeing me
alone.

What an altered appearance had the streets now as
I walked lightly along them, leaning on that arm
which was hereafter to be my stay and protection
through life! How gaily glittered the shops! How
merrily rang the bells as we passed the Cross!—
How happily beat my heart, on which my betrothed's
snowdrops still reposed, and had for many months,

though a sadness did steal across it, when I thought of her state to whom I could now unshrinkingly offer a daughter's affection. William was to present me to her the following evening in my new character; and I promised that when I left Mrs Ronald's, I should share Annie's cares.

We must have walked for a long time about the streets, though it seemed short to us, for it was ten o'clock when I entered Mrs Ronald's lobby. She, I found, had got tired of sitting up, and had gone to bed,—very luckily, I felt, for I could retreat to my own room immediately. When there, what a host of feelings had I to review!—What a sudden access of happiness had I to contemplate! I had left that room some hours earlier, pale, sad, and desponding. I entered it again beaming and hopeful. I was no longer an orphan and homeless. I had a mother and sisters,— a home ready and eager to receive me. And in future—" Oh! my dear father," I murmured, suddenly bursting into tears, " it is true what you said,—God has indeed tempered the wind to the shorn lamb. Is it not enough that I have secured his affections to whom I have so unhesitatingly committed my own ?— But am I really to be restored to my own home, to spend my future days where my earlier ones were passed ?" Well might I adore the goodness of God, who had so marvellously cared for me and dispelled the gloom of my prospects. And that night I could freely utter *his* name in my supplications.

I kissed little Helen that night when I lay down, instead of crying over her as before, and thought how happy I should be to have her visit me at Auchter-muir.

CHAPTER XII.

How tumultuous were my spirits the following day—
how free from care and apprehension! No anxieties
for the future, except that natural one to continue to
deserve William's disinterested affection. How I
romped with the children one moment, and the next
sat pensively down unheeding their play. That was
when I thought of Mrs Campbell. Then I could not
help going up to Mrs Ronald and kissing her cheek;
my heart was so full of all kind affections, that I
required to give vent to them : she had always been
kind besides to me. She looked surprised, but she
smiled placidly. The children were delighted at the
sudden change in my spirits; and I believe we made
it a complete holiday, for I scarcely was sensible how
they got through their lessons.

How cheerful did the day seem to me, though a December rain was pattering heavily against the windows;
though the streets were clogged with black mud, the
natural consequence of a smart shower on the pave-
ments of Glasgow; and though the constant sight of

dripping umbrellas whenever one looked out, might reasonably have made the lightest hearted dull! But there was sunshine within my breast.

I had requested permission to spend the evening at Mrs Campbell's, which had been granted, though with some surprise that I should wish to go there two evenings in succession. When Mrs Ronald saw how heavily it rained, however, in the forenoon, she said she supposed I would not venture. Honest, unsuspecting woman! she did not know that I would have gone even through a thunder storm. I said I was not afraid of a wetting.

How nervous and fluttered was I, when, during the forenoon, the door was opened by Kathrine, and Mr Campbell walked in, ostensibly to call upon Mrs Ronald, who pocketed the compliment very pleasantly, receiving him in her most gracious manner, and expressing her regret that he should have come through the rain for such a purpose. I was obliged to stoop my head very low over Helen's grammar to conceal my smiles and blushes, till the child looked wondering up into my face with those intelligent eyes of hers, as if she read my secret.

Mrs Ronald was very earnest that Mr Campbell should advise me to remain quietly at home on the evening of so inclement a day, as I could easily go any other night to Mrs Campbell's, she said. She did not know that William required to go back to his parish next day. I was obliged to have recourse again to the grammar when he answered her objec-

tions, trying to persuade her that the day was not so
very bad after all; and that his mother and sisters
would be grievously disappointed if I failed in keeping my engagement. If it would be any relief, however, to Mrs Ronald's mind, he himself would be
happy to call for me, and shelter me from the storm
by carrying my umbrella for me. Mrs Ronald was
very sensible of Mr Campbell's attention. It was
very kind and thoughtful indeed, and would relieve
her mind,—but it was giving him so much trouble.

"Oh! not at all,"—and I caught an arch glance
of his eye as he spoke that made me laugh in spite
of myself. Then Helen laughed to see me laugh,
and her sister and brothers laughed also because
she did so. Mrs Ronald could not understand why
we were all so merry, but she looked quite unsus-
picious.

Mr Campbell sat about an hour with us, directing
almost all his conversation to Mrs Ronald, though his
eyes kept up a busy communication with mine whenever I met them. The children would not remain
away from him, and followed him even out of the
room when he went away. He ordered them back as
little incorrigible rebels who ought to be whipt, declaring that Miss Douglas was not fit to be a governess, as she could not keep them in order, and ought,
therefore, to look out for some other occupation. Mrs
Ronald could never distinguish joke from earnest, so
she immediately entered upon a serious and lengthy
defence for the purpose of proving that I was really

not deficient in the art of governing. Mr Campbell
affected to listen with attention, and at length con-
fessed himself perfectly convinced. He then took
leave, promising that he would certainly call for me
at six o'clock.

Mrs Ronald, when he was gone, said that certainly
he was the most obliging young man she knew, and
that his politeness in offering to come for me just to
relieve her mind was really—she did not know what
to call it—was beyond praise. It put her in mind of
poor Mr Ronald during their courtship,—he was always so attentive, and so afraid she would catch
colds. But almost everything put Mrs Ronald in
mind of her deceased husband.

" Miss Douglas," whispered little Helen, coming
up to me as her mother left the room, " Is the gentleman really coming just to please Mama?—You
remember he brought you the snowdrops."

" Did you not hear your Mama say he was, my
dear?" answered I, amused by the quickness of the
child.

" Yes—but I am not sure," said Helen thoughtfully.

I was quite ready by six o'clock, and punctual to
the hour Mr Campbell rang the bell. He again promised Mrs Ronald to take great care of me, and we
set off together. But at the foot of the stair he would
pause and examine if I were warmly clad.

" It is a sad night after all," he said ; " and I
must take care that my little Rose is not withered

by the storm." He was satisfied when he saw the thick cloak and shawls, and the stout boots I had on.

The night was very wet,—the rain was heavy, constant, and searching,—and the lamps and shop windows glimmered faintly through the moisture that clung to them. The few passengers hurried quickly on, as if anxious to get under shelter as soon as possible. The men had their coats buttoned up to the chin, and their hats drawn over their brows. Even the beggars seemed to have deserted the streets. There were a few stragglers sheltering themselves under the piazza at the lately erected Tontine newsroom, when we passed it. Our hearts were probably the happiest on the streets that night. We were not able to say much to one another, for the sudden gusts came in swirls under the umbrella, nearly reversing it at times, and bringing rain, mixed with sleet, on its wings. William hurried me quickly on, for fear I should suffer from exposure to the damp. I was reared in the country, however, and could bear to face the blast.

When we arrived at his mother's, he instantly consigned me to the care of Marion, bidding her pull off all my wet things immediately. Marion looked at us both deliberately.

" Deed," she answered, " I think ye are the maist drookit like o' the twa.—There 's been little o' the umbrella on your side, I wis.—See to yoursel', Mr William, and I 'll look to the leddy here."

She stript off my wrappings and boots, and took them to the kitchen to dry for me.

Mary and Annie sought me in the bedroom. I was a little fluttered at the prospect of meeting William's mother and sisters, now that I stood in a new position to them; not that I had much doubt about my reception. They came to me whenever they knew I had arrived, and each gave me silently a sisterly kiss,—and then they smiled archly at my confusion.

"Why were you and William so long in coming to an understanding, Rose?" asked Mary with matronly composure. "We have been expecting to hear of this so long."

"Have you indeed?" I said with surprise, to find that it had been no new intelligence to them.

"Yes, for months," said Mary smiling; "indeed, we suspected William liked you from the first; but we have been certain of it for a long time, and have been wearying till you chose to inform us of it. It has made us all so happy now." And we all embraced again with tears in our eyes. It was so delightful to know that they wished me to be their sister, and to think that I had found relations.

"Come away now to Mama," said Annie; "for she is expecting to see you." I felt my heart beginning to beat quickly again at the thought of meeting Mrs Campbell.

The sisters led me into the parlour. Mr Grey was sitting there reading. He got up immediately, and shook hands warmly with me. William was with his mother. When I entered her room he hastened to me, and led me up to his mother's bed-side. I raised my eyes timidly to Mrs Campbell's face. She smiled sweetly, but was a little agitated at first.

" God bless you, my dear," she said, putting out her wasted hand to draw me closer to her, and giving me a motherly kiss. " I have long had the affection of a mother for you, and I am happy I am now to have the title of one.—God bless you and her, William."

William affectionately kissed his mother's hand, and then placed his arm round me. " I did not think she would have been so afraid of you, mother," he said, smiling to restore her composure, and glancing at me; " but she is all trembling."

" I was not afraid of Mrs Campbell," I said blushing.

" No, she did not need to be," said his mother: " it is an arrangement we have all been expecting and hoping for; and I will say this of your little wife that is to be William, that she has good and rare qualities, well calculated to make you happy. She has tenderness to make your home pleasing, and energy to meet any trials that God may be pleased to send on you. I have observed her character.

I coloured again with pleasure and emotion to hear such a woman as Mrs Campbell thus speak of me, and her son looked much gratified. Mary and Annie now came in, for they had lingered behind with Mr

Grey, leaving William and me alone with their mother for the first few minutes. We all remained and conversed with Mrs Campbell for some time. But she was easily fatigued, and at last we went to the sitting-room. I had, however, some conversation alone with her farther on in the evening. She then spoke with the freedom and openness of a mother to me, and talked plainly of her own condition,—more plainly than she had yet liked to speak to her daughters.

She said that she felt herself rapidly sinking, and that she did not expect she would see the spring. But if she was alive when my engagement with Mrs Ronald was finished, she wished I would come and reside with her. " She did not know, of course," she said, " what arrangements William and I might propose making ; but let her house be my home till the time of our marriage. Annie would be the better of my company."

I could only, in broken accents, utter my thanks. It pained me to the very heart to hear her speak so decidedly about her own failing state. It threw a gloom over my otherwise happy prospects. I tried to persuade her that she might be mistaken, more because I could not bear to admit the idea, than because I considered her so. I felt, indeed, that she was in all likelihood speaking the truth.

" No, no, my dear," said she, shaking her head ; " there is something here " (putting her thin hand on her breast) " that tells me my hours are numbered.

But what of that?—my earthly cares are all over, my family are grown up, and all but Annie settled in life, and she will have a home either with her sister or with you. You are each walking, I trust, in the ways of the Lord. For me, I am like a weary pilgrim longing for the day's journey to be over, and for the shadows of the evening to fall. I am willing to go in the Lord's good time."

I could not restrain my tears.

"You must not weep, my love," she said kindly. "I should not like to grieve you to-night. William will reproach me if he sees you with red eyes. And after all, Rose, my dear, what is death that we should so dread his approach? Have I not been dying for years? It will be the putting off, perhaps with a pang, of a poor diseased body.—But it will also be," she added, pausing and raising her eyes solemnly upwards, "the admission for ever into the presence of my precious Saviour—such mercy has he for a helpless guilty sinner!"

On our way back to Mrs Ronald's at night, I told William, when he was speaking of our future plans, what his mother had proposed to me. "It is like her," he said; "she thinks of everything. But it is decidedly the best arrangement: for I do not suppose that you would like to go to your aunt's."

"It was quite true," I said.

"Neither should I like you to go there, my own Rose. But this engagement to Mrs Ronald ends this month, does it not?"

"I supposed so," I said, "for Mrs Ronald had written to that effect to her niece, and that young lady had agreed to come by the commencement of the ensuing year."

It was finally settled then, that when I was released from my engagement, I should go to his mother's. He was soon to return to town, so I declared it needless to talk of any further arrangements in the meantime. I decided in my own mind, however, that if Mrs Campbell's life was only to be shortly prolonged, I should not leave her, but share with Annie in the duties of a daughter. She well merited this at my hands.

William and I had to bid one another farewell for a fortnight. It was as soon as he could conveniently leave his parish again. "I shall carry a light heart back with me, Rose," he said, "and I shall besides have the pleasant occupation there of preparing your old home to receive its mistress. Sir Robert Crawford has given Mr Grainger directions to have it all painted and repaired. Shall I say anything for you to Miss Menie?" he added with a smile.

"As you please," I answered smiling too.

"It must be in strict confidence then," he said, "or we shall have bonfires blazing through all the parish in honour of your expected return."

We were obliged to part at last, though he lingered as long as he durst at the outside of Mrs Ronald's door. It was sad to bid him farewell; but I had sweet remembrances and hopes to live on till we met again. There were bright prospects before me now, instead of the gloomy uncertain ones I had lately pictured. Still, even parting for a fortnight is a painful thing when the heart is strongly attached. We had just learnt, too, to understand each other's feelings.

A few days after this, I paid Mrs Ronald the compliment of confiding my secret to her. She had been making inquiries as to how I meant to dispose of myself. She was gratified in no small measure. My communication took her very much by surprise, " though she had thought," she acknowledged, " that I certainly went very often to Mrs Campbell's, and wondered I did not prefer staying at home. But it now turned out to be quite natural, and just what might have been expected in the circumstances. She would, however," she said, " give him a teasing when he came back, for being so sly; he had not spoken half-a-dozen words to me that day he called, though, to be sure," she added, " he might not have liked to speak to me in her presence. She would take care and leave the room the next time."

I rather regretted afterwards that I had been so hasty in my confidence, for from the looks of both Kathrine and Jenny, I could easily see that Mrs Ronald had been unable to keep from sharing her knowledge with them. I was to blame, for I knew the nature of the woman.

The month wore on. I had proposed to Mrs Ronald that she should write again to her niece, and request her, if possible, to arrange matters so as to be able to leave home a few days before the end of December, that she might be that time in the house before I left it. To have taken her away from a fireside surrounded, as it generally is at this season of the year, with happy kindred faces, would have been selfish; but in her altered home there was no festivity. Mrs Craig was too thankful to have one of her family provided for to regard mere feeling as to the time at which she was called to part from her. I thought it would make a less decided change to my little pupils if Miss Craig arrived before I left them. It would afford me also an opportunity, if I found her such a person as I could venture to offer a hint to, to give her some useful advice how she should order her own conduct in this house, so as to have that degree of influence with her aunt which was absolutely needful for the children's benefit. Of course, she was a relation, and I was only a stranger introduced by circumstances into the family; but I knew the ground by this time, and she did not. The servants had much ascendency over their mistress; and they, I saw, were not over pleased at the prospect of a relation of Mrs Ronald's being settled as an inmate in the house. They had no objections to me; but I suppose they expected she would take more liberties. I saw it would require both prudence and good temper on Miss Craig's part to make her new home a comfortable one to her.

Mrs Ronald did not receive an answer till a week

had gone by. It came at last, and was as I wished. Miss Craig would manage to come at the time her aunt requested. I forgot to mention before, that the school scheme which she had talked of in her letters had come to nothing. The old school was too well established, and the mistress of it too great a favourite with the public, for Mrs Craig's daughters to have a chance of succeeding. Mrs Ronald's proposal (as I expected) had been eagerly embraced. The second daughter was needed at home, as Mrs Craig had now been fortunate enough to get two little children recently sent home from India as boarders, and she was to attend to their education.

William made his appearance again at the time appointed. I counted the days till then. He had no sooner seen his mother than he hastened to me. Mrs Ronald was in the room when he entered, and she was all smirks, and nods, and sly looks, while she remained in it. She claimed great credit to herself afterwards for the adroit manner in which she first managed to get rid of the children (no easy task, for they all as usual crowded round him), and then followed them herself, leaving us alone together. William was amused, but was very glad of her manœuvre, for he was anxious to have some conversation with me about the future.

It only wanted ten days now till the time I must leave my situation. William was very urgent that our marriage should take place in the course of the following month. The manse would be in readiness

by then, for the painters were there already, and
had made considerable progress under his superinten-
dence. But I would not consent to any such hasty
proceedings. He pleaded his loneliness — I would
not admit that plea. At last, to put a stop to his
entreaties, I told him all that his mother had said
to me—of my apprehensions that she had spoken the
truth, and my resolution not to leave her while she
lived, and I could be useful to her and Annie.

William was silent for a few moments when he
heard this. I suspect he had been cherishing hope
like Annie about his mother's state. But there
was no wonder—they had seen her revive from so
many serious attacks. He said at last, that he trusted
she was deceived in her opinion of her symptoms;
but he ceased to press our immediate marriage. I believe he went directly after he left me to Mary, and
she, who evidently suspected her mother's danger
more than Annie, burst into tears immediately on
being questioned, and said she feared I was right.
So William told me, when he came to escort me to
his mother's that night. I could observe that his tenderness towards his mother after this was, if possible,
increased. He returned to his parish, consenting that
all should be as I wished.

He had informed me, by the bye, that the Misses
Weir had been no less gratified than amazed by the
secret he had communicated to Miss Menie. They
now thought it the most likely thing to have happened,
and were quite astonished at their own want of pene-

tration. He had recommended silence on the subject at present, and Miss Menie had promised it in the name of her sisters. In spite of the promise, however, I was certain the news would reach the Jennies, through the younger ladies; and then,—to be sure it would only create a sensation a little before the proper time, and William would be oppressed with congratulations.

It was now so clearly settled, both with the Greys and Annie, that I was to assist the latter and Marion in nursing Mrs Campbell, that we all made our arrangements accordingly. I was to step into Mary's place. It was a great relief to Mary, for she was apprehensive about her sister. Mrs Campbell could scarcely turn herself now in her bed, and her attacks were so frequent, that they dreaded leaving her alone a moment. Marion had house work to do, for the Campbells' house consisted of two flats, and Mary Lowrie was not fit to keep it all in proper order without assistance, so Marion could only occasionally relieve Annie. They were therefore very anxious for the end of the month to arrive, and indeed I was the same, though I still felt deeply at the thought of parting from the children. I hoped, however, to be able at times to run down to see them—I could not bear that they should forget me.

I had by this time prepared them for my going away. The younger ones when they heard of it cried and clung to me; but I knew this grief would soon pass away from their young hearts. Helen went

and wept apart. I found her again and again sobbing
by herself in a corner of our bedroom. I could reason
with Helen. I told her the necessity for my leaving
her; said that the young lady who was coming to fill
my place was her own cousin, who had met with
various sorrows lately, and that therefore she ought to
exert herself to receive her with kindness and cheerfulness. I described to her the poor afflicted lady
whom I was going to help to nurse, observing with
interest, as I proceeded, the various changes on Helen's
expressive face; I then asked her if she would not
make an effort for my sake, for the sight of her sorrow
made me more sorrowful, and I am very grieved to
part with you, my own Helen, I said.

Helen fixed her eyes steadfastly on my face while
I spoke. Her little features still worked—her bosom
heaved, and she sighed deeply, but she shed no tears.
I lifted her up on my knee and kissed her,—the little
scene took place in the solitude of the bedroom.

" And now that I see you are going to be composed
and courageous, Helen," I said, " I shall tell you a
little secret, which however you must be careful to
mention to no one, for I would not like you to do so."
Then I told her that I was shortly to be married to
the gentleman she and the others were so fond of,
and when that took place I would go back with him
to Auchtermuir, which she had heard me so often describe; " and then, Helen," I added, kissing her once
more, " if your Mama pleases, and I think we shall
prevail upon her, you shall come and visit me there,

and see old John and Mrs Johnstone, who I know will dearly love you for your affection for me, and you shall play among flowers all day."

" Shall I indeed ?" said Helen with a radiant countenance ; " and shall Jessie and the rest come also ?"

" Perhaps they shall," I said.

" Then," said Helen, jumping off my knee, and clapping her hands with delight, " I shall not cry once, Miss Douglas, till you go away. But won't you be married soon ?"

" It will not be very long, Helen."

And Helen kept her word, for she behaved quietly all the time afterwards, and when Miss Craig arrived, mindful of my injunctions, she was neither shy nor fretful. Besides, she scrupulously kept the secret I had intrusted to her.

Miss Craig arrived punctual to the time fixed. I anxiously expected her arrival, hoping that I should be favourably impressed by her appearance. Her aunt was also in a state of nervous trepidation all the afternoon she was to come, while the children, dressed for the occasion, and seated on their little stools, were perfectly silent, as if they shared our feelings.

It was the evening when she reached us. Mrs Ronald and I had, for some time before, ceased all conversation, our spirits being too much fluttered to speak. She knew almost as little, personally, of her niece as I did—both of us were only acquainted with her through her letters. Jenny had been despatched to the coach to meet and conduct her to the house.

She was to travel by Edinburgh, staying a night with a friend there on her way. At length there came a ring to the bell. Kathrine quickly opened the door, and immediately after there was a bustle of bringing luggage into the lobby.

Mrs Ronald rose mechanically to go and receive her niece. But as she was slowly and nervously approaching the door for that purpose, it was opened by Jenny, and Miss Craig walked in. She was a plain homely-looking girl, with a stout under-sized figure, and a sensible good-humoured face. She looked a little jaded and fatigued with her journey. Her manners were very frank, and like one accustomed to mix pretty freely in society. She seemed a person who would make her way in life, I thought, in spite of obstacles, for she had health, cheerfulness, and energy, besides talent, in her countenance.

"How do you do, Aunt Ronald?" she said in a pleasant voice, kissing the cheek of the agitated Mrs Ronald.

"How are you, my dear?" she managed to answer, "and how did you leave your mother?"

"Mama is well, thank you, and desires to be kindly remembered," said Miss Craig. "Ah! these are the children. Will you not come and speak to your cousin, my dears?"

Helen rose and went forward, the others sat still and looked shy. Miss Craig kissed Helen, and said that she would soon make acquaintance with the rest.

I was standing beside the fireplace a little embar-

rassed; for Mrs Ronald, in the tremor of her spirits at
the arrival at length of her long talked of niece,
seemed to forget altogether the necessity of introducing us to one another. Miss Craig I saw was a little
near-sighted, and was straining her eyes across the
room to enable her to discern my features. I felt
obliged at last to step forward, and as I proffered my
services to help the new comer off with her travelling
things, I took an opportunity of casting an admonitory look at Mrs Ronald. She had perception enough
to comprehend its meaning, so she now made us known
to each other, and we shook hands. I then proposed
to take Miss Craig to my bedroom, which she was
to share with me till I left Little Helen was to
return to the nursery till then.

Miss Craig looked better with her bonnet off. Her
face and figure were still plain enough, but her air
was smarter and more easy. She was a pleasant
frank-looking girl, without affectation of any kind, and
evidently anxious to make herself agreeable. In this
she perfectly succeeded during the evening. She in-
gratiated herself with the children, though Helen
could not be tempted to leave my side, but sat still
there, with her eyes constantly directed to her strange
cousin. I saw that she was endeavouring to satisfy
her mind about her.

When the children had gone to bed, Mrs Ronald,
her niece, and I, had a long confabulation over the
fire, with our feet on the fender. I would have retired, and left the aunt and niece alone, but was re-

quested by both to remain. Miss Craig seemed to
take it for granted that I must understand all the circumstances of the family, and talked of them freely
before me. I was pleased with her views, as I had
formerly been with those she expressed in her letters.
I was still more convinced of her shrewdness and good-
feeling.

She was fatigued with her journey, and we went
early to bed in consequence. When we were alone
in our bedroom her cordiality continued. We had
a kind of confidential chat while we were undress-
ing. I found to my great relief that I did not require
to insinuate the hints I meant to give her. Miss
Craig bluntly asked me what my experience in the
family had been. I answered her with equal
frankness. A certain delicacy, besides good-will, led
me to be as brief and succinct as possible in speaking
of Mrs Ronald. I knew that she would soon discover
her aunt's peculiar faults of herself. But I managed
to give her some idea of the balance of power in the
household, of which I have no doubt so shrewd a girl
as she seemed availed herself. I alluded to the treatment—physical treatment—of the children at the time
I entered the family, and to the different system
I had prevailed upon Mrs Ronald to adopt, at which
she nodded her head repeatedly in an approving manner, and said, she knew a lady in her native town
who greatly resembled her aunt in the respect I had
mentioned.

We next talked of the children, and I spoke most

encouragingly of them, describing Helen as a child of a rare and most lovable nature. I told her what progress they had made in their learning, but offered to explain this more particularly the following day.

Miss Craig thanked me warmly in the end, apologizing for the curiosity she had shown, but excusing it, because, though so near a relation of theirs, she yet knew little of them, and was desirous to adopt a line of conduct at first that might be agreeable. This emboldened me to say, that I myself had been most anxious to have some conversation with her such as we had had; and I advised her to begin from the very first to do as much for her aunt as possible, so that she might have no trouble, and get soon attached to her, and, for the sake of her own comfort, carefully to avoid giving offence to the servants. She said she would be careful to follow my advice. My mind was much relieved by this conversation.

CHAPTER XIII.

I saw the spots where once we played, the walks where once we ranged,
And still they looked the same to me,—my heart alone was changed;
The churchyard walls rose grey and cold beneath the noonday sun,
And shadows rested on the graves, as they of old had done.

I saw each old familiar face, each old familiar thing;
I felt once more upon my cheek my native breeze of spring;
And gladsome murmurs reached mine ears of many an ancient strain;
And kindred voices welcomed me unto my home again.

I LEFT Mrs Ronald on the morning of new year's day.
A year all but a few days had passed away since I
had entered her family. The year was ushered in
soberly in her quiet dwelling, for she was a pious
woman though a weak one,—besides, the family were
in mourning for a near relation. The children were
allowed a full holiday on "Hogmanay," and Miss
Craig and I took them up to see the old Cathedral in
the forenoon. Miss Craig was quite a stranger to
Glasgow, and was much interested by this first view
of the venerable pile. Little Helen too looked up

with wondering admiration, not unmixed with awe, at the dark arched roof and massive pillars, as we walked slowly on through the echoing aisles. Her imagination was impressed by what she had seen all that day, and she was never weary of questioning me on the subject.

In the evening the little ones had a good romping game, in which we joined them. Miss Craig's robust figure and cheerful spirits enabled her to be the life of it. The children, I was sure, would soon get fond of her. Perhaps she was a little too bustling and vigorous in all she did, to suit so quiet-loving a nature as her aunt's. That good lady in the meantime, however, seemed perfectly contented with her niece. I felt it would be more trying when there was no third person present to ward off any annoyances. I saw that Jane Craig exerted herself with earnest good-nature to be agreeable to her aunt. But I thought it was a pity that, with so pleasant a voice, she did not speak in rather a lower key, and that her movements were so abrupt and startling in the presence of one who complained so often of her nerves. Miss Craig, I was sure, could have little sympathy, from personal experience, with such ailments. It was a delicate thing to allude to, however, and I held my peace.

I had bought some toys for the children, and I presented them before I left. I took leave of Mrs Ronald with rather a full heart. I had grown attached to her. I had been a year under her roof, and its quiet and

simplicity had been a pleasant change after the pomp-
ous bustle and vain pretension of my aunt's house.   I
had been an honoured and kindly treated inmate of it.
Mrs Ronald, with all her little weaknesses (and those
were easily endured), was a motherly good woman.
She had been kinder to me than my own flesh and
blood.   I hoped to be able to repay her friendliness
in my own home.

Then the children—But really my parting from
them was too sad to allow me to say much about it,
—and so I had better pass it over.   I told Helen to
be upon honour, and remember her promise, and said
I should run down to see them all in a very few days.
Miss Craig and I shook hands cordially, and she
said she hoped we would continue friends.   Poor
thing, she was just landed on a strange shore, where
all faces were alike unfamiliar to her; and I have no
doubt she felt a little dispirited and solitary.   But I
had no fears for her; she would fight her way on, and
overcome.   Her nature was resolute.

I was received with a kind welcome at Mrs Campbell's, as one of the daughters of the family returning
to her home.   I felt now, indeed, that I was one of
them.   Poor Annie's sad looks revived in my company, and Mary, who was in the house when I
arrived, could not earnestly enough express her thankfulness, it seemed, that I had at last come to them.
But it was a sad day that new-year's day in the
afflicted house.   Mrs Campbell had one of her usual
attacks that very night.

Annie and I now waited closely upon the poor invalid. To her other complaints was now added a cough, which still more exhausted her weak frame. She had to be supported in bed when a fit came upon her,—night and day we were in her room. She was very gentle, very patient, and most unwilling to give trouble. As Marion said, and we felt, the instructions which fell from her lips were worth a thousand times all our fatigue. Annie soon became as persuaded as I was that her mother was dying. The first bitter burst of grief over, she became quiet and resigned. With such a picture of suffering before us, day after day, and night after night, we could only wish for a speedy release for her.

She struggled through the whole of January, and the greater part of February,—and a sore struggle it was. Her lungs were failing, and the cough and difficulty of respiration were consequently often painful to witness. How thankful were poor Annie and I when William came to us! His presence did us both so much good. He strengthened our drooping spirits, and left us always in better frames. How tender and considerate he was to us both, and we were truly in want of it then, and what a comfort to his dying mother! His conversation, his prayers, were so precious to her. It was beautiful to see the son guiding and comforting the parent who had been his own spiritual teacher formerly! But her faith was seldom clouded; for she had had a long experience of the faithfulness of God, and her views were

ever clear and scriptural. Free grace and undeserved
mercy were ever the burden of her song. Ah! those
were trying days.

I occasionally managed, when Marion was disen-
gaged, to run down for a few minutes to Mrs Ronald's.
I never left Annie alone, for when the cough attacked
Mrs Campbell, it required two to raise her properly
up. I always found things going on satisfactorily at
my old quarters, and every one glad to see me. Miss
Craig had not been long an inmate when she had
every one in the house under her rule,—even the servants succumbed to her authority. She seemed to
manage everything well too; but I think her aunt
stood a little in awe of her. She was kind to the
children, though she would scold them heartily at
times, and she brought them on quickly in their
studies. She and I continued very good friends, and
she occasionally called upon me with the children.
Helen still clung to me when we met. I do not
think that Miss Craig suited Helen so well as I did.
She was so active herself, that she did not like
the child to follow the bent of her nature,—perhaps
I was too indulgent that way, for I had a sympathy
with Helen's turn of mind. She wished her to
run about, instead of sitting quietly by herself reading. However, they all continued healthy and
cheerful under her charge, and that was the essential
point.

At last, poor kind Mrs Campbell's sufferings drew
to a close. When it became unmistakably evident

that death could not be very distant, William managed to get a friend to undertake his labours at Auchtermuir, and remained with his mother. It was such a privilege to have him constantly with us. He was deeply affected, for he was a most affectionate son. Mrs Campbell continued sensible to the last, and during the twenty-four hours previous to her death, was perfectly free from pain. She was, however, unable to speak; but she understood what was read and said to her. She often looked smilingly on us, as we stood around her bed; and once when William and I were standing together, she turned her eye upon us with peculiar meaning. It was as if she were invoking a blessing on our future union.

At length, in the latter end of February, she died, while we were all gathered round her bed. A slight raising of the hand a few minutes before death, showed that the spirit was in prayer before departure. And when her son affectionately closed her eyes, I doubt not but the language of every bereaved heart present was,—" May I die the death of the righteous, and may my last end be like hers."

After the funeral was over, and all necessary business attended to, William was obliged to return to his parish. His grief was deep, but he bore it as a man and a Christian. He was most devoted and affectionate to me—soothing my distress with the most anxious tenderness. To his sisters, also, especially Annie, whose situation was different from Mary's, he was most loving and considerate. Nothing of course was yet said in allusion to our marriage. We had a consultation among ourselves after the funeral, the Greys, Annie, William, and I, about what arrangements must take place. It was at last settled that Annie and I should remain together in the house with the two servants till May, when another tenant would probably come in. What should be arranged afterwards, and how the furniture should be disposed of, was left for future consideration. William was forced to leave us the following day.

And so Annie and I were left to live by ourselves in the altered house. How empty and dreary did it seem! It was long before we got accustomed to the change. The days, though we were often at Mary's, and she and her husband with us, hung heavy on our hands. We deserted the old parlour and sat in the dining-room, for poor Mrs Campbell's unoccupied bedroom was too near the former for composure of spirits. We would have been going in and out of it all hours of the day, and brooding over the scenes of the past months. Annie of course felt the blank more than Mary, for Mary had learnt to look upon another place as her home. Her mother she could not but miss and deeply grieve for, but poor Annie had never been away from home, except for the short time she had spent with William. Annie's spirits were very depressed for some time, and Mary and I had to soothe and watch over her. She seemed to take pleasure in nothing except visiting her mother's grave. We went there several times every week at first. Mrs Campbell was buried in the High churchyard beside her husband and several of their children who had died in early childhood. Many a sad stroll had we through the ancient burying-ground. Ah! how many thousands slumber there, beneath the shadows of the old cathedral walls? It was even a more solitary spot then than now, for dark fir-trees covered the brow of the modern burying-ground.

Her brother's visits were what most benefited Annie's state of mind. With much tenderness he remonstrated with her on fostering and indulging her grief. He warned her against repining and fretting over God's providential dealings, and rendering herself thereby weak in body and incapable of useful exertion. Annie at all times only required to have the path of duty clearly pointed out. She meekly acknowledged her error, and, what was better, immediately strove to overcome it. With the aid of stated employment and daily exercise, besides a mind hourly attaining to more resignation and composure, the days began to pass more quickly.

By the time April was over and May had set in (a bright sunshiny May), we had got tolerably accustomed to our quiet solitary life. We had met with much kindness and attention from various friends of the family. Marion, the servant, had also carefully watched over us, as if we were a couple of children. At times we did feel the house dull, especially after William had paid us a visit, and was gone. But though we had still sorrow in our hearts, grief with all of us had lost its first freshness. We were getting more reconciled to our loss.

We had now made all our final arangements. There was a good deal of business to be transacted, but Mr Grey managed it for the whole family. Annie was just one-and-twenty out; so each had their portions assigned to them, according to their father and mother's will. As for the furniture, William took most of it at a valuation, for some of the rooms at the manse were still unfurnished. It was good and substantial, and little the worse for wear. It was conveyed in due time by the carrier to Auchtermuir.

Annie and I took up our abode at the Greys on the servants' term-day. Her residence was to be permanent, she paying them of course a handsome board, which she could well afford to do. Mine was but temporary, till my marriage, which was now fixed to take place in the beginning of the following month. I had not much trouble in preparing for it, for of course I was in mourning for Mrs Campbell, and did not mean to put it off. I got many valuable and useful presents from my two future sisters, Mrs Ronald, and various friends of the Campbells, with whom I had become intimate during the few last months. Dr Balfour gave me a handsome Bible, with my name written in it by his own hand. I have preserved it carefully to this day, in remembrance of that worthy good man. My aunt and cousins were not so liberal.

I called for my aunt when my marriage was fixed, and informed her of it. It took her by surprise, but it was evidently an agreeable one, for it was getting rid of all cares and thought about me for ever. To be sure she had not given herself much trouble heretofore; but I was willing to allow her to possess some conscience, which must occasionally, I think, have admonished her about her neglect of me. I wonder she did not try at this time to balance all such uncomfortable reminders, by making a stout effort to draw her purse-strings for a bridal present. But my aunt could be liberal to none but herself and daughters. She was, however, very inquisitive and condescending in the inquiries she made concerning the marriage, and thought it a very equal match on both sides. No doubt she privately exulted in the superior alliances one of her family had already made, and the others would probably make. I saw she did. Ah! poor woman, she little knew what the future had in store.

None of my cousins were at home when I called. I invited neither her nor them to my wedding, though I had no other relations. But the invitation would have been an empty ceremony. I said I should not likely see her again before I left Glasgow, and bade her farewell. I trust I did it in charity. I left my best wishes for Mr Dalgleish (who, by-the-bye, paid my three hundred pounds into Mr Grey's hands when he learnt of the marriage) and for the rest of the family, and came away. We parted apparently good friends;

but of course we were both aware in what estimation
we mutually held each other.

And now every thing was got in readiness.   I
paid farewell visits to every body who had shown
me attention.   Mrs Ronald I saw repeatedly, and
invited her to visit me at Auchtermuir; and I asked
little Helen to the wedding, which almost over-
whelmed her with joy.

I must not forget to mention the disposal of old
Marion and Mary Lowrie.   Mrs Grey wished the
former to come to her, to take charge, I believe, of the
baby when it made its appearance.   But Marion had
her own fancies.   Though she loved her young
mistress, she did not think of going into servitude
again, and " she was feared, at her time of life, that
she couldna staund the skirlin' o' bairns," she said,
" though she liked to keep them at a time.   Mrs
Grey, too, would be thinking in the end that she
spoiled them."   Marion had saved money.   But she
had much activity about her still, and could not bear
to be idle.   At length her intentions were made
clearly manifest to us.

" Ye see, my dears," she said one evening, when
she paid us a visit at Mary's, for she had hired a
small room, and moved to it at the term, the family
presenting her with sufficient furniture from their
mother's house to furnish it comfortably, " ye see, it
wad never dae for me to be idle.   I never could
thole idleset a' my life; sae, as the doctor and me saw
muckle o' ane anither in my mistress's room, he was

sae kind at last as to say, that if I was weary o'
service — I couldna be that, ye ken — but if I
didna care to tak' a new ane, he thocht he could
secure me a very good opening as a nurse to attend
upon sick folk, for he had often sic things in his
power."

"And did you really accept his offer, Marion?"
said Mary.

"Atweel did I, Mrs Grey, and thank ye tae. Ay,
ye are thinkin' that it's no a pleasant trade; but I
had aye a turn someway for nursin' and watchin' the
sick,—it comes kindly to me. I dinna need, ye ken,
to tak' a place that I think 'll no shute, for, thank
my Maker, I hae twa three pounds in Carrick's
bank that 'll aye keep me frae bein' obleeged to ony
body. I'm gaun to a place the morn—that's the
raison I'm here the nicht, as I mayna be able to see
ye for a while again, and I wanted to bid the bride
(nodding kindly to me) God-speed. She 'll be
married and awa' before I can get back. Mind ye
gie my gude wishes to the young maister."

"And where are you going to, Marion?" we asked,
with some curiosity.

"It's to an auld gentleman," she answered, "that's
sairly crippled up wi' the rheumatism, and his ain
family canna manage him. He's a wee hasty in the
temper. But I hae had it mair than aince mysel' in
my neck and shouther, and, deed, I ken it's very trying. We 'll sort fine, I've nae doot, for I 'll gie him
a' his ain way when he scolds, and tak' my ain after-

hend.   It's no ill managing cankry folk, if since ye
ken the way."

Marion was quite cheerful in the prospect before
her, so we felt it needless to dissuade her from trying
the new life that she proposed.   She bade us all
good-bye heartily, showing some feeling when she
shook hands with me.

Mary Lowrie was gone home to her father's at
present; but she was to accompany me to Auchtermuir.   We were to pick her up in Hamilton on our
way home.

We were married on the second of June—pleasant,
cheerful June,—just a year and a day after Mary.
Dr Balfour performed the ceremony before breakfast,
for we had a long journey in prospect.   There were
no strangers present, as Mrs Campbell's death was
so recent, except little Helen Ronald, who slept in
the house the previous night, and the bridesman,
an old friend of William's—Annie was bridesmaid.
After breakfast, and after many tears and kisses had
been lavished upon me both by my new sisters and
little Helen, to whom I renewed my promise of an
invitation, we stepped into the chaise, which had
been hired for our journey from the Saracen's head,
and set off.

My spirits were fluttered and excited to the last
degree on the journey—I seemed in a dream.   Was
it possible so many things had happened to me during
the year and a half that had passed since I left my
home? and was I really returning to it at last, and

in company with my husband? William laughingly complained that I was absent, and that he could not get me to talk. But no wonder, I told him, I could only think and anticipate. The carriage seemed to me to move so slowly; but that was owing to my impatience to see familiar scenes again. We really got over the ground in a very different sort of manner from what we did when I travelled the same road in the caravan.

Ah! what a change had taken place in my fortunes since that day! How hopeful and happy were my spirits now!—how low and anxious had they been then, with the prospect before me of entering into a strange home, and amongst people I was unacquainted with! No wonder I could not arrange my thoughts, for the images of the past and the present pressed upon and confounded one another. I had had my trials since that time; but how little cause had I to complain of those crosses, when there was so much happiness in store for me. I trust I felt grateful to God.

We stopped at Hamilton to change horses. Currie's inn was the only posting-house then. I peeped out as we were proceeding down the Muir towards it, and had a sight of my old quarters. And there was Mrs Eglinton herself at the door, still in her white dress; but though she looked at the chaise as it passed, she did not seem to recognise me. We paused for a moment, as we drove through the town, to take up Mary Lowrie at her father's door. He came out of his house with bare head and grateful looks, and assisted his daughter to mount beside the driver. I was glad to see that the poor weaver looked less gaunt and care-worn — a token that things were prospering with him.

And now we soon left Hamilton, its crooked narrow streets, with their low-browed shops, its ducal residence, and fair spreading parks, behind us, and were speedily winding along by the lovely banks of the Clyde. How I enjoyed the scenery now! When I travelled through it formerly, it was the season of winter, and there was then a winter in my soul too, which deadened me to the charms of nature. Now my eye and imagination were both filled with the many beauties before me. My husband was with me, and his spirit was congenial with mine. We constantly kept pointing out to each other every new and striking object. William was familiar with the road, he had travelled it so often for some months, but he was all the more alive to its beauty. He was amused, however, with my enthusiasm. The chaise was stopt for ten minutes to allow me a peep of Stonebyres. "Ah!" I said, as we returned along the pathway, after viewing the fall, "when I heard the roar of that water formerly, I was too heart-sick to get out and look at it." It was again a reminder for thankfulness.

At length we entered Lanark, toiling first up the long steep hill at the outside of the town. In mercy to the horses, we all alighted and walked up, leaving the driver to accompany his weary steeds. I was glad to get my limbs stretched by exercise, and so was William, for we had now been confined a number of hours to the chaise. When the hill was surmounted, we got into our vehicle again.

Now I began to recognise familiar objects, and my heart beat rapidly with expectation. I could not help feeling agitated. In my former simple days, Lanark had been "the town," a place of first-rate importance in my eyes. Its shops seemed handsome, and I thought it a busy thriving place. Everything is relative, of course, and I had contrasted it with Auchtermuir. Now, as we rattled along its principal street to the inn, I wondered where all the people had gone to. The streets seemed deserted, though several individuals came to their doors on hearing the noise of our chaise. One or two of them appeared to recognise me. And the shops—had I only imagined their splendour all the time? or had it vanished too? Lanark was an altered place, and was now only a small dull country town, with little trade, and a scanty population. I knew it possessed its own genteel society, however, and I had several acquaintances there.

After again changing horses, we struck across the country towards the hills,—and now every turn in the road was well known to me. I sat with my eyes fixed upon the landscape, straining them in a tumult of feeling to discern objects before they appeared. William tried to divert my thoughts, which he saw were all in commotion, but it would not do. I could not even speak to him now, but sat with my hand in his, breathless and expectant. He too at last became silent, looking out as I did.

We had taken a long time to our journey; but the roads were not so well attended to in those days. It was considerably past five when we reached the moor that belongs to the parish. How sweet it was to breathe my native air! Ah! how keenly had the November wind, which blew over the moor, been felt by me a year and a half ago! It had swirled into the cart where I sat, pale, weeping, and cheerless.. It was in character with my melancholy departure. But now, the bright June sun, just beginning to decline a little in the west, was as much in unison with my home-coming.

Along the rough uneven road,—along the black heathery moor,—stretched long lines of slanting sunshine, broken and mingling with the shadows; little sparkling rills leaped up by the way-side, and murmured a soft welcome to the returning pilgrim; joyous insects were buzzing out their feeble life in the warm summer air; and moorland birds were skimming along on every side. How sweet the small clusters of cottages looked that dotted the moor, though their walls were built of unhewn stones mixed with turf, and though their heath-thatched roofs were green and uneven! Groups of sun-burnt urchins were playing in front of them, who, at sight of our chaise at a little distance, instantly deserted their sports, and honoured us with a loud huzza, thus bringing out many of their mothers and *grannies* to the doors, who, screening their eyes from the sun, gazed earnestly after us, some of them vigorously waving their aprons in the air, in sign of welcome. " That is all for you, Rose," said William smilingly. The cottages were generally situated a little off the road, and I could not recognise any of the people distinctly, though I was certain that I saw old Lowrie Walker (for one of those clusters contained his cottage) standing in front of his own door, with red cowl and woollen apron, as if he had just left his loom.

On we went, leaving the moor behind us, and presently the doctor's trim domicile appeared in sight, with its smart green gate and gravelled walk, and Mrs M'Whirter evidently on the watch at the window. And after we left it behind, we approached in a short time dear hospitable Burnside, with its old trees grouped around it, and its white walls peeping so picturesquely through the foliage. Oh! how my heart warmed to them and their kind inmates. But just as we drove past the gate, who should be there, for no other purpose apparently than to watch for our appearance, but the two Jennies, who were so vociferous in welcoming us, and in waving of handkerchiefs, that they scarcely attended to my hasty demand as to their mistresses' welfare.

" Ah! William," I exclaimed, my mind still busy with retrospects, which every object in the road recalled, " the last time I walked by that fence I had to cover my face with my veil for fear any one I met should see my tears."

"But I think there are tears in your eyes yet—let me see, Rose—Yes! you are positively weeping."

"Ah! but they are tears of joy," I said; "that makes a great difference." A few minutes more brought us close to the Craiglands. My breath came thick and fast, and the tears which formerly had only stood in my eyes now came rushing down. William tenderly soothed my agitation; but he knew the cause as well as I, and that it was impossible not to be moved in the circumstances. There was no one in waiting at the gate here, for the old inhabitants of the solitary mansion could not be expected to make such an exertion as to walk all the way to the head of the long avenue, for the chance of seeing us as we passed. The grey mossy pillars and massive arch were lonely, as they had formerly been; but I thought, as I caught a glimpse of the avenue, that it looked more grass-grown than it used to do—the path traced through it by occasional footsteps seemed less distinct. How long it was since mine had helped to wear it!

But one glance at the Craiglands gate, and one thought of my kind old friend sitting happy and thankful in the ancient matted parlour, now sufficed, for I knew that in a minute more we should come to that turn of the road where my old home would be visible. My impatience to arrive at it was so great, that I could scarcely bear to remain in the chaise, it moved so slowly in comparison with my feelings. If I had yielded to them, I should have sprung out and rushed down the hill.

The turn was gained—there was the quiet nest-like manse—there was the stately range of trees leading towards it (every one of them familiar to me)—there was the bending river,—and there the old church, beside which was my father and mother's grave, with its graceful sycamores and birches drooping over the churchyard wall. I hid my face on my husband's shoulder and wept quietly.

"Welcome home, my love," he whispered, drawing me closer to him; "welcome to your own home."

It took only a short time to descend the hill and reach the gate. It was wide open for our reception. A glimpse of figures hurrying out of the house caught my eye, as we turned in to the little shrub-bordered approach (oh! how deliciously the honeysuckles and the sweet-briar smelt); and before I had time to collect my thoughts, which were strangely excited, and to think of whom I was to meet (I almost expected to see my father's figure at the door), the chaise stopped. William quickly wrenched open the door and lifted me out. I threw a hurried glance around me as my feet touched the ground. There was Nanny, who, to her own great joy, had been engaged by my desire to return to her old place, looking half ready to cry, half to laugh; and there was honest old John, drest in his Sunday coat, with his blue bonnet in his hand, and a thousand emotions struggling for the mastery in his furrowed countenance—old friends both —no one but themselves was there. The neighbours had had the delicacy to allow us to arrive quietly, though an hour afterwards I noticed some curious heads peeping through the hedge.

I shook hands hastily with John—"Ah! John, I said, "do you remember how you deserted me?" The old man attempted to smile, but was compelled to draw his sleeve across his eyes, and afraid, I suppose, that he might betray more emotion if he remained, he fairly vacated the spot, and made his way back to the kitchen. I could not help kissing Nanny in my delight at seeing her again. "Ah! Miss Rose—Mrs Campbell, I mean," she said, quickly correcting herself, "I am sae glad to see ye back again at your ain hame."

But William would not let me linger longer at the door; so I just asked Nanny to be kind to Mary, and cast one hasty look on the familiar scene around before I allowed him to lead me into the house.

And oh! how sweet and fresh the old parlour looked, with its pretty new carpet, green-stained walls, and bright windows, (shaded with neat muslin curtains as white as snow,) against which the roses clustered, as if they too wanted to be within. And there was the ancient Dutch cabinet in its former place, and my father's large easy chair in its place, and my mother's screen standing just in the corner as it used to do,—all most thoughtfully sent back by Mrs Johnstone, when she was fully aware of the marriage being settled. The parlour certainly looked little altered,—more spruce and fresh perhaps,—for Nanny,

well acquainted with all my habits, had placed the new
furniture in such a way that I was almost deceived,
and thought there was no change at all. But in the
recess of the window in which I had always sat, there
was a pretty new work-table,—very handsome it was,
—with a green bag to it, which suited the colour of
the carpet exactly: and this was a present from the
good ladies at Burnside to me. The room was perfectly lovely, and I could not enough admire it, nor
the bright clean lobby, nor the little study, where
William's books were carefully arranged in handsome bookcases. He pretended to smile at my ex-
tasies; but he was evidently deeply moved himself,
and followed my movements with loving eyes. I
could not help a sigh, however, from occasionally
breaking forth in the midst of my happiness, especially when my eyes turned towards one corner in
the parlour. But it would not have been kind to
William to indulge sad recollections in the home he
had just brought me to; so I restrained my feelings,
and looked to him and smiled.

He pulled a bunch of keys out of his pocket and
handed them to me, declaring himself now happily
emancipated from all such cares. I took them smiling and blushing, and promised to take good care of
them.

The table was set out for tea, and there was the
Greys' handsome silver tea-equipage which they had
presented to us, and the beautiful china which had
been Annie's bridal present—making quite a goodly

show in honour of our home-coming. And when I
opened the cupboards, and took a peep into them,
(William was nearly as curious as I was,—it was
quite evident that Nanny had managed everything,
not he), I cannot but say the sight was a pleasant
one, for there was abundance of both crystal and china,
and indeed everything necessary and suitable for
housekeeping for one of William's means and calling.
It was really very gratifying to a young housekeeper.

William and I strolled about later in the evening.
It was impossible for me to remain in-doors. How
lovely everything looked! How quiet and peaceful
after my city life!—and I was to spend my life here.
Our hearts were truly happy—too happy sometimes
for words—looks sufficed to communicate our thoughts
to one another. Here we were then to be companions
through existence—fellow-helpers to one another.

The flower-beds were in perfect order and beauty,
more particularly my old garden, of which great care
seemed to have been taken, and the roses and honeysuckles, which clothed the walls and porch, were
sweet in the soft dewy evening. How inexpressibly
pleasing were all the sounds and sights of the country—the distant lowing of the cattle, anxious for their
return to the homestead—the cawing of the rooks, returning in large flocks to their nests among the old
trees at Burnside—the rich foliage, and the green turf
where the daisies had now closed their eyes till the
next morning's sun would rise to waken them up!
As we were walking about, I saw Nanny go down

with the milk-pail to the stables, and Mary was with her, to get her first lesson in milking a cow, I suppose. And presently Nanny made her appearance at my side with a smile on her face, and a glass of the sweet foaming milk in her hand—the draught I used to love. I thought it the sweetest milk I ever tasted.

William as well as I thought the spot a little paradise. There was a tender sadness in my heart, though, in the midst of those familiar scenes, which he did not experience, albeit he could sympathize with me. Former days arose before me, and I thought of my father and sighed. How he had loved this spot, which his own hands had helped so much to beautify!

My husband kept the key of the churchyard himself, for he loved to stroll there occasionally — no wonder, it was a sweet and solitary place. I drew him at length gently there, and he could not resist me

In the grey of the summer evening, as it had been the grey of the winter's morning before, I stood again at the grave of my parents. My husband was by my side. We were far removed from all stir and intrusion; perfect silence was around us, unbroken even by our voices. There was calm on the earth and in the air,—the still dewy calm of a summer eve. The evening star had just begun to twinkle in the fading west: and, as I raised my eyes and saw it, it seemed to whisper of a calmer and more peaceful future. The trees were clothed in the graceful foliage of summer, and the bat darted between them in airy circles. Winter was gone from the face of nature, and from my heart.

I stooped down as before, and perused the epitaph with tears of tender remembrance. I had stood formerly beside that stone, a poor, forlorn, homeless orphan, about to go forth to earn her bread in a world she was ignorant of, and with a heart full of grief for the heavy loss she had newly sustained. I had stood beside it, solitary and unsupported, with no hope that I would ever more re-visit the spot. How was it now?—Naomi's case and mine were reversed. I had gone forth empty, and the Lord had brought me back full. I had gone sorrowing, and the Lord had made me return rejoicing. He had thought fit to remove the beloved father who now slumbered there. He had thought fit to try me with various afflictions, but these were all now passed away; and instead of a father by my side, I had a loving and most tender husband. Henceforward I was to be a helper with him in the Lord's vineyard—to labour with him side by side, and I was to dwell among my own people. Truly saith the Psalmist, " I have never yet seen the righteous forsaken, *nor his seed begging their bread.*"

CHAPTER XIV.

No, we can ne'er regret the hours
Of youth, though thickly strewn with flowers :
A calmer life will now be ours ;
And then to age is given
Hopes which re-animate the breast
Of never-ending holy rest,—
Eternal youth in heaven.

AND now, reader, you must endeavour to transform the young hopeful bride into an old feeble woman, for such a one it is who has written this history. And I trust that, knowing this, you will excuse the garrulity to which advanced years are liable, and which, I doubt not, is visible in these poor sketches of my early life.

I have been anxious, dear reader, to bear testimony to God's goodness, through a most trying time for a young inepxerienced girl, and which has never once failed me during the long course of my pilgrimage. I have always had a turn for writing, even from my early years, and it occurred to me that it would be a mournfully pleasing and even profitable occupation, if I could occasionally set down the more striking portions of the history of my youth, interspersed with a few sketches connected with the parish and my former friends. It is some years since I commenced doing so, and now my work is all but completed.

Dear reader, what are your retrospects? Can you also bear testimony for God, and say,—" It is good for me that I have been afflicted?" or, if you are young in years, and have experienced little of this world's cares and disappointments, are you willing to trust the future to His ordering, and to leave all in His hands? You must bear the cross yet as well as others,—but the weight of the burden depends much on how it is borne. Our Saviour bore His, and it is this truth alone received into our hearts which can lighten ours to us. My life was a very trying one for a certain period; but I can now say, that not one stripe was given me more than I needed. Insensible and blind of heart, I would have rested content in the creature, if he had not brought me to feel what an unsatisfactory portion it was.

And now I must go back once more, that I may say just a few words still about the parish and many dear friends of my youth, some of whom have long been in the grave. I hope the reader will bear with me for in some degree resuming my narrative.

It was a sweet peaceful summer that first one I spent with my dear husband at Auchtermuir. We were most truly united in heart; and I may say we went hand in hand together in all exertions for the benefit of our poor people. He had a clear vigorous intellect, and a most enlightened piety. He was no lazy careless minister; but he fed the flock, and he taught me also to aid him. He was, indeed, the poor man's friend,—patient, gentle, and persevering in all his attempts to benefit others. He followed in my father's footsteps, or rather he excelled him, for his nature was more energetic. However, when he succeeded to the parish, he was a younger man than my father was when I was able to observe him. At this late period of my life, it would be superfluous modesty to hesitate to acknowledge, that both he and I were much beloved.

That first summer was a busy though a pleasant period. There was the change to me of marriage, and of a return to all old habits. Then we had many invitations, for the young minister and his little wife were much sought after—more than we liked; and all the farmers and the old miller got up tea-drinkings in succession in honour of us. I had my little household to organize; but that was not difficult to do, for the girls were both attached to me, and remained with me till they were married. And John never had the heart to contradict one of my orders now, but grew like a lamb. He lived till he was near eighty; and all that time he occupied his old cottage, doing little jobs about the place when he could. We would not have sent him away for the world. My children became his pets, as I had formerly been, and many a posy and apple he gathered for them, and many a ride in his wheel-barrow he gave them. He

died at length, and we all mourned for him as for
one of ourselves.

During that summer we had a visit from Annie, who
soon afterwards managed to get married herself; and
dear little Helen Ronald was allowed to accompany her.
How Helen did enjoy the country! living like a bird
among flowers and in shady nooks under trees the
whole day, though I did not permit her to neglect her
studies either. Closer and closer Helen clung to me;
and for many years, every summer, we were gladdened by her presence at the manse; and once or
twice, when I was ill, she nursed me so tenderly!
Helen grew into a charming young woman, with the
most engaging disposition I almost ever met with.
During the summer succeeding to the one in which I
was married, while Miss Craig was paying a visit to
her friends, Mrs Ronald herself and the rest of the
children came to us. They staid a month; and Mrs
Ronald enjoyed her visit. Her niece was never
married, but resided with her aunt till Helen was
nearly grown up, when she returned home, one of her
brothers having been very prosperous in business, and
being able to assist the family.

Good old Mrs Johnstone lived five years after I
returned to the parish; and when she died, old Mysie
and Bauldy were removed and pensioned off, while
Sir Robert's gamekeeper and his wife and family
were placed in the house. It was allowed to fall more
and more into disrepair, till now it is a mere ruin.
But still the old gateway stands, and the avenue

remains, though it is very grass-grown and more gloomy-like than ever from the increasing size of the trees. I sometimes wander in it still, and muse sadly over old times, and sometimes I meet the game-keeper's children—another gamekeeper than the first-mentioned—playing about in it. But all the children around are familiar with the appearance of the " old leddy," as they call me, and so I pat their heads, and speak kindly to them, and wander on.

I remember well my first meeting with Mrs John-stone after I returned a bride to Auchtermuir. I stole away from William after breakfast the next morning to pay her a visit, for I was longing to see her, and she, I knew, would be equally anxious to see me. I ran through the kitchen to her room, greeting Mysie as I passed, who uttered a loud shriek of welcome. The idea had come into my mind, as I approached the house, to try the dining-room window again, which was probably still unmended, and give them all a thorough surprise ; but I happily reflected that I was now the " minister's wife," and that it would not be decorous. So I entered the usual way. And there was Mrs Johnstone seated in her room in the old window recess, and at the same employment as when I parted from her a year and a half before. But this was a meeting,—not a parting ; and tears, and smiles, and kind embraces were all mingled to-gether ; and she did not look a bit older than when I had seen her last. " Ah ! Rose," I remember her say-ing, " do ye mind what I said that weary morning when I bade ye fareweel, that the Lord would surely bring ye back again in his own good time?" And so He did, blessed be His name.

And I took a peep at the library too before hurrying home to William, who had only consented to let me go for a very short time, and whom I expected to meet me somewhere in the avenue. How ancient and ghostly-like it looked! It seemed as if no one had entered it, even to dust it, since I had gone away, for the dust was lying quite thick. I did not think I should disturb it much more now, but would read at home quietly like a good housewife.

When Mrs Johnstone died I attended her, and performed the last offices for her. Her illness was a short one. She was a second mother to me. Peace be with her memory!

And many a happy evening did William and I spend at Burnside, which continued the same hospitable place for many years. Miss Menie was still a kind friend and counsellor to me. They are all gone now; and the old house is turned into a farm-steading, and all the trees are cut down. Such changes as one sees in a long life! And many such besides these there have been in the parish. All the old people that I knew in my youth are gone, and their children have grown up and filled their places. One generation cometh and another goeth. Even so. But we are still a simple people.

Ah! well do I remember that Sabbath on which I was churched after my marriage. What a full congregation it was for one thing! But all the old faces were there,—the miller, with his floating grey locks and kindly eye—the farmers with their wives and daughters—old Lowrie Walker, who continued to teach the Sabbath school for many a year afterwards —the doctor and his ancient helpmate—and William the bellman, as pedantic and respectable-looking as ever. Almost all of these are now gone!

There was much interest excited among them by my return, and many kindly greetings I received in the churchyard when I left the church. It was strangely sweet to sit in my old corner in the minister's seat, with John and Nanny opposite me once more, and so many friendly faces in the little congregation around me, and listen to my own husband as he expounded the Word of Life to his simple flock. My heart was full of happiness and peace. I felt that the Lord had dealt very bountifully with me.

Mary, Annie, and I have preserved our early friendship—not a cloud has ever darkened it. We love one another's society, and a visit from them and their husbands makes sunshine at Auchtermuir. Their young people are often with us, and mine visit them often in Glasgow. I have not been able to pay many visits to that city of late years, for I am growing feeble, and do not like to leave home, neither does Mr Campbell. But I am told it is wonderfully improving; and, indeed, the last time I was there, if one of my nieces had not been in waiting for me at the coach (for we have now a coach from Lanark, reader,) with a noddy,

I think I should not have found my way. The Greys
now live in a handsome house in St Vincent Street,
and the Mackays (Annie and her husband) somewhere
about the Sauchiehall road—both new localities. Both
families have prospered in the world.

And now I must say a few words, before closing,
about the Dalgleishes, my own relations. I have but
a melancholy tale to tell of them. Perhaps the reader
may be struck to hear that they were subjected to sad
and unexpected reverses. My poor aunt, so ambitious
and worldly-minded; it was a bitter change to her.

I think it was about two years after my marriage,
—during which time little communication took place
between us, though when I was in Glasgow visiting
my sisters I made a point of calling for them,—that
Mr Dalgleish unexpectedly became a bankrupt. He
had, contrary to his usual prudence in mercantile matters, involved himself in large and doubtful specula-
tions, and even induced his son-in-law so far to join
him. These proved ruinous, and poor Mr Dalgleish
had the pain of communicating to his incredulous and
finally horror-struck family, that he was a broken man.
He lost energy afterwards, and never retrieved himself. But the family—what a fearful change it was
to them! Everything had to be given up to the creditors, even their very furniture. I was sadly shocked
when I first heard of it through my sister Mary's
letters.

Mr Dalgleish did not survive his fall many months.
They said that the heartless frettings and constant

reproaches of his family for his imprudence were more than he could bear, and killed him. I was deeply grieved for him. He was a kind-hearted man, as I can testify.

Poor Eliza, in spite of her worldly advantages, had a sorrowful fate. She did not live long to enjoy these, for she died of her second child. Mr M'Callum lost a considerable sum by his father-in-law's failure, which seemed to have rankled in his mind; for after his wife's death, he did not do much for her friends; besides, he very soon married again.

I called for my aunt the first time I was in Glasgow after Mr Dalgleish's death, and found her in a small dingy uncomfortable flat in an obscure part of the town. What a change! And she had sunk by that time into a mere querulous old woman. She seemed rather mortified that I should see the contrast between her present and past condition; but it was kindness brought me there. She could talk of nothing but their misfortunes, and peevishly bewailed the privations she was now exposed to, blaming her departed husband with little delicacy; and this continued without intermission, till, with a sickened heart at this display of repining and discontent for mere worldly fortune, I came away.

Her sons, poor woman! were no comfort to her. Robert went off to America immediately after the failure, and Matthew, after leading for some years a very idle dissolute life about town, followed him, and she was left alone, with her two daughters, to subsist

upon a small pittance allowed them from sympathy
by the creditors. The aunts either could or would
not help them. The friends of their prosperity, of
course, all forgot them. My husband generously permitted me to assist them, and I still continue to do
so. My assistance was accepted by my aunt, but she
testified no gratitude. However, I did not expect it.

She at last sunk, poor woman! into a state approaching to imbecility, in which condition she continued till her death. Her daughters, Margaret and
Jemima, having no mental resources nor religious
principles to support them, felt the change in their
condition very painfully. They are alive still, a pair
of peevish, backbiting old maids, with few friends and
many enemies. Their afflictions have not taught
them patience, nor forgetfulness of the world. Margaret, however, is the least fretful of the two, and the
best endured. Their fate truly affords a lesson on the
uncertainty of worldly things. When their aunts
died, it was found, to their nieces' sore disappointment and indignation, that they had jointly settled
their little property on Eliza's children, who truly
had no need of it. The two families have not spoken
since.

And now what more have I to say? Something
merely about my own family. God has been very
kind to us. Two dear lovely infants sleep near their
grand-parents in the churchyard; but we have four
dutiful children left. My sons were educated at the
same university as their father, and are both, I be-

lieve, excellent scholars. My second son is now settled in Glasgow, and is in partnership with a son of
his uncle Grey's in the old business,—the old gentleman has retired. My eldest son, who was bred for
the church, was last year, at the earnest petition of
the parishioners, which was graciously granted by our
old acquaintance Sir John Crawford (Sir Robert has
long been dead), ordained assistant and successor to
his father, which has lightened his labours considerably. My eldest daughter is happily married to a
neighbouring minister, and my youngest keeps house
at home, and attends to her parents.

The manse is growing old and frail like ourselves,
and some of our friends occasionally hint to Mr Campbell that he should apply for a new one; but we have
experienced too much peace and happiness within its
walls to think of pulling them down. The rooms are
sadly old-fashioned and incommodious, they tell us—
but my husband and I are old-fashioned too. The
house will last our time; and when we are gone,
James can apply for a new one if he pleases. They
say, too, that our little church cannot be allowed to
stand much longer; but I trust I shall never live to
see it taken down. It is sadly cold and damp, to be
sure, in winter; but it is sweet to worship in the
same spot still, as I did in my girlhood, and look up
at my husband or son in my father's old pulpit.

My husband and I are fast declining into the vale
of years. God has spared us yet to one another.
But I now often gaze from my window, as I sit alone,

upon the two or three green mounds in a certain part of the quiet churchyard, and think that erelong I shall be laid there too, among kindred dust.—And I am ready in the Lord's good time.

THE END.

Printed by Oliver & Boyd,
Tweeddale Court, High Street, Edinburgh.

January 1851.

A CATALOGUE OF BOOKS

IN

VARIOUS BRANCHES OF LITERATURE,

PUBLISHED AND PREPARING FOR PUBLICATION BY

SMITH, ELDER AND CO.,

65, CORNHILL, LONDON.

CONTENTS.

WOMEN EXEMPLARY FOR PIETY AND CHARITY.

By JULIA KAVANAGH,

Author of " Woman in France," &c.

In One Volume, post 8vo. *(In preparation.)*

ROSE DOUGLAS;

or, the Autobiography of a Minister's Daughter.

Two Volumes, post 8vo. *(Nearly ready.)*

MILITARY MEMOIRS OF LIEUTENANT-COLONEL JAMES SKINNER, C.B.

Commanding a Corps of Irregular Cavalry in the Hon. E. I. Company's Service.

By J. BAILLIE FRASER, Esq.

Two Volumes. Post 8vo., with Portraits. *(Just ready.)*

THE KING OF THE GOLDEN RIVER;
or, The Black Brothers.
With Twenty-two Illustrations by RICHARD DOYLE.
Price 6s. in an ornamental cover.

"This little fairy tale is by a master-hand. The story has a charming moral, and the writing is so excellent, that it would be hard to say which it will give most pleasure to, the very wise man or the very simple child."—*Examiner*.

"Full of exquisite little pictures, with an under-current of humour floating through, and bearing a moral which can never be repeated too often."—*Fraser's Magazine*.

"It has humour, fancy, grace, tenderness, and the moral purpose of shewing the superiority of kindness to riches. Richard Doyle shines in the illustrations."—*Spectator*.

CONVERSATIONS OF GOETHE with ECKERMAN.
Translated from the German by JOHN OXENFORD.
In Two Volumes, post 8vo., price 24s. cloth.

"These conversations present a distinct and truthful image of Goethe's mind during the last ten years of his life. And never was his judgment more clear and correct than in his closing years. The time spent on the perusal of this book will be usefully and agreeably employed. Mr. Oxenford's translation is as exact and faithful as it is elegant."—*Spectator*.

"These conversations contain a rich vein of wise thoughts upon a great variety of subjects."—*Westminster Review*.

"We cannot praise these volumes too highly. They a most valuable contribution from German literature, and rank with the most delightful productions of our own."—*Examiner*.

THE BRITISH OFFICER:
His Position, Duties, Emoluments, and Privileges:

Being a Digest and Compilation of the Rules, Regulations, Warrants, and Memoranda relating to the Duties, Promotion, Pay, and Allowances of the Officers in Her Majesty's Service, and in that of the Honourable East India Company; with Notices of the Military Colleges, Hospitals, &c.; and a variety of Information regarding the Regular Regiments and Local Corps in both Services, and the Yeomanry, Militia, and other Volunteer Corps.
By J. H. STOCQUELER.
One Volume, 8vo.

THE KICKLEBURYS ON THE RHINE.
A new Picture Book, Drawn and Written by MR. M. A. TITMARSH.
Second Edition, with a Preface, entitled, "An Essay on Thunder and Small Beer."
Price 5s. plain. 7s. 6d. coloured.

PIQUE.
A NOVEL.
In Three Volumes. Post 8vo.

"'Pique' is a brilliant novel. There is grace and refinement everywhere."—*Critic*.

"In this clever book, the enforcement of a sound, social moral, gives energy and purpose to the exercise of the author's powers of observation and description."—*Globe*.

"The narrative is so easy, earnest, and pleasant, as to have enticed us on from chapter to chapter, —with a charm which is by no means of every week's experience."—*Athenæum*.

"'Pique' is well exposed in the character and conduct of the heroine of this story. The interest of order is closely engaged throughout."—*Morning Post*.

WORKS OF MR. RUSKIN.

(THE "OXFORD GRADUATE.")

I.

THE STONES OF VENICE.

Volume the First.   THE FOUNDATIONS.

By JOHN RUSKIN, Author of "The Seven Lamps of Architecture," &c.

With numerous Illustrations.   (*Just ready.*)

II.

THE SEVEN LAMPS OF ARCHITECTURE.

By JOHN RUSKIN, Author of "Modern Painters."

1 vol. imp. 8vo., with Fourteen Etchings by the Author.   Price One Guinea,
bound in embossed cloth, with top edge gilt.

" By the ' Seven Lamps of Architecture,' we understand Mr. Ruskin to mean the seven funda-
mental and cardinal laws, the observance of and obedience to which are indispensable to the architect
who would deserve the name. The politician, the moralist, the divine, will find in it ample store of
instructive matter, as well as the artist."—*Examiner.*

" This eloquent and deeply-instructive volume is a book for amateurs to read; for it will make the
thoughtless thoughtful, and open new fields of contemplation and sources of interest, and suggest and
strengthen important principles to all."—*Ecclesiologist.*

" Mr. Ruskin's book bears so unmistakeably the marks of keen and accurate observation, of a true
and subtle judgment and refined sense of beauty, joined with so much earnestness, so noble a sense of
the purposes and business of art, and such a command of rich and glowing language, that it cannot
but tell powerfully in producing a more religious view of the uses of architecture, and a deeper insight
into its artistic principles."—*Guardian.*

" From the series of works upon which Mr. Ruskin is engaged, we can scarcely hope too much for
art. The brilliant manner by which the present and other works of Mr. Ruskin are adorned has
placed them at once amongst the books that *must* be read. The views broached in this volume con-
stitute the most significant piece of criticism which has appeared in the English language for very
many years."—*North British Review.*

III.

MODERN PAINTERS.

By A GRADUATE OF OXFORD.

Volume the First.   Fourth Edition, imp. 8vo., price 18*s.* cloth.

Volume the Second.   Second Edition, imp. 8vo., price 10*s.* 6*d.* cloth.

" A generous and impassioned review of the works of living painters. A hearty and earnest work,
full of deep thought, and developing great and striking truths in art."—*British Quarterly Review.*

" A very extraordinary and delightful book, full of truth and goodness, of power and beauty."
North British Review.

" This work is the most valuable contribution towards a proper view of painting, its purpose and
means, that has come within our knowledge."—*Foreign Quarterly Review.*

" One of the most remarkable works on art which has appeared in our time."—*Edinburgh Review.*

WORKS OF CURRER, ELLIS, & ACTON BELL.

I.

JANE EYRE: an Autobiography. By CURRER BELL.

4th Edition, 1 vol. post 8vo., 6s. cloth.

"'Jane Eyre' is a remarkable production. Freshness and originality, truth and passion, singular felicity in the description of natural scenery and in the analyzation of human thought, enable this tale to stand boldly out from the mass, and to assume its own place in the bright field of romantic literature. We could not but be struck with the raciness and ability of the work, by the independent sway of a thoroughly original and unworn pen, by the masculine current of noble thoughts, and the unflinching dissection of the dark yet truthful character."—*Times.*

"A very pathetic tale—very singular: and so like the truth, that it is difficult to avoid believing that much of the characters and incidents are taken from life. It is a book for the enjoyment of a feeling heart and vigorous understanding."—*Blackwood's Magazine.*

"A book of decided power. The thoughts are true, sound, and original. The object and moral of the work are excellent."—*Examiner.*

II.

WUTHERING HEIGHTS and AGNES GREY.

With a Selection of the Literary Remains of ELLIS and ACTON BELL,

and a Biographical Notice of both Authors by CURRER BELL.

One volume. Crown 8vo., cloth. Price 6s.

III.

SHIRLEY: a Tale. By CURRER BELL,

Author of "Jane Eyre." 3 vols. post 8vo., 1l. 11s. 6d. cloth.

"'Shirley' is an admirable book; totally free from cant and affectation; genuine English in the independence and uprightness of the tone of thought, in the purity of heart and feeling which pervade it, in the masculine vigour of its conception of character, and in style and diction. It is a tale of passion and character, and a veritable triumph of psychology."—*Morning Chronicle.*

"'Shirley' is very clever. The faculty of graphic description, strong imagination, fervid and masculine diction, analytic skill, all are visible. Gems of rare thought and glorious passion shine here and there throughout the volumes."—*Times.*

"The book possesses deep interest and an irresistible grasp of reality. There is vividness and distinctness of conception in it quite marvellous. There are scenes which, for strength and delicacy of emotion, are not transcended in the range of English fiction."—*Examiner.*

"There is something in it of kin to Jane Austen's books, or Maria Edgeworth's, or Walter Scott's. There is human life as it is in England, in the thoughtful and toiling classes, with the women and clergy thereto appurtenant."—*Globe.*

IV.

POEMS. By CURRER, ELLIS, AND ACTON BELL.

Fcap. 8vo., 4s. cloth.

"A volume of poems which will not detract from the fame of the authors. The poems bearing the signature of Currer Bell exhibit the impress of a matured intellect and masterly hand."—*Morning Herald.*

WORKS OF MR. LEIGH HUNT.

I.

TABLE TALK. By LEIGH HUNT.

One Volume. Crown 8vo., cloth guilt. Price 7*s.*

II.

THE AUTOBIOGRAPHY OF LEIGH HUNT;

WITH REMINISCENCES OF FRIENDS AND CONTEMPORARIES.

In 3 vols. post 8vo., with Three Portraits, price 31*s.* 6*d.* cloth.

"These volumes contain a personal recollection of the literature and politics, as well as some of the most remarkable literary men and politicians, of the last fifty years. The reminiscences are varied by sketches of manners during the same period, and by critical remarks on various topics. They are also extended by boyish recollection, family tradition, and cotemporary reading; so that we have a sort of social picture of almost a century, with its fluctuations of public fortune and its changes of fashions, manners, and opinions."—*Spectator.*

"The 'Autobiography of Leigh Hunt' ought to be a valuable and interesting work. His life has been a long and varied one; the hero has played a tolerably distinguished part on the literary stage, has seen and suffered much, and has mixed in his time with notabilities of every kind. * * * In spite of the many faults of the work, there are chapters to be found in these volumes worthy of Mr. Hunt's pen, and very delightful to read. Beautiful fragments of criticism shine here and there with unmistakeable lustre."—*Times.*

III.

THE TOWN: its Memorable Characters and Events.

By LEIGH HUNT.

2 vols. post 8vo., with Forty-five Illustrations, price 24*s.* cloth.

"We will allow no higher enjoyment for a rational Englishman than to stroll leisurely through this marvellous town arm-in-arm with Mr. Leigh Hunt. He gives us the outpourings of a mind enriched with the most agreeable knowledge. There is not a page of this book which does not glow with interest. It is a series of pictures from life, representing scenes in which every inhabitant of the metropolis has an interest far greater than he suspects."—*Times.*

IV.

MEN, WOMEN, AND BOOKS.

By LEIGH HUNT.

Two vols. post 8vo., with Portrait, price 1*l.* 1*s.* cloth.

"A book for a parlour-window, for a summer's eve, for a warm fireside, for a half-hour's leisure, for a whole day's luxury; in any and every possible shape a charming companion."—*Westminster Review.*

"Mr. Leigh Hunt never writes otherwise than cheerfully. He *will* have sunshine, *will* promote gay spirits, *will* uphold liberal truths; blithely, yet earnestly. He is the prince of parlour-window writers."—*Athenæum.*

V.

IMAGINATION AND FANCY.

By LEIGH HUNT.

VI.

WIT AND HUMOUR.

By LEIGH HUNT.

Bound in cloth, with gilt edges, price 10*s.* 6*d.* each, or in boards 9*s* each.

WOMAN IN FRANCE during the 18th Century.

By JULIA KAVANAGH.

In 2 vols. post 8vo., with Eight Portraits of Remarkable French Women, price 24s. in embossed cloth.

"Which among us will be ever tired of reading about the women of France, especially when they are marshalled so agreeably and discreetly as in the pages before us ?"—*Athenæum.*

"The subject is handled with much delicacy and tact, and the book shows often an original tone of remark, and always a graceful and becoming one."—*Examiner.*

"Miss Kavanagh has acquitted herself with artist-like skill; her picture of the manners of a most remarkable epoch is drawn with boldness, precision, and delicacy."—*Globe.*

"Delightful volumes, not only of immense interest, but of permanent value."—*Britannia.*

"An attractive and pleasant book on an important subject, teaching history in a delightful manner."—*Economist.*

"A work of more than common interest."—*Atlas.*

MACFARLANE'S GLANCE AT REVOLUTIONISED ITALY.

2 vols. post 8vo., price 1l. 1s. cloth.

"These two amusing and unpretending volumes give more insight into the present state of the Italian peninsula than can be collected from all the voluminous speeches, pamphlets, reports, and letters with which the press has been inundated."—*Quarterly Review.*

"These volumes afford the fairest view yet given to the public of Italian affairs during the last few eventful months."—*Britannia.*

THOMPSON'S AUSTRIA.

One Volume, post 8vo, with Portrait, price 12s. cloth.

"We find in every page evidence of personal acquaintance with his subject, and an honest desire to tell the truth without fear or favour."—*Athenæum.*

"A useful volume for those who wish to investigate the condition of the Austrian empire."—*Spectator.*

ROSS'S ADVENTURES ON THE COLOMBIA RIVER.

1 vol. post 8vo., with a Map, 10s. 6d. cloth.

"One of the most striking pictures of a life of adventure which we have read for a long time, and as full of information as of amusement."—*Athenæum.*

"This narrative ought to be a companion volume to Washington Irving's 'Astoria.'"
Westminster Review.

"A work of permanent value, as well as interesting, from the novelty and variety of the life and scenery it describes."—*Globe.*

ROWCROFT'S TALES OF THE COLONIES; or, the Adventures of an Emigrant.

Sixth Edition, fcp. 8vo., price 6s.

"'Tales of the Colonies' is an able and interesting book. The author has the first great requisite in fiction—a knowledge of the life he undertakes to describe; and his matter is solid and real."—*Spectator.*

Works of Practical Information.

SCRIVENOR'S ACCOUNT of the RAILWAYS of the UNITED KINGDOM.

1 thick vol. 8vo., price 1l. 1s. cloth.

"A work embracing the entire statistics, so far as they can be gathered from authentic documents, of the railways of the United Kingdom. The financial history of each company, and its dependencies, is detailed in a well-arranged form, together with their present position, and every point of useful official information."—*Times.*

SCRIVENOR'S HISTORY OF THE IRON TRADE.

Demy 8vo., price 15s. cloth.

"Mr. Scrivenor's History is written with elaborate research and anxious care, and goes into and exhausts the entire subject."—*Tait's Magazine.*

GILBART'S HISTORY OF ANCIENT COMMERCE.

Post 8vo., price 7s. 6d. cloth.

"A work useful to students of political economy, and interesting to the general reader."—*Economist.*

VAN SOMMER'S TABLES OF CONSOLS,

Exhibiting the various Fluctuations in 3 per Cent. Consols from 1789 to 1849 inclusive.

4to., price 1l. 1s. cloth.

PIDDINGTON'S SAILOR'S HORN-BOOK OF STORMS.

1 vol. 8vo., price 10s. 6d., with Charts and Storm Cards.

"A valuable manual of the law of storms. We wish we could be sure that it would be in every ship in which English is read."—*Athenæum.*

"A valuable practical work."—*Nautical Magazine.*

"An exceedingly useful manual on an important subject, interesting to the meteorologist as well as the mariner."—*Westminster Review.*

"The law of storms and the mode of evading them are very fully handled by Mr. Piddington."—*Spectator.*

THOM ON STORMS IN THE INDIAN OCEAN

SOUTH OF THE EQUATOR; with Suggestions on the means of avoiding them.

1 vol. 8vo., with Map and Plates, price 12s. cloth.

"The work before us is most valuable to seamen."—*Nautical Magazine.*

SMALL'S MERCANTILE TABLES OF BENGAL PRODUCE.

1 vol. 4to., 2*l.* 10*s.*   Any Table may be had separately, price 7*s.* 6*d.*

THE FARMER'S FRIEND:

A Record of Recent Discoveries, Improvements, and Practical Suggestions in Agriculture.

1 vol. post 8vo., price 7*s.* 6*d.* cloth.

"The design of this work is excellent, and calculated to do good service to agricultural science. The editor has performed his task well."—*Morning Chronicle.*

HUGHES ON THE DUTIES OF JUDGE ADVOCATES.

Post 8vo., price 7s. cloth.

"Captain Hughes's little volume will well supply the absence of that full and particular information which officers suddenly appointed to act as ' deputy judge advocates ' must have felt the want of, even though tolerably well versed in military law."—*Spectator.*

"This book may be emphatically called ' The Hand-book of Military Justice.' "—*Atlas.*

KENTFIELD ON BILLIARDS.

4th Edition, small folio, with 93 Diagrams, price 31*s.* 6*d.* cloth.

" The work is sanctioned by the name of the highest authority and best player of billiards—*Edwin* Kentfield, better known as ' Jonathan' of Brighton."—*Literary Gazette.*

" A treatise, scientific and practical, with the rules and descriptions of twenty-two different games, and diagrams of all the strokes and hazards, *coups* and canons, which can be made. The instructions are very clear and precise."—*Morning Post.*

POCOCK ON ASSURANCES UPON LIVES;

Including the different Systems of Life Assurance now in use ; the Principles, Terms, and Tables of Seventy London Assurance Offices, &c.

1 vol. post 8vo. price 7*s.* cloth.

" Those who are likely to have recourse to life insurance, will do wisely in consulting this familiar explanation of its nature and advantages."—*Globe.*

LIFE CONTINGENCY TABLES.

By EDWIN JAMES FARREN.

Part I. price 5*s.* 4to.

" In these Tables Mr. Farren has investigated the subject in a systematic and scientific way, and thrown some curious light upon it."—*Spectator.*

Illustrated Scientific Works.

Sir J. HERSCHEL'S ASTRONOMICAL OBSERVATIONS.

Made during the Years 1834-5-6-7-8, at the Cape of Good Hope; being the completion of a Telescopic Survey of the whole Surface of the visible Heavens, commenced in 1825.

In 1 vol. royal 4to., with Eighteen Plates, price 4*l.* 4*s.*

Under the Auspices of H. M. Government, and of the Hon. the Court of Directors of the East India Company.

FAUNA ANTIQUA SIVALENSIS:

The Fossil Zoology of the Sewalik Hills, in the North of India. By HUGH FALCONER, M.D., F.R.S., F.L.S., F.G.S., &c. &c., and PROBY T. CAUTLEY, F.R.S., F.L.S., F.G.S., Lieut.-Colonel in the Bengal Artillery, &c. &c. Edited by Dr. HUGH FALCONER. The Fossil Bones drawn from Nature and on Stone by G. H. FORD and Assistants.

*** The work will be completed in about Twelve parts, each containing twelve folio plates. The descriptive letterpress will be printed in royal octavo. Price of each Part One Guinea. Parts I. to IX. have appeared.

"A work of immense labour and research.....Nothing has ever appeared in lithography in this country at all comparable to these plates; and as regards the representations of minute osseous texture by Mr. Ford, they are, perhaps, the most perfect that have yet been produced in any country."— *Address of the President of the Geological Society of London.*

ILLUSTRATIONS OF THE
BOTANY OF THE HIMALAYA MOUNTAINS,
And of the Flora of Cashmere.

By J. FORBES ROYLE, M.D., V.P.R.S., F.L.S. & G.S., M.R.A.S., Professor of Materia Medica and Therapeutics, King's College.

2 vols. imperial 4to., 100 coloured Plates, price 5*l.* 5*s.* cloth.

Published with the Approval of the Lords Commissioners of Her Majesty's Treasury.

DARWIN'S GEOLOGICAL OBSERVATIONS; made during the Voyage of H.M.S. Beagle.

PART I.—ON CORAL FORMATIONS.

8vo., with Plate and Woodcuts, 15*s.* in cloth.

PART II.—ON THE VOLCANIC ISLANDS OF THE ATLANTIC AND PACIFIC OCEANS.

8vo., with Map, 10*s.* 6*d.* cloth.

PART III.—ON THE GEOLOGY OF SOUTH AMERICA.

8vo., with Maps and Plates, 12*s.* cloth.

ILLUSTRATIONS of the ZOOLOGY of SOUTH AFRICA

By Dr. ANDREW SMITH.

Complete in Twenty-eight royal 4to. Parts, comprising 277 Plates of Quadrupeds Birds, Reptiles, Fish, and Insects, drawn on Stone by Mr. G. H. Ford, and nearly all beautifully coloured from Nature, with Descriptions of about 60 Species. Price 16*l.* in Sewed Parts; or 18*l.* bound in Five Quarto Volumes cloth, lettered.

Each division of the work may be purchased separately, bound in cloth lettered, at the following proportionate prices, viz. :—

MAMMALIA	50 *Plates*	.	£3 0s. 0d.
AVES	114 „	.	7 0 0
REPTILIA	78 „	.	5 0 0
PISCES	31 „	.	2 0 0
INVERTEBRATÆ	„	.	1 0 0

₊ Subscribers are respectfully urged to complete their sets without delay, in order to prevent disappointment.

THE ZOOLOGY of the VOYAGE of H.M.S. SULPHUR.

In Ten royal 4to. Parts. Complete, price 5*l.*; or in cloth binding, 5*l.* 10*s.*

THE BOTANY of the VOYAGE of H.M.S. SULPHUR.

Complete, in Six sewed Parts, price 3*l.*; or in cloth binding, 3*l.* 5*s.*

———

CAPT. THOS. BROWN'S WORKS ON NATURAL HISTORY.

RECENT CONCHOLOGY OF GREAT BRITAIN.

In 1 vol. royal 4to., illustrated with 59 coloured Plates, price 63*s.* cloth.

FOSSIL CONCHOLOGY OF GREAT BRITAIN.

Complete in 1 vol. royal 4to, price 5*l.* 10*s.* coloured; 3*l.* 15*s.* plain.
Separate Numbers may be had, 3*s.* each, coloured; 2*s.* plain.

ILLUSTRATIONS OF THE GENERA OF BIRDS.

Now publishing in Numbers, royal 4to., each containing 4 Plates, price 3*s.* coloured.
Part I. is just completed, price 36*s.* cloth.

ELEMENTS OF FOSSIL CONCHOLOGY.

12 Plates, fcap. 8vo., price 5*s.* cloth.

ALPHABETICAL LIST OF SHELLS.

On a Sheet, price 1*s.*

Oriental and Colonial.

THE MOOHUMMUDAN LAW OF SALE.

Selected from the Digest of the Emperor Aurungzebe, and Translated from the original Arabic; with an Introduction and Explanatory Notes.

By NEIL B. E. BAILLIE,

Author of the "Moohummudan Law of Inheritance."

1 vol. 8vo, price 14s. cloth.

"A valuable addition to juridical and even to general literature. It is the best specimen of a really good Mahommedan law book that has yet been published."—*Spectator.*

A HISTORY of the REIGNING FAMILY of LAHORE.

With some Account of the Sikh Soldiers and their Sirdars.

Edited by MAJOR G. CARMICHAEL SMYTH, Third Bengal Light Cavalry.

8vo., price 12s. cloth.

ANNALS OF INDIA:

An Outline of the Principal Events which have occurred in the British Dominions in India, from January 1848 to March 1849.

By GEORGE BUIST, LL.D. F.R.S. L. & E., F.G.S., &c.

8vo., price 3s.

THE BOMBAY CALENDAR AND ALMANAC for 1850.

8vo, price 12s. bound.

A SKETCH OF ASSAM.

With some Account of the Hill Tribes. By an Officer of the E. I. C. S.

1 vol., with 16 Coloured Plates and a Map, price 15s. cloth extra, or 20s. elegantly bound in calf.

Dr. Wm. GEDDES on the DISEASES OF INDIA, &c.

8vo, price 16s. cloth.

"To the medical officers in India, and especially to those about to proceed thither, this will be found a valuable book of reference."—*British and Foreign Medical Review.*

"Dr. Geddes has done for the symptoms of the diseases which he describes what Louis has done for the microscopic phenomena of fever."—*Medico-Chirurgical Review.*

"This work must be referred to as a source of correct information on most questions relating to the diseases prevalent among Europeans in India."—*Edinburgh Medical and Surgical Journal.*

HURSTHOUSE'S ACCOUNT OF NEW PLYMOUTE

Post 8vo., with a Plan and Five Views, price 6s. cloth.

"No one should emigrate to New Zealand without first having perused this valuable lin volume."—*Westminster Review*.

"The work of a shrewd and observant man. It is clear, precise, and full in detail, and tempera in tone."—*Globe*.

"The merit of this book consists in the full and impartial account it gives of the settlement, a: the sound advice which accompanies it."—*Spectator*.

WRAY'S PRACTICAL SUGAR PLANTER:

1 vol. 8vo., with numerous Illustrations, price One Guinea.

"'The Practical Sugar Planter' is a most useful book, containing more condensed and soli general information than we have ever before found collected on the subject of which it treats. T: the actual planter it will be found a most valuable work."—*Colonial Magazine*.

"Mr. Wray's work is of commanding interest. It is full of practical details, and will be an exce lent guide to planters."—*Economist*.

"Immeasurably the best practical work which has been written on the subject."—*Atlas*.

"Mr. Wray is well qualified to write on this subject; and it has been his especial object to intro duce such improvements in the culture of the cane and manufacture of sugar as a long series c experiments demonstrated to be judicious."—*Athenæum*.

FORBES'S HISTORY OF CALIFORNIA.

Illustrated with a Map, Plans of the Harbours, and Plates.

8vo, price 14s. cloth.

COOPER'S INVALID'S GUIDE TO MADEIRA.

Fcp. 8vo., price 4s. cloth gilt.

"A work which may be consulted with advantage."—*Sir James Clarke on Climate*.

ROYLE'S PRODUCTIVE RESOURCES OF INDIA.

Royal 8vo., price 14s. cloth.

PORTER ON THE SUGAR CANE.

New Edition, revised, with Plates, demy 8vo., price 12s. cloth.

WELLS'S GEOGRAPHICAL DICTIONARY OF THE AUSTRALIAN COLONIES.

8vo., with Maps and Views, 16s. cloth.

𝔈𝔡𝔲𝔠𝔞𝔱𝔦𝔬𝔫𝔞𝔩.

OF HAPPINESS in its RELATIONS to WORK and KNOWLEDGE.

By JOHN FORBES, M.D., F.R.S.

Fcap. 8vo, price 2s.

WORKS ON ANGLO-SAXON LITERATURE.

By B. THORPE, Esq.

I.

ANALECTA ANGLO-SAXONICA.

Post 8vo., price 12s. cloth.

II.

ANGLO-SAXON VERSION of APOLLONIUS of TYRE.

Post 8vo., price 6s.

III.

RASK'S GRAMMAR of the ANGLO-SAXON TONGUE.

8vo., price 12s.

ELEMENTARY WORKS ON SOCIAL SCIENCE.

Uniform, in fcap. 8vo., half-bound.

I.

PROGRESSIVE LESSONS IN SOCIAL SCIENCE.—1s. 6d.

II.

INTRODUCTION to the SOCIAL SCIENCES.—2s.

III.

OUTLINES of SOCIAL ECONOMY.—1s. 6d.

IV.

QUESTIONS and ANSWERS on the Arrangements and Relations of Social Life.—2s. 6d.

V.

OUTLINES of the UNDERSTANDING.—2s.

"The author of these various manuals of the social sciences has the art of stating clearly the abstruse points of political economy and metaphysics, and making them level to every understanding."—*Economist.*

JERMYN'S BOOK OF ENGLISH EPITHETS.

Imperial 8vo. price 9s. cloth.

"The plan pursued in this volume is to take a substantive, and give all the epithets which have been employed by our best writers to qualify it. What Mr. Jermyn has done he has done well."—*Britannia*.

PARENTS' CABINET of Amusement and Instruction.

6 vols. price 2s. 6d. each. Each volume is complete in itself, and may be had separately.

"This little work contains just that description of reading which will be beneficial to young children."—*Quarterly Journal of Education*.

LITTLE STORIES from the Parlour Printing Press.

By the Author of the "Parent's Cabinet." Royal 18mo., price 2s. cloth.

"A very nice little book for children."—*Weekly Chronicle*.

Religious.

THE NOVITIATE; Or, a Year among the English Jesuits.

By ANDREW STEINMETZ.

Third Edition, with Memoir and Portrait, 1 vol. post 8vo., 6s. cloth.

"This is a remarkable book. It describes, with a welcome minuteness, the daily, nightly, hourly occupations of the Jesuit Novitiates at Stonyhurst, their religious exercises and manners, in private and together; and depicts, with considerable acuteness and power, the conflicts of an intelligent, susceptible, honest-purposed spirit, while passing through such a process."—*British Quarterly Review*.
"If it be desirable to know what is that mode of training by which the Jesuit system prepares its novices for their duties, this is the book to inform us, for it is a chronicle of actual experience."
Britannia.

THE JESUIT IN THE FAMILY: A Tale.

By ANDREW STEINMETZ.

In 1 vol. post 8vo., 9s. cloth.

"A well-written and powerful novel, constructed for the development of Jesuit practices, and to show the Jesuit in action. The interest in some parts is intensely wrought up."—*John Bull*.

SERMONS BY THE REV. DR. CROLY.

1 vol. 8vo., price 10s. 6d. cloth.

"Of all the theological productions of Dr. Croly which have fallen under our notice, we think this volume, in many respects, the most striking, and the most likely permanently to establish his fame as an original, effective, and eloquent preacher."—*Britannia*.

TESTIMONY TO THE TRUTH;

Or, the Autobiography of a converted Atheist.

2d Edit. fcap. 8vo., 4*s.* 6*d.* cloth.

" A very interesting account of the experiences of an intelligent and sincere mind on the subject of religion. We can honestly recommend the book to the notice of our readers."—*Eclectic Review.*

" The work we trust will obtain a wide circulation, especially amongst classes exposed to the contagion of sceptical association. Even to firm believers it is calculated to be very profitable."
Evangelical Magazine.

" The history of the conversion of an individual mind has never been more minutely traced : the psychological phenomena revealed have never been more curious and suggestive ; and the incidents have never been described with more minute fidelity."—*Atlas.*

THE RECTORY OF VALEHEAD.

By the REV. ROBERT WILSON EVANS.

Fourteenth Edition, price 5*s.* cloth.

" Universally and cordially do we recommend this delightful volume. We believe no person could read this work and not be the better for its pious and touching lessons."—*Literary Gazette.*

RECORDS OF A GOOD MAN'S LIFE.

By the REV. CHARLES B. TAYLER.

Ninth Edition, fcap. 8vo., price 6*s.* bound in cloth.

THE CHURCH OF GOD.
A Series of Sermons.

By the REV. ROBERT WILSON EVANS.

8vo., price 10*s.* 6*d.,* boards.

REASON, REVELATION, AND FAITH.
By A BENGAL CIVILIAN.

12mo., price 4*s.* 6*d.,* cloth.

SCRIPTURAL EPITAPHS:

A Selection of Passages from Scripture suitable for Christian Epitaphs.

Price 2*s.* 6*d.* cloth lettered. An Edition on large paper, price 4*s.* cloth.

THE CALCUTTA REVIEW.

Published Quarterly, and received regularly by the Overland Mail.

Nos. I. to XXVI., price 6s. each.

The articles, written by gentlemen long resident in India, connected with the Civil and Military services, the Missionary establishments, the Bar, the Church, Commerce, the Press, &c., contain, in a condensed form, an immense mass of information relating to the contemporary History and Biography of India, Eastern Ethnography, Philology, Topography, Statistics, Science, Literature, Missionary labours, Society, Manners and Customs, and a large body of original intelligence of the most authentic character. The Review is the organ of no party and no sect, and is supported by men of all shades of opinion.

BOOKS FOR THE USE OF THE BLIND.

Printed with a very distinct Raised Roman Letter, adapted to their Touch.

THE HOLY BIBLE, in 15 vols. 4to bd. Any volume separately:—

			£	s.	d.				£	s.	d.
Vol.	1.	Genesis	£0	10	0	Vol.	9.	Job, Ezra, and Nehemiah	£0	9	0
—	2.	Exodus and Leviticus	0	13	0	—	10.	Psalms	0	13	0
—	3.	Numbers	0	9	0	—	11.	Proverbs, Ecclesiastes, Song			
—	4.	Deuteronomy	0	7	6			of Solomon and Esther	0	8	6
—	5.	Joshua, Judges, and Ruth	0	10	0	—	12.	Isaiah	0	10	0
—	6.	Samuel	0	11	0	—	13.	Jeremiah and Lamentations	0	11	0
—	7.	Kings	0	11	0	—	14.	Ezekiel	0	10	0
—	8.	Chronicles	0	11	0	—	15.	Daniel, to the end	0	11	0

The NEW TESTAMENT, complete, 4 vols. bound £2 0 0

The Four Gospels, separately:—

	£	s.	d.		£	s.	d.
Matthew	£0	5	6	The Acts of the Apostles	£0	5	6
Mark	0	4	0	The Epistles to the Ephesians and			
Luke	0	5	6	Galatians	0	4	0
John	0	4	6	The Epistle to the Romans	0	4	0

	£	s.	d.		£	s.	d.
The Church of England Catechism	£0	1	0	The Psalms and Paraphrases, 2 vols.			
Church of Scotland Shorter Cate-				(Scotch version)	£0	16	0
chism	0	2	6	Psalms and Hymns (English version)	0	12	0
Selections from Eminent Authors	0	1	6	The Morning and Evening Services	0	2	6
Selections of Sacred Poetry, with				The History of the Bible	0	2	0
Tunes	0	1	0	Musical Catechism, with Tunes	0	3	6
Arithmetical Boards	0	10	6	English Grammar	0	5	0
Map of England and Wales	0	2	0	Tod's Lectures, vols. 1, 2, and 3, each	0	2	6
Ruth and James	0	2	6	Description of London, by Chambers	0	3	0
Report and Statement of Education	0	2	0	Meditations on the Sacrament	0	4	0
First and Second Book of Lessons	0	1	6	Scottish Songs	0	3	0
A Selection of Æsop's Fables, with				Introduction to Astronomy	0	3	6
Woodcuts	0	2	0	Alphabet, on Card	0	0	1
Lessons on Natural Religion	0	1	6	Types for Writing (per Alphabet)	0	3	6

LONDON: PRINTED BY STEWART AND MURRAY, OLD BAILEY.